"A riveting true story of friendship between two boys—one black, one white—during the racially polarizing years of the Deep South. This book will inspire and touch the hearts of young and old alike."

—**Roscoe Orman**, actor; entertainer; and for forty years played Gordon on *Sesame Street*

"*More Than Rivals*, a book based on a true story from the 1960s, allowed me to reflect on how far we have come in this country and how far we still have to go. This book will make you laugh, cry, and want to get to know people who don't look like you or come from your same background. Unity is what will bring us together as a people, if we just take time to reach out and get to know others from a different race. I have learned over the years that real friendships are based not on the color of your skin but on the love and respect you have for one another. This book is a must-read for adults and teens."

—**Yolanda Conley Shields**, CEO, Let's Go Innovate; author, *Letters to Our Sons*

"One of the best heartwarming and inspiring books I have read. Wow, powerful. Amazing how one act can change everyone's tone as it did that night in Gallatin."

—**Mark White**, Tennessee state representative

"Simple, direct, and powerful—this is a story about how human kindness and understanding transformed a community. One act of kindness helped a community heal and transcend into a better, more inclusive town in the heart of America. A story of compassion that survives the decades of time . . . and the eternal truth that in the end, love wins. Add *More Than Rivals* to your library!"

—**Jack E. Pattison**, lieutenant colonel, infantry, US Army (retired); president and owner, Pattison Enterprises

"*More Than Rivals* holds a candle with true light to a dark place we wish had never been. While it shares a painful journey, it also hints at a promise of the silver lining within the cloud, an engrossing history lesson in which spiritual redemption, sports, leadership, and brotherhood can bring young men and their town to an important crossroads. An informative and engrossing read that grabbed me in the first pages and never let me go."

—**Catkin Kilcher Burton**, colonel, US Marine Corps (retired); president, Alaska Humanities Forum Board of Directors; CEO, Eagles Enterprises

"*More Than Rivals* offers a rewarding reading experience. You are taken back in time to witness the nostalgia of small-town America and the struggles of the segregated South. I strongly recommend that you purchase a copy of *More Than Rivals* and read it immediately. It is truly an outstanding story and shows me that Eddie and Bill (now adult friends) continue to have an important role in the lives of children and youth in Gallatin and throughout the New South."

—**Charles Martin "C.M." Newton**, former basketball coach, Transylvania University, the University of Alabama, and Vanderbilt University; former athletic director, University of Kentucky; former chair, NCAA Rules Committee

"Ken Abraham is one of my favorite writers. *More Than Rivals* is a monster slam dunk that will impact your life in a powerful fashion."

—**Pat Williams**, founder and senior vice president, Orlando Magic; author, *It's Not Who You Know, It's Who You Are*

"A championship basketball game was much more than what it appeared. The year was 1970, and this game was a reflection of a community on edge, at the crossroads of racial tension and hope. *More Than Rivals* is a true story about a friendship that transcended the past, reconciled the present, and imagined a new future."

—**Skip Prichard**, CEO, OCLC; leadership insights blogger at Skipprichard.com

"I think the best stories in the world are the ones you'd never expect. Leave it to Ken Abraham to keep finding true stories that absolutely must be told."

—**Dave Ramsey**, *New York Times* bestselling author and nationally syndicated radio show host

"Dick and I played high school basketball in Indiana in the '60s, so *More Than Rivals* brought back many great memories for us. We loved the diversity of sports and loved playing, traveling, and living with teammates of a different color. If everyone would love like that, despite differences in skin color, it would be a better world. The players accepted and loved and appreciated one another. Most of all, we understood one another. The relativity of the blending of sports and race relations is more important today than ever before. *More Than Rivals* gives the reader a little of both sides."

—**Tom & Dick Van Arsdale**, Indiana University All-Americans; twelve-year NBA players; three-time NBA All-Stars

MORE THAN
RIVALS

A Championship Game
and a Friendship That Moved a Town
Beyond Black and White

KEN ABRAHAM

Revell

a division of Baker Publishing Group
Grand Rapids, Michigan

© 2016 by Ken Abraham

Published by Revell
a division of Baker Publishing Group
P.O. Box 6287, Grand Rapids, MI 49516-6287
www.revellbooks.com

Printed in the United States of America

Library of Congress Cataloging-in-Publication Data is on file at the Library of Congress, Washington, DC.

ISBN 978-0-8007-2722-2

Published in association with the literary agency of Mark Sweeney & Associates, Bonita Springs, Florida 34135

This book is a retelling of a true story and is based on actual events. Certain items or incidents have been adapted for dramatic effect, and some artistic license has been taken to assist in the flow of the storyline. In some cases, for the sake of the narrative, conversations have been created, composite characters combined, or chronologies adjusted. Some names and details have been changed to protect identities.

16 17 18 19 20 21 22   7 6 5 4 3 2 1

Dedication in Memorium

The
MORE THAN RIVALS
team
wishes to honor
the following individuals:

Anna Bransford Ligon
(mother of Bill Ligon)

Jimmy H. (Bo) Sherlin Jr.
(brother of Eddie Sherlin)

Dan P. Herron
(former principal of Gallatin High School)

Professor John V. Malone
(former principal of Union High School)

Acknowledgments

THE DREAM FOR *MORE THAN RIVALS* originated in the heart and mind of Eddie Sherlin, one of the key figures in the story, when he realized that people are still longing for the hope this story inspires. Eddie took his ideas to Nancy Bailey, president of ACT 2 Films, a film development company in Nashville, Tennessee. Nancy worked with indefatigable determination for more than seven years to bring this story to the world. She shared the idea of a book with Regina Moore, owner and CEO of Moore Casting, who connected Nancy with me. Thanks, Regina! I am deeply grateful to Eddie, Nancy, and Regina for entrusting this powerful story to me. Thank you, Nancy, for believing and for all your hard work!

Eddie Sherlin is a personal inspiration to me. His humility and kindness are traits I hope to emulate. Thank you for sharing with me not only your story but also your heart. Eddie says he can teach almost anyone how to shoot a basketball better. Maybe someday you can teach me how to shoot as well as you! Thank you, Eddie.

Bill Ligon was also tremendously helpful in telling this story. Bill graciously granted personal interviews with me and continued to answer my questions throughout the writing process. I deeply appreciated Bill's honest perspectives. Thanks, Bill!

Special thanks and kudos to Jennifer Easton, an education reporter for the *Tennessean* and the *Gallatin News Examiner*, who served as the project's primary research specialist. Jennifer has published numerous articles about these events, and she conducted many of the initial interviews with people who knew the inside details of the story. Your contributions were invaluable, Jennifer, and much of the credit for the success of this book goes to you!

Kevin Shaw, director of photography, did an outstanding job conducting interviews with the people in Gallatin and drawing out their true feelings surrounding the events in the story. Thank you, Kevin!

Johnnie Scoutton did a fantastic job creating a website that conveys the concepts of *More Than Rivals*. Thank you, Johnnie!

A special thank-you goes to Bonnie Bailey for her skillful blogging and tweeting!

We are also indebted to every person who graciously granted interviews for this project, many of which were conducted by Nancy or Jennifer. Your contributions make this story work. Special thanks to:

John Alexander	Mary Malone
Benny Bills	George Offitt
Frank Brinkley	Betty Carol Purcell
Velma Brinkley	Jordan Scott
Buddy Bruce	Betty Sherlin Shaw
Julian Buford	Jacob Sherlin
William Buntin	Jim Sherlin
Susan Dalton	Andrew Turner
Sue Herron	Jerry Vradenburg
Joseph Malone	

Heartfelt thanks to the marvelous editorial and marketing teams at Revell—Andrea Doering, Vicki Crumpton, Amy Ballor, Twila Bennett, Claudia Marsh, and Brittany Miller—bless you for taking this story to the world!

Most of all, thanks to the One whose peace, forgiveness, and reconciliation we all need: the Lord Jesus Christ.

1

THE MOURNFUL WAIL of a distant train whistle pierced the afternoon calm as eleven-year-old Eddie Sherlin and his brother, Bo, two years his senior, struggled to pull a heavy 4′ × 4′ wooden pallet along the track.

"Hurry up, Eddie," Bo urged, "or we're gonna get caught."

The two brothers had just stolen the large pallet from the storage area of the local shirt factory. They were hauling it to their backyard, more than two miles away, where they planned to hoist it onto a pole and use it for a basketball backboard. The pallet wasn't worth much, and had they asked the manager if they could have it, he might have given it to them for nothing. But that would have meant going inside the factory and searching out the shift foreman—something Eddie was far too shy to do. Besides, the boys figured it would be easier to seek forgiveness than ask for permission, so they opted to steal the used wood.

Although the pallet was too heavy and bulky to carry, Eddie and Bo had managed to drag it to the railroad tracks, where once they hoisted it onto one of the rails, they could slide it along the shining track as fast as they could walk or run. As long as they kept at least part of the cumbersome pallet on the rails, it skimmed along. But when the pallet slipped off, the friction from the coal and dirt between the railroad ties quickly grabbed the pallet, jerking it out of the boys' grasp, slicing their fingers or stabbing their hands with rough splinters.

Another wail of the approaching train split the air. The sound was clearer and the train much closer.

"Hurry, Bo! It can't be far away," Eddie prodded his brother, just as the pallet skidded off the track again. Eddie reached down and grabbed the left-hand corners of the pallet, lifting and dragging it back onto the rail at the same time. The pallet rotated slightly, and for a moment Eddie thought it was going to twist his entire wrist with it, but quickly, Bo took the pressure off by grasping and lifting the right-hand corners. The boys precariously balanced the pallet on one rail as they yanked it farther up the track and toward a trestle, where the rails and railroad ties formed a bridge over the creek below. They could have pulled the pallet down into the thistles and briar patches on one side of the tracks, but that was sure to be painful, so with a hastily exchanged glance, both boys knew what they had to do.

They tugged and strained with all their might, hoping to get the pallet over the trestle before the train came. Nothing but empty space and air were on either side of the trestle. Nowhere to dive into the weeds should the train come around the turn before the boys got the pallet to the other side and back onto solid ground.

"Pull, Eddie!" Bo yelled, his eyes wide.

Eddie glanced back toward the warehouse. Around a large tree-covered curve, he saw what had prompted Bo's outburst. The cow-catcher of the locomotive had just rounded the bend and was fast approaching, less than a couple hundred yards away. Struggling to keep his feet from slipping between the railroad ties spaced about twelve inches apart, Eddie tugged on the pallet with every ounce of his strength. He cast a wary glance to the dirty creek waters swirling below the trestle.

"I'm pulling, Bo! We can do it. Only another ten or fifteen yards to go. Come on!" Eddie looked over his shoulder. The train was in full sight now. The engineer was leaning out of the side window. He sounded the shrill whistle, warning them to get off the tracks.

Eddie knew there was no stopping the locomotive. They were running out of time. The train had picked up a head of steam coming around the bend and down the straight stretch. Even if the engineer slammed on the brakes, the train would roll over him and Bo if they didn't clear the tracks.

The engineer laid on the train whistle, its steady blast urging the boys to run faster, to get off the trestle and away from the track.

The whistle screamed as the train bore down on Eddie and Bo. "Five yards, Bo!" Eddie yelled. "Just five more yards. Don't give up. Don't let go. We can do it!" Splinters from the rough-hewn wooden pallet pierced Eddie's fingertips as he clutched the wood, dragging it down the vibrating rails. They had hauled it this far; he wasn't going to let it go now.

"Almost there!" Bo grunted, his words barely audible over the roaring locomotive. "Roll to the right!" he called to his younger brother.

With one foot still on the trestle and one off, Eddie gripped the pallet and lunged.

Bo gave a mighty heave of the pallet, lifting it off the track and toppling it in Eddie's direction as both boys dove for the weeds and rolled down the embankment just as the train's cowcatcher cleared the trestle, thundering past them. The long line of boxcars clacked along the tracks as Eddie and Bo scrambled to their feet and began tugging thistles off their clothing.

"Whew! That was close. You okay?" Bo said.

"I think so." Eddie studied his bloody fingertips. "My set shot's gonna be a little rough for a week or so, but I'll live. How's the backboard?"

Bo trudged up the embankment where the pallet was lying on the ground, just clear of the tracks. "Looks like it's still in one piece. C'mon. Let's get it home."

"Help me get it back on the track," Eddie said, "and we can slide this thing all the way to the house."

"Yeah, I don't think another train will be coming through for a little while."

The boys lugged the pallet back onto the rail and resumed dragging it toward their home.

The train tracks stretched all the way through the boys' hometown of Gallatin, Tennessee, passing within twenty feet of the Sherlin family's backyard, behind their two-bedroom home at 225 Morrison Street. Eddie and Bo, along with their two younger sisters, Delilah and Debbie, heard trains rattling down the tracks so often, even at night, that they rarely paid them much attention. Eddie loved hearing the trains at night. In fact, the clacking sound of a train rolling past his bedroom was a soothing balm, a reminder that all was well with the world, even when things weren't so good at home, which they often weren't.

Just short of their house, Eddie and Bo lugged the pallet off the railroad track and over an embankment. The boys picked it up and slowly walked it through the brush and trees behind the Sherlin home, inching their way along, shifting their grips every thirty seconds so the splinters wouldn't catch in their hands. They finally dragged the pallet to a light pole their dad had installed near the garage at the end of the gravel driveway. That pole was going to be the brace for the Sherlin boys' new backboard.

Bo found a ladder in the garage, and Eddie grabbed a hammer and some eight-penny nails from the toolshed. "Do you think these nails will hold it up?" Eddie asked. "That pallet is pretty heavy."

Bo eyed the nails skeptically. "I guess we'll find out. Is that all you can find?"

"These are the biggest nails Dad has. There are a few spikes in there too. They're a little longer, but we only have a couple of them."

"Better grab those too," Bo said. "We'll probably need them. This backboard is going to take a beating, so we need something strong to hold it up there on the pole."

The boys slid the heavy pallet up the pole, carefully measuring so that the spot on the wood where they planned to attach the basketball rim would be ten feet off the ground. They secured the backboard to a makeshift crossbar and then attached the whole thing to the light pole. They nailed it from every angle, making sure the backboard wouldn't fall down.

When the pallet seemed strong enough, Eddie scampered down the ladder and grabbed the basketball rim. "Now we need to make sure this is level with the ground."

"I know, Eddie. You think I'm a dummy? It needs to be ten feet high and parallel to the ground. No problem. Now, hand me the bolts so I can attach the back of the rim. You hang on to the net until I make sure the goal is strong."

Bo drilled three holes in the pallet and tightly fastened the base of the rim to the wood with strong bolts. "This baby ain't goin' nowhere." He flashed a grin at his younger brother. "Toss that net up here, Eddie."

As though unwrapping a priceless gift, Eddie slowly removed the nylon net from the plastic package. They had never owned a net for their basketball hoop, so it was a precious commodity. He and Bo had been saving their lunch money for several months so they could purchase the new net. The old rope nets never lasted long in the outdoor elements, and this new nylon net was supposed to last until the boys graduated from high school. Eddie passed the net up the ladder to Bo, who carefully attached each loop under the corresponding metal hook.

"How's that, little brother?" he called down to Eddie.

Eddie looked up. He'd never seen anything so beautiful as that white net hanging from the rim. "It's perfect, Bo. Come on down. Let's give this baby a try!"

Bo replaced the ladder in the garage as Eddie bounced the ball on the grass in front of the backboard. The grass deadened the bounce, but Eddie didn't mind. He knew it wouldn't take long before they'd wear the grass down to the dirt and be playing on hardpacked Tennessee clay. He dropped back fifteen feet or so and lofted a shot into the air.

Swish! Eddie fell in love with the sound of the ball slashing through the nylon net. It was the first of thousands of shots Eddie would fire through the net over the next few years.

"Feed me," Bo called as he ran out of the garage toward the goal. Eddie retrieved his rebound and tossed the ball rim high. Bo leaped into the air and tipped it into the basket. Bo was an incredible athlete. A great baseball player and a budding star in football, basketball, track—any sport he put his mind to, and Eddie idolized him. He hoped that someday he'd be half the athlete his big brother was.

Eddie was already well on his way to surpassing Bo. Eddie could run faster, and his natural physical abilities went far beyond Bo's, but Bo was the big brother—the standard against which Eddie measured himself.

Bo grabbed the ball before it hit the ground and fired it back to Eddie. The younger Sherlin dropped back another five feet and effortlessly lobbed a set shot from twenty feet out. *Swish!*

"Good shot, Eddie. You keep working at this thing, and you just might make a good ballplayer one of these days." Bo smiled as Eddie fired the ball back at his brother.

"Come on, superstar. Let's see *you* hit a twenty-footer," Eddie challenged.

Bo slid smoothly to the exact spot where Eddie had shot from, bounced the ball once, and put it in the air, banking it high off the backboard and into the net.

"Do you mean like that?" he asked good-naturedly.

"Yeah, somethin' like that. Too bad you needed some help from the backboard, but I'll give it to you."

The brothers laughed and kept pouring in shots from all over their makeshift court. Not yet in his teens, Eddie Sherlin was already one of the best basketball players in Gallatin, Tennessee.

2

ON THE "COLORED" SIDE OF TOWN, just a few hundred yards away from the Sherlin home, eleven-year-old Bill Ligon and his brother, Tyree, three years younger, climbed through some bushes leading to the railroad tracks. Along with two other black boys, Leslie Gurley and Walter Lee, the Ligon brothers snuck across the tracks and into the "white" side of Gallatin.

Bill reached down and felt the tracks. They were still warm from the last passing train. "Come on, let's hurry before another train comes." He waved his arm, urging the boys to follow him.

"Grandpa Ackerson is never home during the afternoons," Bill said, stepping across the first rail and walking on a railroad tie toward the parallel rail. "And he has a great rope swing that stretches all the way over the pond in his backyard. You guys are gonna love it!"

"How did you find out about the swing, Bill?" Walter asked, pushing some of the thick bushes aside so he could slip through without getting scratched.

"I've seen it!" Bill answered. "My mom worked over here one day last summer, and I helped her carry in some food trays. I think the old man put in the swing so his grandchildren can use it when they come to visit. I've seen them swimming in the pond behind the house. They hold on to the rope and swing all the way out over the pond and then drop right into the water. It's the best ride in town!"

"But Old Man Ackerson is *white*." Leslie stopped at the first rail, clearly reluctant to cross the tracks. "We can't swim in his pond. If he catches us, he might just shoot us or string us up on that rope!"

"Oh, don't be silly, Leslie." Bill tried to reassure his friend, even though he knew Leslie was right. "There hasn't been a lynching in Gallatin for at least"—he paused and raised his eyes skyward, as though trying to remember—"oh, I'd say at least a couple of years."

"A couple of years!" the other boys shrieked, their eyes wide as they stopped in their tracks.

Bill smiled broadly. He loved to tease, and the boys were so gullible. "I'm just kiddin' ya. They haven't lynched a colored around here for a long time."

Leslie eyed his friend, seemingly unconvinced. "If white folks don't allow us in their park, and they don't let us in the town swimming pool, Old Man Ackerson sure ain't gonna be happy if he comes home and finds four coloreds in his pond."

"Yeah, Bill," Tyree said. "What if he shows up? What'll we do then?"

"Then we hightail it outta there. That's what we'll do."

"Quit being a bunch of sissies," Walter said to Tyree and Leslie. "I can't wait to ride that swinging rope. Come on, Bill. Even if these guys don't want to go, I sure do."

Tyree stroked his chin. "I don't know. Mom's not gonna like it."

Bill crossed his arms. "Who's gonna tell her?" He paused a few seconds. "Not me."

"Me either!" Walter added.

The boys turned and looked at Leslie.

"Hey, I ain't no tattletale." Leslie shoved his fists into his pockets. "Don't be lookin' at me like that." He straightened. With a burst of apparent courage, he shouted, "Let's go ride that swing!"

"Oookay," Tyree said, as he fell in step with the other boys. "But somethin' tells me this ain't gonna turn out good."

16

The boys crossed the tracks and hurried to the edge of town, trying to be as inconspicuous as four colored boys could be while traipsing through a white section of Gallatin. Luckily, they reached the Ackerson property without incident. A stone slave wall, a three-foot-high gray stone fence built by Negro slaves more than a hundred years earlier, surrounded the large field behind the house. Between the wall and the house was a beautiful tree-lined pond. And hanging from one of the largest trees—the infamous rope swing.

The boys slipped up to the wall and crouched behind it. "Okay, I'll go first," Bill whispered. "Then you guys come behind me. Tyree, you keep watch, and if you see anyone coming, whistle fast so we can hit the dirt."

"Okay, Bill, but—"

"No buts about it. Just keep your eyes open. Once Walter and Leslie are over the wall, you come on in too." Bill didn't wait for any more protests from his brother. He put his right foot on one of the stones and hopped on top of the wall. For a moment he stood there, his arms stretched out like Superman ready to fly. "Here goes nuthin' now." He looked over his shoulder at the other boys as he jumped off the wall and into Old Man Ackerson's field. Walter and Leslie quickly followed. Bill watched as Tyree took one last nervous look around and then joined the other boys.

For a few seconds, they knelt on the ground next to the wall, just to be certain that the old man wasn't home.

"Okay, all clear," Bill said. "Let's go!"

The boys raced across the field to the pond. Bill was the first to grab the rope and swing out over the pond and back. The large tree limb barely budged at Bill's slim body weight. One by one, the boys all gave the rope a try, out and back, out and back.

"Hey, did any of you guys wear a swimming suit?" Bill asked.

"Naw, no way I could put on a bathing suit at home," Walter said. "Not without my mom knowin' that somethin' was up."

"Not me," Leslie said.

"Yeah, me neither," Bill concurred. "But that water looks mighty inviting, you follow me?"

Walter smiled broadly and nodded. "I sure do!" Without another word, both he and Bill began unbuckling their belts. They peeled off their pants and shirts and stripped down to their underwear.

"Now we're really gonna have some fun!" Bill called.

"Are you guys crazy?" Leslie yelled.

Too late. Bill was already swinging on the rope like Tarzan, taking a long ride forward, then back, and then swinging high over the pond again. When he was about six feet above the pond, Bill let go of the rope and plunged into the water. For a second or two, he remained under the dark water. Then his head popped out with a big splash. "Whooweee! That is fantastic!"

"I'm next," Walter yelled. He scrambled up and grabbed the rope, swinging even higher than Bill had. Walter, with a loud "whoop!" let go of the rope and dropped into the water beside Bill. Leslie and Tyree didn't waste any time. They were out of their clothes in a flash, vying to see who could get to the rope first.

For the next half hour, the boys laughed and squealed as they took turns swinging out over the pond before plunging into the cool water. Tyree even tried some acrobatic moves on a couple of his jumps. They were having so much fun they never gave Old Man Ackerson a thought. They didn't notice the old Chevy pickup pull in beside the house. Nor did they see the old man dressed in coveralls and a farm hat ease out of the truck and grab a broom. In fact, they didn't pay a lick of attention until they heard the barking of two large German shepherds as they shot out of the truck bed, bound for the boys in the pond.

The dogs raced down the field with Old Man Ackerson hobbling behind them as fast as he could, looking like Mr. McGregor in *The Tale of Peter Rabbit*, and wielding the broom high in the air as he ran. "Hey, you . . . ! Get out of my pond right this minute!"

The dogs reached the pond first, growling and barking at the boys from the water's edge.

"Uh-oh!" Walter said.

"We're in trouble now!" Leslie called to his cohorts.

"I told you this was a bad idea," Tyree whined.

Bill quickly assessed the situation. "Run for the wall!" He swam in the opposite direction of the dogs and attempted to scramble up the back edge of the pond, but his foot slipped, and he slid back into the water. Meanwhile, the other boys swam in three directions, hoping the dogs couldn't cover the ground between them. But they too discovered that the sides of the pond were much more slippery than the front. And the dogs were quicker than they figured. The old man threatening them with the broom was getting closer by the second.

One by one, the boys pulled themselves out of the water, but then they realized they had another problem. "We gotta get our clothes!" Bill shouted from the back side of the pond.

Leslie ran to the right, with a German shepherd nipping at him. Walter scrambled in the opposite direction with the other dog barking and chasing after him. Tyree started to grab their clothes, but then Old Man Ackerson reached the pond and began swatting Tyree with the broom. Still in their wet underwear, the boys ran first in one direction, then another, with the dogs right behind them and the old man swatting at each boy as he passed by.

Round and round the pond they went, looking like a three-ring circus, with the boys screaming for dear life, Old Man Ackerson hollering obscenities, and the dogs barking incessantly. At last, Bill eluded the dogs long enough to swoop in close, under the big tree, where the clothes were lying on the ground. He gathered an armful of shirts and pants and sneakers and hustled toward the wall. The other boys raced behind him. Still barefoot and wearing nothing but his underwear, Bill vaulted over the wall. Tyree tumbled over behind him. With his underwear torn and soiled, Walter followed. Leslie grazed his knee on the stone wall as he clambered over. Scared and scraped but otherwise unharmed, the boys escaped.

"And don't you ever come back! Ya hear?" Old Man Ackerson yelled as they sat on the ground a safe distance away and threw on their clothes and slipped on their shoes.

Leslie frantically searched for one of his sneakers. "My shoe's missing!"

Bill jumped up. "Come on, hurry! Leave it! We gotta get outta here before he calls the cops."

The boys ran for the tracks, with Leslie running barefoot. They crossed the hot tracks just as they heard the distant sound of the train whistle. They squeezed back through the bushes, the thicket scratching their arms, but they didn't care. They were just glad to be back safe and sound—on the colored side of town.

3

GALLATIN, TENNESSEE—a town of less than thirty thousand residents today and half that number in the 1960s—is located twenty-five miles north of Nashville. Situated along the banks of the meandering Cumberland River, Gallatin has a Mayberry-like look and feel to it. It was founded in 1802 as an industrial town with both railroad and river access, and by the mid-1960s many of the local blue-collar workers were employed in the shirt or shoe factories.

Most of the population was white. Negroes comprised less than 10 percent of Gallatin's population; therefore, few people in town talked much about the racial tension seething in the South in places such as Montgomery, Selma, Birmingham, and, of course, Memphis. Quite the opposite seemed to be the norm. Ask any of the fellas congregating in downtown Gallatin at the whites-only pool hall, and one of them would quickly tell you, "We don't have any problems with coloreds around here. We all get along just fine. Coloreds know their place."

And they did.

The lines were clearly delineated, drawn on the basis of skin color. Gallatin had white stores—stores in which Caucasians were welcome and African Americans were not, although nobody used those terms. They were simply "white folks" or "coloreds." On one side of Main Street stood white stores; on the other side, colored stores, where blacks could shop. Whites could shop at the colored stores if they wanted to, but they rarely did. The town had a white park and a black park in which kids could play. The black children were not permitted to play in the park for white kids—ever.

Like most towns in the Southern United States during the mid-1960s, Gallatin maintained elements of segregation long after the dark-robed judges in Washington, DC, ruled otherwise. Gallatin still had separate water fountains for whites and coloreds. It wasn't unusual to see a sign prominently posted above one of the fountains: WHITE ONLY. Gallatin also had segregated swimming pools. Whites refused to get into the water if a black person had somehow been invited to swim in the white pool. And a young black man could find himself in jail, beaten or, in years past, hanging from a rope if he dared stare at a white woman in a bathing suit.

Blacks purposely avoided walking down the sidewalk in the direction of whites. An unspoken rule demanded that if a white person or a black person inadvertently approached someone of the other race, somebody must veer off in another direction. Usually that somebody was the black person. Most colored people avoided even stepping into certain sections of Gallatin.

Instead, they stayed in their familiar neighborhoods, two or three streets off Main Street where the black businesses were located. There they could relax at Joey's Place, the pool hall for blacks.

The barbershop for blacks was also downtown, in addition to a shoe-shine business up the street and the dry cleaners. Clothing worn by black people was never permitted to mingle with clothing worn by white folks. The black people also had their own dance hall in that part of town. A grocery store stood nearby, where only coloreds shopped.

———————————

Both Eddie Sherlin and Bill Ligon attended Sumner County schools, of which Gallatin schools were a part. By the early 1960s, the county had seven public high schools, six of which were predominantly attended by white students, and one school—only one—Union, a county-wide school, was designated as a "colored" school. Students walked great distances to get there; others rode a school bus for more than an hour each way.

The US Supreme Court's *Brown v. Board of Education* landmark decision in 1954 declaring that schools should be fully integrated swept through the South like a raging tornado, often leaving a path of emotional turmoil and destruction. In many Southern cities, the white power base balked. "Over my dead body will I let a colored boy in the same classroom as my daughter." Many of the whites opposed to integration simply didn't want change. Others were deadly serious in their resistance. The long-entrenched attitude of community leaders was "Blood will flow in the streets first." And in many Southern towns and cities such as Birmingham, Montgomery, and even "sophisticated" Atlanta, it did.

In Tennessee, school boards, as well as teachers, were reluctant to give up racial segregation in the classrooms. The Sumner County school district dragged its feet; it was one of the last in the South to open its doors to students of all races.

"We're doin' just fine. Why do we want to mess with a system that is working?" was a question posed mostly by whites but also frequently voiced by blacks who were willing to maintain the status quo. Many of Gallatin's Negro population were reluctant to speak out about racial issues.

White folks were equally intimidated. White people who spoke in favor of integration would quickly be tagged with a pejorative, tarnishing their reputations in town and making them the targets of horrendous verbal abuse. Such a label had an impact on a person's ability to get a job, open or maintain a business, and, in some instances, it could be life-threatening.

This was the racially charged environment in which Eddie Sherlin and Bill Ligon lived the first eleven years of their lives.

Few people thought it would ever change.

4

THE BLOND-HAIRED, BLUE-EYED, eleven-year-old Eddie Sherlin lay asleep in his bed. Although he maintained a quiet and serene exterior, the dreams playing in his head were vibrantly active. His eyelids moved slightly as the sight and sound of another twenty-five-footer from well above the key swished through the net. Eddie Sherlin lived to play basketball. He not only ate and drank basketball during his waking hours, but he also lived it in his sleep. Almost every night, all night long, Eddie played basketball in his mind, planning his moves against the opposition, seeing himself executing perfectly the difficult corner shot, feeling the defensive guard lose his balance as Eddie gave a slight head fake to the left and then drove the lane for an easy layup. Eddie never worried about what the other players were doing. Instead, he let the defense react to him.

As the sun peeked through Eddie's bedroom curtains, the young boy's eyelids fluttered. He rubbed his eyes with his fingertips and stretched, bumping his brother, Bo, who was still sound asleep in their shared bed. Across the room in bunk beds, Eddie's two younger sisters, Delilah and Debbie, nine and seven, respectively, also slept soundly.

Eddie bounded to his feet, still wearing the basketball shorts in which he fell asleep late the previous evening. He quietly moved around the room, locating his clothes without waking his slumbering siblings. He found his favorite worn-out Converse sneakers, donned some white athletic socks, and changed into a fresh, clean shirt. He picked up his dirty shirt from the floor and wadded it into a sphere. In perfect form he shot the balled-up clothing into the clothes hamper. *Swish!*

Eddie slipped out of the bedroom and went out to the side of the house to shoot some hoops before breakfast. The makeshift banking board hanging from the post out back served Eddie well. Where grass had once grown, the ground in front of the basket was now well worn, pounded into a firm surface from Eddie's feet and the myriad bounces of a basketball.

Before long, Eddie had worked up a sweat, shooting baskets from every angle on the "court," careful to avoid getting too near the bushes inhabited by unfriendly red wasps. Eddie had received more than a few nasty bee stings when his rebounds veered too close to those vicious bees.

He continued shooting as the world around him came to life with the hum of cars carrying adults to work, the occasional roar of a school bus barreling down the street, and, of course, the consistently on-time clickety-clack of the morning freight train churning past the backyard.

Concentrating on his outside set shots, Eddie paid no attention to the buzz of activity in the neighborhood. His mind was focused on the rim. Nevertheless, he knew the rest of the family was getting up and around because he could hear the radio playing in the kitchen.

"It's 8 a.m. here on WHIN radio in Gallatin," the morning show announcer droned. "The weather today . . ."

Eddie tuned out the man's voice and dribbled toward the basket, whirling around on the clay as though an invisible man stood in front of him attempting to block his shot. Bouncing the ball off the

26

clay surface had caused his fingertips to develop an almost innate sense for where the ball was. He didn't have to see it; he could *feel* it.

"Ed-die!" his mom called as she peeked her head out the door. "Breakfast is ready. Hurry up now, or you will be late for school."

"Be right there, Mom." Eddie picked up the ball and slid over to the periphery of the lot, dangerously close to the bees' nests. He lofted a fifteen-footer, with a perfect arc, toward the rim. The ball barely touched the net as it slipped through. Eddie jogged under the rim and caught the ball before it hit the ground. He moved to the opposite corner and fired in another perfect fifteen-footer. Now totally disregarding his mom's call, Eddie bounded from one corner shot to another.

In the kitchen, thirty-seven-year-old Betty Sherlin, dressed in a raggedy blue bathrobe, hummed a gospel song as she stirred a pot of oatmeal large enough to satisfy the appetites of her growing kids. On the Sherlins' tight budget, oatmeal and a few slices of toast were the only breakfast foods they could afford.

Delilah and Debbie, still rubbing sleep from their eyes, slipped into the tiny kitchen and climbed onto their usual chairs at the Formica and chrome kitchen table.

"Morning, Mama," Delilah said.

Despite her unusual name, Delilah was one of the most delightful children any parent could imagine—sweet, innocent, always upbeat and positive no matter what the circumstances, with a smile that lit up every room she entered.

Debbie was also a sweetheart, but she often deferred to Delilah and let her lead the way.

Betty looked up briefly from the pot of oatmeal. "Good morning, baby. Sit up straight at the table now. You too, Debbie. I'll have your breakfast in a minute." She glanced out the window just as Bo bounded into the kitchen, ready for school with his hair neatly combed. "Bo, tell your brother to get in here. Now."

"Good morning, Mom," Bo replied, stepping over to the door. "Eddie! Give it a break. It's oatmeal time."

Eddie waved his hand high in the air to let Bo know he had heard him. He took one last long shot. The ball swished through the net. Eddie retrieved it and dribbled to the porch. Because he couldn't resist, he bounced it one more time before tucking it under his arm and entering the kitchen.

"Wash your hands, Eddie," his mother shot at him without turning away from the stove. "And please put down that ball!"

"Yes, ma'am," Eddie responded. He put the ball under his chair at the kitchen table and strode over to the sink, where he ran some water over his hands and then dried them on his shirt. He sat down at his usual place at the table as Betty evenly distributed the hot oatmeal into four bowls, adding a bit extra to the one in front of Bo, her rapidly growing teenager.

"Say the blessing," Jim Sherlin said, as he stepped into the kitchen and went straight to the coffeepot, while still fumbling with a necktie that didn't want to cooperate with his stark, dark suit.

"Good morning, Daddy," Delilah and Debbie chorused.

"Mornin', Dad," Eddie said.

"Hey, Dad," Bo added.

"I'll pray!" Debbie offered. "Dear Lord, please bless this food to our bodies. Amen!"

"Amen," the other family members echoed.

"Bo, what does it mean to bless the food to our bodies?" Debbie asked.

Bo scowled at the usual mess of oatmeal in his bowl. "I'm not sure that even God can bless this stuff," he said just above a whisper.

Still in "shooting mode," Eddie picked up a ball of used rolled-up duct tape and tossed it into a cardboard cutout of a basketball rim hanging on the kitchen door. Eddie shot anything and everything whenever he could, and his parents and siblings had long ago stopped paying attention. As long as he didn't shoot in the direction of the kitchen table, Betty simply went about her business of getting breakfast for her family.

Jim poured himself a cup of coffee and took a sip as he casually watched Eddie sink another shot. An avid baseball fan, Jim had coached Eddie early on by standing on one side of the house and tossing a baseball over the roof, forcing his son to quickly spot the ball and move into position to make a catch. Eddie rarely missed. He was a standout player in Little League, and if Jim could work with him, Eddie probably had a great future as a second baseman.

Bo was an excellent baseball player too. Named James H. Sherlin Jr. at birth, Bo was just a toddler when Jim saw potential in his son and began calling his namesake "Bo," after baseball star Bobo Newsome. The nickname stuck. Jim Sr. dreamed of helping his boys develop their athletic abilities. But these days, Jim was far too busy trying to make a living, eking out barely enough income to buy food and clothes for the kids. He didn't have time to play catch with Eddie or Bo.

Jim and the family had moved to the Nashville area from Cleveland, Tennessee, an industrial town near Chattanooga. At first they stayed with relatives who lived so far out in the country they had no indoor bathroom, and four or five of the children all slept in the same bed. Then they found a small home in the government-funded projects in East Nashville. Jim found work with a local casket company, and for years his claim to fame was that he had hand-built the casket in which Elvis Presley's mother was buried. Although it made for an interesting line on his résumé, Jim's casket-making provided insufficient income for his growing family.

Before long, they moved to Gallatin, where Jim took a job with an insurance company collecting the monthly fees from policyholders. His work took him all over town (the poor, colored sections as well as the affluent, white sections), throughout the county, and often around the state, causing him to sometimes be away from home for days at a time. Although Jim was a good man with godly parents and devoutly Christian extended family members, his faith had been sorely tried as he struggled to make life work in Gallatin.

He had come close to giving up or giving in to various temptations he'd met along his insurance route, but he was hanging on, hoping against hope that something good would happen soon—something that could turn things around for him and his family. Until then, he resigned himself to working the insurance collection route.

Jim finished his coffee and planted a cursory kiss on Betty's forehead as he headed toward the door. "I'll probably be late tonight."

"So what's new about that?" Betty replied.

Jim stopped and turned to her. "Just letting you know not to hold dinner for me."

"No danger of that," his wife said.

"I'll see y'all tomorrow," he said to the kids around the table.

"'Bye, Daddy!" Delilah called after him.

Betty reached for the radio dial, found a music station playing upbeat music, and turned up the volume. She busied herself cleaning the pot in which she had cooked the oatmeal. She had calls to make as well. She worked as a sales representative for World Book Encyclopedia, and as soon as the kids got off to school, she planned to make her rounds, offering the expensive set of books to any parents willing to invest in their children's future. Betty didn't make a lot of money from selling encyclopedias, but in addition to getting her out of the house, the commission-based sales job provided her with enough cash to purchase the few "luxuries" her family possessed, including Eddie's basketball shoes and Bo's baseball cleats and uniforms.

"Let's get this day hoppin' with a blast from the past," the bombastic local radio deejay thundered. "Sponsored by Randy's Records right here in Gallatin, here's Pat Boone on Dot Records with a remake of Little Richard's hit 'Tutti Frutti.'"

The song's introduction was already playing in the background, growing louder under the deejay's ebullient banter. The deejay's voice disappeared and the music filled the kitchen as the Sherlin kids hurriedly finished their oatmeal.

Bo caught Eddie's eye and gave him an inquisitive look, as though asking, "Are you going to school today?" Bo knew Eddie always went out the door with his siblings, but if their mom and dad had already left for work, he sometimes skipped school to stay home and shoot baskets in the backyard.

Eddie nodded toward their mother and frowned. Betty was running behind schedule this morning, so it would be more difficult for Eddie to play hooky today.

"Get dressed quickly, girls," Betty instructed. "Bo, wait for your sisters. Eddie, please put that ball down! You are in the house, young man."

Eddie quickly put down the ball he had picked up only seconds earlier. "Yes, ma'am." He hurried to his bedroom and changed into his school clothes. The girls also hurried off to change out of their pajamas and into their school clothes.

"Aw, Mom," Bo whined, slamming his school books on the kitchen table. "Why do I have to be the one to walk the girls to school? Eddie can do it. Nobody else walks their kid sisters to school. It's embarrassing."

Betty bristled. "Bo Sherlin, don't you give me no back talk. I said you wait for your sisters, and I mean it. Don't you go running off on them, either. Especially when you go walkin' near the coloreds. I don't want to hear that you took off and left them for some colored boy to grab."

"Oh, Mom. Ain't nobody gonna grab Delilah or Debbie."

"I'll be the judge of that. You just listen to what I say, young man. And you stay near to your kin."

Bo recognized the fire in his mother's eyes and, despite the growing rebellious streak running through him, knew better than to mess with Betty Sherlin when she was mad.

"Aw, okay, Mom. I'll stick with them all the way to school."

"That's more like it." Betty placed a pot in the cupboard a little more loudly than necessary, as though to emphasize her point.

Bo hustled the girls out the door and escorted them up the road toward school, right through "black town." Eddie followed closely behind, dribbling the basketball in a figure eight pattern and pausing every time he spotted a garbage can or anything that looked like a rim along the way, pretending to shoot. Then it was back to the figure eight, dribbling the basketball over the gravel on the side of the road, his fingertips adeptly controlling the ball regardless of the rough terrain on which he bounced it.

At the corner crosswalk, Bo stretched out his arms, stopping the procession while a dilapidated pickup truck huffed by. The tobacco farmer driving the truck nodded at Bo in a cordial but meaningless greeting. Everyone in Gallatin said hello or acknowledged one another, especially if they had the same skin color.

With his arms still extended, Bo looked to his left, then to his right. Meanwhile, Eddie dribbled incessantly behind his sisters and brother while standing on the corner waiting to cross. A 1953, beat-up Cadillac driven by a black man roared down the street. Bo shook his head. It was obvious that the old Caddie's mufflers must have worn out a long time ago, because the enormous car sounded like a Harley-Davidson motorcycle. The driver had lowered the windows and the radio blared, ironically playing the original version of "Tutti Frutti" recorded by Little Richard.

Instinctively, Bo backed up slightly as the car slowed to turn the corner in front of him. The black man behind the wheel looked at Bo then quickly looked away while Bo glared at him. Bo eyed the car suspiciously as the driver gunned the engine before driving up the street.

"Nice car, eh?" Eddie said, dribbling up behind Bo.

Bo spun around and gave Eddie a dirty look. The Sherlins lived only one street away from the coloreds, so it was not unusual for them to be there. Nevertheless, Eddie always grew anxious when he and his siblings were the only white faces to be seen anywhere in the neighborhood. Eddie's fear motivated him to run from one place to another. He didn't think so much about color as he ran; his fear stemmed from early childhood, when his family first moved to Nashville and he had been picked on by one of the other white boys who, like Eddie and his family, lived in government housing. Nobody else was aware of Eddie's fear, but it was always there, just below the surface in his heart and his mind.

"Come on, Debbie." Eddie put one hand on his sister's shoulder and dribbled the basketball across the street with his other hand. He gently nudged Debbie forward as Bo took Delilah's hand and pulled her safely into the white side of town.

5

EDDIE SQUIRMED IN HIS SEAT in the middle of his all-white class of eleven- and twelve-year-olds at Guild School, part of the Gallatin elementary school system. Mrs. Lee, his strict but wonderfully kind teacher droned on, making some point about the American Revolution. Eddie had tuned out at least fifteen minutes before Washington crossed the Delaware. His focus was on a gray trash can located in the front corner of the classroom. Holding his hands behind his history book so his teacher couldn't see them, Eddie caressed the invisible basketball in his palm. Unlike many coaches and players who insisted on keeping the basketball in their fingertips, Eddie was convinced he could get a much better sense of touch by cradling the ball in his hand. He subtly shifted his head, as though ducking a defender. Then when the teacher's back was turned, Eddie pump faked and then shot his imaginary basketball toward the trash can.

Swish! In his mind, he heard the glorious sound of the ball going through the net.

Eddie's teacher moved slightly to the left. He leaned far out of his seat to the right, trying to maintain eye contact with the trash can in the corner. The teacher was writing on the blackboard, her body blocking Eddie's view of the metal basket. Eddie leaned even farther out of his seat, so far that the wooden desk and chair tipped and came off the floor several inches. Eddie quickly moved his body to the left in an attempt to regain his balance. Too late. The desk and chair slammed back down, hitting the hardwood flooring with a loud thud.

Mrs. Lee whirled around and looked in the direction of the noise, just in time to see Eddie retrieving his history book from the floor.

"Eddie, are you all right?"

"Yes, ma'am. I was just leaning over too far," he said truthfully, careful not to mention that his teacher had been blocking his shots.

"Well, good posture is important, Eddie. Sit up straight, please. Class, backs pressed up against the back of your chair, feet on the floor."

"Yes, ma'am," Eddie said quietly.

"Now, where was I?" Mrs. Lee said to herself more than to the students. "Oh, yes, Valley Forge." Mrs. Lee stepped to the middle of the blackboard and picked up a piece of chalk, tossing it up and down in her hand, momentarily capturing Eddie's attention. "Washington's troops were emaciated and freezing," she began, turning toward the board. "And they were surrounded by the enemy." She drew a large circle on the board.

Eddie smiled. He'd found another rim. He was back in his game.

School was not Eddie's forte. He didn't lack intelligence and probably could have made better grades had he applied himself, but he didn't. In fact, if it weren't for the physical education classes, Eddie might have skipped more school than he did.

The dismissal bell had barely rung before Bo and Eddie were on their way to the whites-only park, with their sisters tagging along. There was no reason to go home yet, since both of their parents were working, so the park became the Sherlins' after-school day care center. Delilah and Debbie ran to the teeter-totters, while Bo and Eddie opened the gate to the basketball court.

Before they even stepped through the gate, Bo and Eddie heard the pounding of tennis shoes on the asphalt court. Some older white boys were playing a game of four-on-four on half of the court, and another group of high school–aged boys were playing three-on-three on the other side. Bo stopped on the sidelines, hoping that someone in either game might want to come out for a rest. Eddie practiced his dribbling, bouncing the ball back and forth between his legs, never losing control.

Eddie studied the much taller and muscular players while he continued dribbling. He didn't need anyone to teach him how to shoot—he was a natural—but he enjoyed trying some of the shots he saw the older boys executing. Whatever he saw them do, he attempted, mimicking their moves on the court and even shooting his basketball at an imaginary basket on the side of the asphalt. One of the high school guys reminded Eddie of his uncle Bob, known around Cleveland as "Boog" Sherlin.

Uncle Bob was Eddie's first role model when it came to sports. He had been a star basketball player for Cleveland's Bradley Central High School, going on to excel at Lee University. Another standout on that Bradley Central team was Steve Sloan, a Christian who later became Eddie's hero.

In 1960, Boog Sherlin and Steve Sloan played on Bradley Central's team for the state championship at Vanderbilt University's Memorial Gymnasium. Eddie and his dad had traveled several hours by car from Cleveland to Nashville to attend that game. From the moment Eddie stepped inside the cavernous gymnasium—built in 1952 to accommodate eight thousand fans and eventually expanded to seat more than fourteen thousand people—he was hooked. The smell of popcorn wafting through the gym, the cheerleaders bouncing in vivacious cheers, the players warming up under the weird glow of the halogen overhead lights—all of the sights and sounds coalesced to captivate Eddie. *This is what I want to do*, he thought.

"Hey, Eddie." Bo's voice brought Eddie back to real life in Gallatin. "Let's go. Time to go home." Bo was already moving toward the park exit, along with Delilah, Debbie, and several of Bo's pals.

"I'll be right behind you, Bo," Eddie called over his shoulder. He watched the action on the court for another few seconds before reluctantly turning away. When the group reached the street separating the white and colored sections of town, Bo stretched out his arms, stopping them just as he had done earlier that morning. The quickest way to get home was crossing through the black neighborhood, but Bo still wanted to step cautiously. He looked in every direction.

"Hold on," he said. His friends must have noticed the pensive tone in his voice.

"What's up?" one asked.

Bo nodded down the street toward four black teenagers in the distance.

"I thought they crossed over by the railroad tracks on Blythe Street," another friend said.

"Not all of 'em." Bo's eyes never left the colored teens. "Wait just a minute." He stared down the street, making sure they were not moving to a position in which his sisters, his friends, Eddie, or he might have to confront them. He waited until they crossed the street and appeared to be going in the opposite direction. "Okay," Bo said. "Go. Go now!"

The group raced across the street and into the black neighborhood, glancing around constantly as they hurried toward Morrison Street. When they crossed over Morrison Street without confronting any black people, everyone breathed a little easier. The girls were giggling and Bo and his buddies were joking, making sarcastic comments to one another. Nobody noticed that Eddie was not with them.

Eddie, while hurrying through the black section of town near the corner of South Boyers Street and East Bledsoe, became distracted by the familiar sound of a dribbling basketball. Then he heard the muffled clunk of a ball bouncing off a backboard. He stopped to listen as Bo and the rest of the group continued down the street. There it was again—the unmistakable thump of a basketball banking off the backboard and through the rim.

Curious, Eddie crept behind some bushes and peeked through to see what was going on. Fear leapt into his mind. *Should I get out of here before I get in trouble?* Eddie heard some kids' voices, and he was sure they were playing basketball. It was too tempting to pass by. *Sure, I'm afraid, but some things are worth the risk. Sometimes a boy has to face his fears head-on.*

Eddie tucked his basketball under his arm and peeked around the corner of the hedge. Through the bush, he spotted some black legs and arms moving in an open space. Like a Vietnam commando, Eddie moved stealthily forward and hid himself behind a large tree on the edge of the corner lot. Holding on to the tree with his suddenly very white hands, Eddie stretched his neck to the right so he could see. Sure enough, there they were—six colored boys that Eddie guessed to be around his age were playing basketball on a hardpacked dirt court. The goal was attached to a lopsided, partial sheet of plywood nailed to a pole, similar to the backboard Eddie and Bo had erected behind their house. This rim, however, was rusty and didn't have a net.

A good-looking, skinny boy seemed to be the leader, chiding his fellow players when they missed a shot or slapping his teammate on the back in the three-on-three competition. Loquacious to the point of being obnoxious, the skinny kid kept up a constant play-by-play commentary, as though he were describing the action for a radio audience.

"Ligon has the ball on the right side of the court," the talker said. "It looks like no one can stop him. Surely not the pitiful excuse for a team he sees in front of him." The "commentator" dribbled toward the basket as though he was driving for a layup, but instead of shooting, he drove right under the bucket and back out to what would have been the top of the key on a regular basketball court. And he was still blabbering.

"Come on, Bill," the stocky boy guarding him groused disgustedly. "Play ball. We don't have all day. The sun will be going down before long."

Bill paid no attention and continued jabbering. "Ligon pumps, fakes, goes up, shoots!" Bill lofted a jump shot, and the ball glided through the air, piercing the center of the rim so well it was almost hard to see whether the ball went through.

But Bill knew it had. "Ligon scores!" he said with a whoop. "Unbelievable! Incredible! Ligon is amazing."

Watching from behind the tree, Eddie smiled and spun his basketball in his hands. He was impressed—he recognized that the skinny kid had some talent. He had good moves and a good shot. Not as good as Eddie's, but not bad either.

Just then, Bill heard a woman's voice calling from someplace down the street. "Leroy! Leroy White. You get on home!"

The stocky black boy who had been guarding Bill stood up straight and cocked his ear in the direction of the woman's voice.

"Leroy White! Where you at?" the female voice called again.

"That's my mama," Leroy said. "I gotta go."

"Aw, man!" Bill looked at Leroy with an irritated expression on his face. "We're right in the middle of the game here. Come on, can't you stay a little longer?"

"Sorry, Bill. You know Mama. Just like yours. When she calls, I gots to go." Leroy looked around at the other players. "Sorry, guys. Catch ya tomorrow." Leroy took off running toward his house.

Clearly annoyed, Bill put his hands on his hips and grunted. "What are we gonna do now?" He paused and looked around at the remaining four boys. "Okay, let's go three-on-two." He nodded toward his teammate. "Walter and I are so good, we'll whup you anyhow." Bill bounced the ball hard on the dirt.

"I can play, Bill," a young boy called from the porch of a nearby house just beyond the basketball court.

Bill spotted his eight-year-old brother, Tyree, waving his arms and standing on the porch steps of a one-story home owned by their distant cousin Ella Lee Rutledge and her husband, Glen.

"Yeah, thanks, Ty," Bill called to his brother. "But I don't see that you've grown eight inches since you asked to play fifteen minutes ago. Your day will come, brother. Don't you worry. But your day is not today."

Tyree sighed and slumped down on the steps to watch the older boys play.

Just then, Eddie shuffled his basketball from one hand to another and stepped out from behind the tree where he had been hiding. "Can I play?" he ventured, his throat dry.

Bill and the other boys spun around to look at Eddie. For several seconds, nobody said a word.

"It's a white boy!" Bill whispered to Walter as he stared at the light-haired, light-skinned kid standing there holding a basketball. "What on God's good earth is a white boy doing here in our neighborhood? And asking to play basketball, no less!" Bill's friends stood with their hands on their hips, as though they were thinking much the same thing.

Eddie stood silently while the five black boys stared at him as though he were a visitor from another planet. And in some ways, he was.

Several more seconds passed in silence, magnifying Eddie's fears. Maybe this wasn't such a good idea. He slowly moved his eyes from one tense black face to another, none of them showing any welcoming signs.

Finally, Bill broke the silence. "Who are you?"

"Name's Eddie. Eddie Sherlin."

"What are you doin' on our street?"

"Just watching. I live right over there." Eddie nodded toward Morrison Street. "Can I play?"

Bill eyed the basketball in Eddie's hands. It wasn't new, but it was a far better ball than he had. He studied Eddie, sizing up his height and slim frame to be a few inches shorter and lighter than his own. He glanced at Walter Lee, Leslie Gurley, and the other two boys, noted their blank expressions and then looked back at Eddie. Bill made a quick decision. "If you can shoot, you can play." His tone carried a challenge.

That dispelled Eddie's fears instantly. "Oh, I can shoot." *I'll show you how I can shoot*, he said to himself, mentally accepting Bill's challenge.

"Well, good. Get in here, then," Bill said.

It wasn't the most gracious of invitations, but Bill had long since learned that he couldn't be too forward with a white person, even a white person who looked to be about his same age. He looked over at Leroy's former teammates. "John and Simon, you take the new guy. I'll take Walter and Leslie."

John, who was standing under the basket, drawing designs on the dirt with his sneaker, looked up and fired back at Bill. "I don't want no white boy on my team," he said bitterly. "Why don't he go over to the white-boy park?" John pointed to the fenced-in park across the way.

Bill nodded, enviously noting the new nets on the basketball goals where the white kids were playing. He understood John's sentiments all too well. After all, Bill and his family lived in the small house adjacent to the gates of the whites-only park. Bill could look out the window and see the white kids playing basketball just a few feet away, yet he was not permitted to step foot on the asphalt court, much less play basketball on the smooth, flat, well-marked surface equipped with the top-quality metal backboards. That's why Bill walked over to the corner lot near Cousin Ella Lee's house every day to play ball. He dreamed of playing in the whites' park, but that's what it was—just a dream.

"Aw, come on, John." He turned his back to Eddie and spoke in a quiet but forceful tone. "I don't care if the kid is orange. If he can play, we need another guy."

John wrinkled his face, as though he was going to say something snide, but Bill ignored him. He turned back to Eddie. "Let's go. Our ball out." He grabbed the basketball and stepped to the back of the court. He fired a sharp pass to his teammate Walter, who bounce passed it to Leslie Gurley, their third guy. The game was on.

It was that simple. For the first time in his life, Eddie Sherlin was playing basketball with colored people. And Bill Ligon and his friends were allowing a "cracker" to join them on their home court, on their territory, and on their terms. Things like that just didn't happen in Gallatin in 1963.

The game quickly grew heated, as all six boys—competitive by nature—fought hard to win. Early on, Bill, Walter, and Leslie tried to intimidate Eddie by bumping into him harder than necessary, setting picks so Eddie was bound to slam into one of them and get jostled. It was obvious that the boys didn't want Eddie to get the better of them, and Eddie was certainly not backing down. He was not about to let the colored players get the best of him either. But it wasn't about color; Eddie and Bill were fierce competitors, and they were much more interested in basketball than any personal battles.

Eddie's teammates, John and Simon, slowly warmed to him. They were reluctant to give Eddie the ball at first, until Eddie snagged a blocked shot that ricocheted to the backcourt. He spun and hit a jump shot from nearly twenty feet out.

John and Simon quickly changed their tune. "The white boy can shoot!" Simon said under his breath to John as he retrieved the ball and bounced it to Leslie after Eddie sank another long one from the corner.

Before long, they were feeding the ball to Eddie on the outside every time they got tangled up on the inside. And more often than not, Eddie sent the ball through the hoop.

The game continued into late afternoon. The boys were so absorbed in playing that they failed to keep score, but it didn't matter. It wasn't about the score. It wasn't about winning or losing. It was about *the game*.

Dinnertime was approaching, and one by one, the boys were called home, slowly breaking up the game.

"Hey, Eddie, good playin' with you," Walter said, as he slapped Eddie on his sweat-soaked back. "Catch ya again sometime."

"Yeah, thanks. Sure will," Eddie responded.

Even John reluctantly gave Eddie a superficial nod before heading off for supper. Finally, only Bill and Eddie remained on the court, playing one-on-one.

Fascinated by the unusual sight of a white boy playing on their court, Bill's brother, Tyree, walked over and watched from the side as Bill and Eddie traded shots, one after another, with most of them going in. Bill recognized that Eddie was the better player, but that didn't keep him from putting on the pressure.

Nor did it reduce his rhetoric.

"Oh, yeah, ladies and gentleman, this is the game. They're pullin' out all the stops now. The light-haired Bob Cousy has his set shot working for the Celtics today, but he can't stop the Pistons' Willie Jones. Oh, watch out! Jones is heading for the basket! The crowd is on its feet as Willie plays keep-away for the final seconds of the game, and Cousy can't do a thing about it!"

Bill suddenly made a move for the basket, and Eddie backed up and quickly moved to the side to block him. Bill didn't slow down but rammed into Eddie full force, sending him flying. He hit the dirt and slid awkwardly on his knees. It was a powerful blow and would have been a clear-cut offensive foul for charging had they been playing a real game with a referee. Bill continued his layup over top of Eddie, banking the shot off the board and through the hoop.

Tyree cringed when the two boys collided. This could be bad news. He was almost certain that the white boy wasn't accustomed to playing that rough. Eddie could be hurt. Or it might turn into a fistfight. Tyree wasn't quite sure what to expect.

"Willie Jones scores and the crowd goes wild," Bill yelled, whipping his arms in the air as though hyping the crowd.

Eddie lay on the ground grimacing. His knee was badly scraped and bleeding, although it was more of a floor burn than a cut.

Bill grabbed the ball as it bounced on the ground below the hoop. He stepped back and looked down condescendingly at Eddie while Eddie glared back at him.

Tyree inched forward so he could see and hear, and so he could be ready to run for help if a fight broke out. *That burn on Eddie's knee must have hurt. Bad.*

"Come on, man," Bill chided Eddie. "You're not hurt. Get off the ground."

Eddie brushed a film of blood and dirt off his knee and looked up at Bill. Anger surged through him at Bill's obvious foul. He was ready to get up and let Bill have a piece of his mind and more, when Bill did something totally unexpected. He reached down his hand in Eddie's direction.

For a long, awkward moment, Eddie simply stared at Bill's black hand. As Bill continued to extend his hand, Eddie's eyes darted back and forth, from the pinkish-white skin on Bill's palm to the almost identical color of skin on Eddie's own palm. He finally reached out and grabbed Bill's hand.

Bill firmly grasped Eddie's hand and yanked him up off the dirt.

Off court, Tyree looked on in amazement and breathed a sigh of relief.

Eddie stood and looked Bill directly in the eyes. "Thanks. Bucket's no good. Charging, on you." He took the ball from Bill's hands and dribbled to the backcourt, where they picked up where they had left off and started the game all over again.

Bill and Eddie played until dusk. By the time they quit, they had developed a strong respect for each other. "You got a nice shot there," Bill said as he wiped the perspiration off his brow.

"Thanks," Eddie said. "You're not so bad yourself."

"I enjoyed playin' with ya," Bill said. "I'm not that good, but the guys here don't give me much competition. I sure had some today." Bill smiled broadly.

"Hey, me too," Eddie said with a laugh as he brushed off his bruised knee. "Let's do it again sometime."

"Okay, let's." Bill paused. "But you know I can't come over to your court." He glanced at the whites-only park just across the way.

"Yeah, I know," Eddie said sadly. "Never have understood all that."

"You mind coming back over here?"

"Naw, I don't mind at all. The ball bounces the same here as it does over there." Eddie nodded toward the park. "I'll be back. But I'd better get goin' now, or I'll be in for a whippin."

"Yeah, same here," Bill said. "My mama is little, but she sure is mighty." He twirled the basketball around his back as though it were a hula hoop, wrapping the ball under his shoulder and around his body and back to his chest.

"Cool trick," Eddie said. "See ya."

"Okay. Hey, what's your name again?"

"Eddie Sherlin."

"Got it. Bill. Bill Ligon. Keep that name in mind," he said with a twinkle in his eye. "You're gonna see me on the court with the greats one of these days."

"Okay, Bill. I'll look forward to that." Eddie waved good-bye and headed over to Morrison Street, a short distance but an entirely different world away.

When Eddie arrived at home, his mom was already preparing dinner. He opened the kitchen door but didn't go in. "I'm home, Mom. I'm just going to shoot for a while until supper's ready."

"All right," Betty said. "It won't be too long." Betty had been out all day long trying to sell encyclopedias, and Jim wasn't coming home until late, so she was not in the mood to prepare much of a dinner. A little ground beef, some fried potatoes, and a vegetable if she could rustle up one.

With a single work light from the back porch as the only illumination on his basketball court, Eddie continued practicing his shots. *Swish!* One after another sliced through the net. Even in the dark, Eddie could tell he was hitting the center of the goal. Between shots, Eddie kept trying to twirl the basketball around his back, as he had seen Bill do. He dropped the ball on a few attempts, but before long, Eddie was wrapping the ball around his back like a member of the Harlem Globetrotters. *Just wait till Bill sees this!* He whipped the basketball around his back again just as Bo came out the back door.

"Hey, fancy move," Bo said. "Where'd you learn that?"

Eddie hesitated. "Oh, I saw some guy doing it this afternoon, so I decided to try it."

"Yeah, where'd you go this afternoon? You were right behind us and then when we got home, you were nowhere to be found. Did you stop to talk to some pretty girl or something? Mom was not happy that you weren't here when she got home from work so late. I covered for you, but where'd you get to?"

"Oh, I just stopped to play some ball."

"Did you go back to the park?"

"No . . ." Eddie bounced the basketball to Bo in an effort to divert his attention from his questions. Bo caught the ball and took a shot, but the ball bumped the rim and bounced off. Bo grabbed the rebound and dribbled back to where Eddie was standing.

"Where were you? I might have wanted to play too. Were you playing at a friend's house?"

"No, not exactly . . ."

"Not exactly? What are you talking about, Eddie? There ain't no basketball courts between here and the park."

"Yeah . . . there is—"

"Don't tell me you were playin' basketball over on the colored side of town!"

"Yeah, I was—"

"Eddie! Are you crazy? You can't be doing that. If Dad knew you were over there, he'd whip you." Bo snapped a hard pass at Eddie, almost catching Eddie by surprise in the dim light. He raised his hands just in time to catch the ball.

"Why not? We were just playing some three-on-three."

"With darkies?"

"Color don't matter none to me," Eddie said. "Don't you remember what we learned in church? Jesus loves 'em all: red and yellow, black and white. They're all precious in his sight." Eddie nonchalantly took a shot. The ball swished through the goal, and Bo picked it up.

"Yes, I remember. But Jesus wasn't playing basketball with a bunch of darkies!"

"It's not about dark or light, Bo. It's about *basketball*. We were playing basketball, and I had a good time. That's all there is to it."

"Not smart, Eddie. That is *not* smart. Haven't you heard about the bad things goin' on down in Birmingham? That Martin Luther King fella stirrin' stuff up? People rioting in the streets? And it could be downright dangerous in this town too. You should know better." Bo fired another hard pass to his brother and stomped toward the house.

"But, Bo—"

Bo raised his hand, shook his head, and kept moving toward the back door. "You shouldn't be over there, Eddie. If I were you, I'd stay away from the dark side."

Bo slammed the back door as he went inside the house.

Eddie shrugged and went back to shooting. He didn't understand why Bo was so upset.

Eddie continued shooting for another half hour before he heard the back door open. In his peripheral vision, he saw Delilah stick her head out while holding the door slightly open. "Eddie! Come on! It's suppertime. Mama said it's hamburger Friday, and if you don't get in here soon, we're gonna eat it all up without you!"

"Y'all go ahead. I'll be there in just a few minutes."

Delilah went back inside the house and Eddie continued shooting. *Some things are more important than eating.*

A lonely train whistle sounded in the distance, reminding Eddie that it was nearly nine o'clock. He took one last long shot and nailed it. *Swish.*

6

"EDDIE! BE CAREFUL!" Bill Ligon called out to his new friend as quietly as possible. Today was Bill's turn to hide behind a tree, along with his younger brother, Tyree, who crouched behind him. They nervously glanced around in every direction, watching for approaching cars or even early rising pedestrians who might be passing by the white Gallatin Junior High School just after sunup on a Saturday morning. From their safe distance in the shadows, Bill and Tyree watched Eddie slowly climb up the outside wall of the school gymnasium, using the strong vines that grew alongside the brick walls for footing and something to grasp.

Every time Eddie's foot slipped from a vine, Bill's heart jumped to his throat. He could envision the headlines already: "White Boy Falls to His Death," with the additional tag line: "Two Negroes Jailed for Encouraging Him to Climb Wall." Bill's imaginary headlines weren't far-fetched. That's the way the justice system worked in the South in the early 1960s. If a black person was involved in an incident, it was their fault.

Fortunately, Eddie didn't fall. He climbed to an upper window that had been left unlocked, pulled it open, and crawled over the windowsill. A few moments later, he was in! He turned and waved to Bill and Tyree. The Ligon brothers raced to the gymnasium's front door, where Eddie met them and let them inside the school.

All three boys ran onto the basketball court and stopped short, gawking in wonder. Eddie had been to the school to watch some junior high basketball games, but he had never before played on this court. Bill and Tyree had never been inside the building.

All three of them stood awestruck as their eyes swept the spacious gym.

"This must be what heaven looks like," Tyree quipped.

The court was replete with brightly shining hardwood flooring. It had real Plexiglas backboards, straight orange rims, and new nets. Even for Eddie, who was accustomed to practicing behind his house, this was a treat.

"You did it, Eddie! Way to go," Bill said. "I was worried when you slipped on those vines out there. But you did it!"

"I just did what you said," Eddie replied with an "Aw, shucks" expression. "After the junior high game yesterday afternoon, while there were still a bunch of people on the bleachers, I went up and unlocked the window. Nobody noticed. I was just hoping Mr. Evans, the janitor, didn't come around and check the windows after I left."

Bill laughed. "I'm impressed. I didn't know a white boy could be so devious."

"Oh, I can be devious," Eddie said seriously. "My heart is as black as yours. Er, uh . . . well, you know what I mean."

Bill slapped Eddie on the back. "Yeah, I know what you mean. Let's shoot some ball." The boys bounce passed the ball back and forth as they crossed center court, and then Bill took it the rest of the way to the top of the key, where he launched a long jump shot. Swish! "Oh, what a beautiful sound!" Bill yelled. "We don't hear that sound over at Cousin Ella's court."

He bounced the ball to Eddie, who sank a long shot from the far side of the gym.

Tyree ran up alongside Bill. "Are we gonna get in trouble for being in here, Bill?"

"Nah, we're with Eddie," Bill said as he retrieved a rebound. "Besides, there ain't nobody else playing basketball this early on Saturday morning. Not whites or coloreds. We can play for several hours before anyone else shows up around here." Bill passed the ball to Tyree. "Let's see whatcha got."

Tyree dribbled back to a position just behind the foul line and executed a perfect set shot. "Whoooweee!" All three boys whooped it up, enjoying the echo of their voices in the large gymnasium. They played for more than an hour and got so caught up in shooting, rebounding, and shooting again that they never heard the door open. They didn't see the imposing figure standing with his hands on his hips, a gun on his right side, and a billy club on his left.

For a moment, Officer Howard Barton, a longtime member of Gallatin's police force, watched the boys totally immersed in playing basketball, oblivious to his presence. He shook his head and almost grinned, but then he straightened and yelled, "Hey!"

Eddie was shooting a jump shot. He seemed to stop, suspended momentarily in midair. Bill was watching the net, ready to retrieve the ball as soon as it ripped through, and Tyree had his back to the officer. All three boys froze.

"Uh-oh," Tyree said under his breath.

"What are you boys doing in here?" Barton bellowed, his voice echoing off the bare walls of the gymnasium.

Silly question. It was quite obvious what the boys were doing. The real question was how they got into the gym without supervision. And who had the audacity to let two black kids into a white school? "Get over here, now!" he barked, pointing at a spot in front of him. "And bring that basketball too."

The boys dutifully obeyed Officer Barton's commands. Eddie scooped up the basketball and joined Bill and Tyree, who stood in front of Barton. Bill and Tyree looked at the floor; Eddie stared at the policeman's gun.

"What are your names?" Officer Barton asked. "You first." He pointed at Eddie.

"Eddie Sherlin, sir."

"And what about you?" He nudged Bill on the shoulder. "Look at me, boy."

"Ligon," Bill said quietly. "Bill Ligon. My mama is Anna Ligon, the schoolteacher," he added, hoping the officer would recognize his mom's name and be aware of her sterling reputation in town.

"And I'm Tyree," the younger brother chirped.

Bill elbowed Tyree, as though to say, "Shut up!"

Officer Barton ignored Tyree and glared at Bill. "And how did you get in here?" There was no question in his mind about who was at fault. Clearly, this black kid had broken into the building.

Bill appeared to weigh his words carefully. "The window was open, sir." He raised his hand slowly and pointed to a window above the bleachers, the same window Eddie had crawled through from the outside wall.

"Hmmph." He looked at the high window and grunted again. "Where do you live, son?" He addressed his question to Eddie.

"Morrison Street, sir. Over behind the railroad tracks."

"Okay. Let's go. Come with me." He nodded toward the exit doors, and the three frightened basketball players moved in that direction. Barton followed closely behind, making sure the gym doors locked behind them. Once outside, Officer Barton nodded toward his black-and-white patrol car parked in front of the school. "Get in," he said, pointing at the car. He looked at Bill and Tyree. "You two get in the back. You get in the front seat with me," he instructed Eddie. The boys quickly followed his orders.

Officer Barton locked the car doors and pulled out. Bill and Tyree sat silently in the backseat, staring out the windows. The officer looked over at Eddie when they stopped at the traffic light downtown. "What's your daddy's name?"

"Jimmy Sherlin."

"Jimmy Sherlin, the fella who leads the church choir over at First Assembly?"

"Yes, sir. That's my father."

Barton nodded, thinking Eddie was going to be in much more trouble with his dad than he was right now. "And is your mama home?"

"Yes, sir. She was when I left this morning."

Officer Barton cast a sidelong glance at Eddie and raised his eyebrows. "And apparently you left rather early this morning."

"Yes, sir. I did."

They drove on in silence and arrived at Eddie's home in minutes. Barton pulled the squad car into the gravel driveway and turned off the engine. "Let's go." He turned to Bill and Tyree in the backseat. "You two stay right here. Don't move a muscle."

"Yes, sir," both boys mumbled.

Officer Barton got out of the car and marched Eddie to the front porch. The officer looked over at the double-seat swing tucked on the right side of the small porch, in front of the double windows. Then he rapped on the door. Eddie stood at his side as they waited for someone to answer the knock.

Betty Sherlin clutched her heart when she opened the door and saw Eddie standing next to the policeman. "Eddie!" she blurted. "What's going on?"

"Mrs. Sherlin?" Officer Barton ignored her outburst.

"Yes. Yes, I am." Betty opened the door wider. "Come in."

"No, thank you, ma'am. We can talk right here. As you might have guessed already, we've had a bit of a problem this morning."

"We have?" Betty looked at him and then at Eddie, who immediately dropped his gaze to the porch floor.

"Yes, ma'am, we have. Seems your son and those two colored boys broke into the school this morning." Barton nodded toward the backseat of his patrol car, where Bill and Tyree sat motionless.

"Eddie?" Betty Sherlin's surprise was genuine. Clearly she was shocked her son would do such a thing.

"Yes, Eddie," the officer said. "Is Mr. Sherlin home?"

"No, he already left to make some rounds. He's an insurance man, and he usually does some collections on Saturday that he can't get to through the week because folks are working, and—"

Barton raised his hand. "Yes, ma'am. I understand." He turned toward Eddie. "Son, I want to speak to your mother privately. You get on inside. And I don't want to see you in my car ever again. You understand?"

"Yes, sir." Obvious relief swept over Eddie.

"You stay out of trouble," the officer said gruffly. "And stay away from those colored boys, ya hear?"

"Ah, yes, sir." Eddie said quietly as he slipped behind his mother and went inside the house, far enough to get out of Officer Barton's sight but probably close enough to still hear what he was saying to his mom.

With Eddie gone, the officer's facial expression and tone softened. "They were just playing basketball, ma'am. They weren't doing anything bad. But they did not have permission to be in the gym. And then there's the matter of those two." He nodded toward Bill and Tyree. "That is trouble just waiting to happen."

"I'm so sorry," Betty Sherlin said. "That isn't like Eddie to get into trouble. He's a good boy."

"I'm sure he is, ma'am." Officer Barton pushed back his hat. "Let's hope he stays that way. I'm not arresting him. But I expect that you and Mr. Sherlin will handle this matter."

"Oh, yes, sir, officer. I assure you that Mr. Sherlin, I mean Jim, will apply the rod of instruction. I'd do it myself right now, but I'm certain Eddie's daddy will want to address it with him."

"All right, that's fine. You have a good day, ma'am." The officer raised his index and middle fingers to his hat in an informal salute. "I have another matter to attend to." He looked toward the backseat of the car.

The officer stiffened and strode to his vehicle. He opened the door and peered at Bill. "And where do you two live?"

"Right over there." Bill pointed out the rear window, toward a small brown house on the edge of the whites-only park.

"Over by the church?"

"Yes, sir."

Officer Barton shrugged, slid behind the wheel, and started the car. He drove down Morrison and turned to the right, driving along the fenced-in whites-only park, all the way to Bill and Tyree's street. The patrol car eased around the corner and up the hill, stopping in front of a brown house. Officer Barton turned around in his seat and glared at the boys. "Get out of my car. And if I ever catch you in the whites' school again, I'll have your backsides out on a work detail faster than you can blink. Now, scram!"

"Yes, sir," Bill said. "Thank you, sir." He and Tyree bounded out of the backseat and away from the patrol car as quickly as they could.

That night Eddie was in his tiny bedroom when Jim Sherlin returned home from work. He could hear loud voices in the kitchen and knew his mother was informing his dad about Officer Barton's visit. He cringed as the voices escalated in intensity. He hated it when his parents argued—especially when it involved him. Eddie knew his dad would not respond well to his breaking into the school, and he might be especially upset about his playing basketball with two colored boys.

A short while later, Eddie heard the familiar strains of George Beverly Shea singing "Amazing Grace" on the family phonograph.

That meant that whatever the conversation between his mom and dad had been, it was now over and his mom was immersing herself in the Bible, trying to find absolution, if not forgiveness, for all the nasty things she had said to her husband.

Jim Sherlin reached inside the coat closet. He moved aside some coats and found what he was looking for—a three-foot-long smooth stick, about the thickness of a thin drumstick, made from hickory wood. Jim ran his hand over the smooth wood and tapped it against his thigh. While the stick rendered less damage and pain than Jim's hand, it could deliver a serious welt.

Delilah was drying the supper dishes near the sink and Debbie was doing her homework at the kitchen table when their dad, with his mouth set in a firm line and his shoulders squared, walked through the kitchen carrying the hickory stick. Neither girl said a word, and each pretended not to notice, but both feared what was about to happen.

Bo looked up as his dad moved through the living room on his way to Eddie's room. His eyes went wide and he swallowed hard, clearly understanding Eddie's coming punishment.

Jim entered Eddie's room without knocking. He shut the door behind him.

Eddie sat on the bed, pretending to read a sports magazine while trying to ignore the hickory switch in his dad's hand.

"Hey, Dad," Eddie said amiably. "Have a seat." He nodded to his bed.

Jim did not sit down. "Son, I want to talk to you about what happened today."

Eddie dropped his eyes. "Yes, sir."

"Bend over." Jim did all the talking from that point. He also did the switching. Jim swatted where he knew it would hurt the most—on the back of Eddie's thighs.

The *whoosh!* of the switch traveling at a rapid speed and the *whap!* of it connecting with Eddie's thighs could be heard throughout the small house. Betty sat in her easy chair, sipping her coffee and reading the Bible. With each swat of the switch against Eddie's flesh, her stomach churned. She closed her eyes and tried not to listen, but Eddie's bedroom door could not silence the hickory stick's contact with her son's flesh or the sounds of his cries. She leaned over and turned up the volume on the George Beverly Shea album playing on the phonograph.

She glanced toward her daughters, who busied themselves in the kitchen, pretending they didn't notice the beating. But they too flinched with every swat. Even Bo grimaced as the hickory stick slapped Eddie's bare skin.

Finally, it was over. Jim emerged from Eddie's room and looked back at his younger son lying on the bed, choking back sobs. He stepped into the living room, glared at Betty and Bo, who briefly looked up and then returned to what they were doing, as though everything was normal. Jim stood motionless for a moment. Then he announced: "I'm going out to the garage." He stormed through the living room and out the kitchen door, as Delilah and Debbie quickly moved out of his way.

It wasn't the first time Jim had whipped Eddie with the switch. Disobedience in the Sherlin home often brought out the hickory stick. When Eddie delayed too long coming in from shooting baskets or one of the girls disobeyed Betty or Jim or Bo back talked once too often, the switch made an appearance. Although the switch was sometimes a reflection of Jim and Betty's own frustrations in life, their sincere desire was to raise children who respected the laws of God and man. They were convinced the biblical proverb "Spare the rod and spoil the child" was true, so they took that aspect of parenting quite seriously.

Eddie didn't awaken on Sunday morning to the *swish* of a basket-ball slipping through a net. Instead, he woke up to the nightmarish memories of the *whoosh* of the hickory switch making contact with his thighs.

Jim Sherlin's voice broke through the quietness. "Let's go, you guys. Time for church. Mom's got your oatmeal on the table. Get a move on."

The sounds of Betty's gospel quartet music playing on the pho-nograph greeted the Sherlin siblings who were still rubbing their sleepy eyes as they slowly made their way into the kitchen. "Mornin', Mama," each one dutifully offered.

"Good morning. Let's go. Eat and then get on your Sunday clothes. We can't be late for church. Daddy's got to meet with the choir be-fore service this morning, so we need to be there even earlier than usual. Hurry, please!"

Eddie gulped down his oatmeal and hurried to his room, where he put on a clean pair of pants, a white shirt, and a necktie. He bent over and crammed his feet into the black church shoes his mom had bought for him last year. They were already too tight and didn't help his gimpy walk one bit.

Bo dressed in much the same way, wearing a slightly larger ver-sion of Eddie's church outfit. The girls, of course, wore their finest flowing cotton dresses and patent leather shoes reserved for Sundays.

Decked out in a dark suit, white shirt, and bright orange tie, Jim Sherlin held the door for his family as they exited the house and piled into their car for the quick drive across town to the Assembly of God church. Wearing a high-necked dress with long sleeves, Betty Sherlin sat stiffly in the front seat and adjusted her beret-style hat that served as her head covering. Most of the "spiritually mature" women who attended the Assembly of God church felt it inappropriate to be seen in a church service without something covering their heads, indicating their respect for biblical doctrine and church traditions. Nobody in the church dared suggest that Saint Paul's admonition that women should not be seen in church without a head covering had a cultural meaning in his day that had long since been lost to believers in the twentieth century. Quite the contrary. "Saintly" members of the church considered women who refused to wear a hat or some sort of covering on their heads as "loose women" who probably went to dances and smoked cigarettes too.

The pressure exerted by his sisters and brother squeezing into the backseat with him exacerbated the stinging in Eddie's legs. He didn't say anything, but he was glad the trip to the church on South Water Street was a short five-minute ride. Jim parked the car between a lined space—their usual spot—in front of a small sign that read *Choir Director*. The Sherlins arrived well before the service began, piled out of the car, and headed inside the sanctuary. Eddie limped along behind the others.

About the same time, across town, Bill and Tyree Ligon, also dressed in their best Sunday suits, were hobbling into the Original Church of God in much the same manner as Eddie. Although Officer Barton had not spoken to Anna Ligon about the boys' escapade, she had somehow heard about it. Anna Ligon was not a woman to be trifled with. She was as strict with Bill and Tyree and their sister, Delores, as the Sherlins were with their kids—maybe even more so. Anna's husband, William Sr., had left the family when Bill was very young, forcing her to be both mom and dad to the kids, and she played both roles superbly. Thankfully, Anna's mama, Callie Bennett Bransford, lived nearby, as did other relatives, so they all watched out for the Ligon children and made sure they behaved. And when they didn't, Anna wielded a strong hickory switch as punishment.

Also, the Original Church of God, the "sanctified" church where Anna's family worshiped on Pace Street, was attended by fewer than thirty people, all coloreds, so everyone knew everyone and everybody watched out for one another. The adults especially kept their eyes on the kids. The congregation was much like an extended family. Bill and Tyree never could have gotten in trouble with the police without their mama finding out.

The Ligon family members were faithful to the Original Church of God and held a profound respect for their pastor, Lula Mae Swanson, a no-nonsense gospel preacher who served three other area churches as well. Pastor Lula Mae, a bishop in her domination, was a small, dark-skinned woman with a slight build. Always impeccably dressed in a black, blue, or white business suit with a matching hat, Bishop Swanson was both a concerned minister and a shrewd business-woman. In addition to preaching, she managed the first Negro-owned nursing home in Middle Tennessee.

Bishop Swanson was a dynamic speaker, and when she preached, people listened; when she sang, they swooned at her beautiful voice. She had a forceful personality and a quick wit, combined with an abundance of charm. She also hosted and preached on a radio show on WHIN for which Bill and his family members sang gospel songs along with her. Bill's grandmother, Callie Bransford, prayed down the glory, and, of course, Bishop Swanson always read the Bible and presented words of encouragement.

Sunday morning church service at the Original Church of God was an exuberant experience. Even for people like Bill, who preferred his religion on the quieter side, the energy and spirit of the people—not to mention the Spirit of the Lord—created a contagious atmosphere of hope.

A Hammond B-3 organ played by a middle-aged Negro man backed up, echoed, reiterated, or otherwise responded to everything Sister Lula Mae said from the pulpit. "Let's have some lively testimonies this morning!" said the pastor, followed by a riff on the B-3 to emphasize her point. "I mean current and lively testimonies," Bishop Swanson said. "I'm glad the Lord saved your soul a long time ago, and we're glad he brought you out of Egypt into

Canaan, but what has he done for you this week? Come on, now, get up and tell us!"

Sister Lula Mae didn't have to beg for witnesses. Men and women popped up all over the sanctuary to tell of what God had done for them over the past seven days.

"I was sick and the Lord made me well," one woman said.

"I got me a new job, glory to God," a man in his forties said.

Punctuating each testimony, the Hammond organ added a musical "Amen."

"My child was having trouble hearing, but Sister Lula Mae and Sister Bransford, thank God for her, prayed for my baby. And today, my little girl can hear!" The small crowd burst into applause and cheers.

With the entire congregation now on its feet, Bishop Swanson looked over the room. "That's so good to hear from the mamas and the daddies, but where are my young-uns? What's the good Lord done for you this week?" Her searing gaze searched the room for a young witness, and finding none, Bishop Swanson was not above calling on someone. "Brother William. Young Brother Bill Ligon. What has God done for you this week?"

Taken aback by Sister Lula Mae's question, Bill did not have a prepared answer. But he knew better than to be silent when the pastor made a special request. "Well, er, uh . . . the good Lord brought me here to church today to hear the Word," Bill finally said.

The B-3 roared its approval and the audience cheered. Sister Lula Mae looked down from the pulpit and smiled at Bill. All was well with the world.

Inside the simply decorated Assembly of God sanctuary, Eddie and Bo Sherlin sat quietly toward the front on one of the pine-colored pews with padded red cushions. "I hate sitting up so close in church," Bo leaned over and whispered to Eddie.

"I know what you mean," Eddie replied. "But you heard what Dad said. He told us to plant ourselves on one of the pews up front." Both boys would have much preferred a back-row seat, but with Eddie's whipping still fresh in their minds, they weren't about to press their luck.

Jim Sherlin stood in front of the choir, composed of about twenty middle-aged women and a few elderly gentlemen, along with two teenage girls and one teenage boy with closely cropped hair. Of course, Betty, Delilah, and Debbie sang in Jim's choir as well. Jim and Betty occasionally sang together with another couple in a gospel quartet, so they had some experience singing in public. And similar to most churches in the Nashville area, a few of the choir singers were quite good—practically professional quality. Many of the others in the choir were mediocre "gospel wannabees" who regularly attended *Wally Fowler's All-Night Singing,* a live radio show broadcast on WSM from the Ryman Auditorium, home of the Grand Ole Opry.

The choir members showed up on Sunday mornings excited to try some of the vocal gymnastics exhibited by the gospel pros. Usually, the results were less than pleasing, but Jim always reassured his choir members. "Christians are instructed to sing and make melody in our hearts," he said, "and to make a joyful noise unto the Lord."

Joyful? Maybe. On key? That was another matter.

Following some lively congregational singing, the choir stood to perform "How Great Thou Art," the number they had practiced especially for the morning service. Jim Sherlin stepped up and smiled at several of the women in the front row of the choir. He didn't use a conductor's wand to lead the choir. Instead, he used his hands to keep time and employed exaggerated physical gyrations of his body to help emphasize the music's swells and crescendos.

The choir sang the majestic anthem as though they were singing at Carnegie Hall in front of thousands of people, rather than in Gallatin before the small but enthusiastic crowd of slightly more than one hundred all-white worshipers. When the choir came to the third verse, Jim nodded toward Violet Johnson, a pretty woman in her late thirties, to sing that stanza as a solo. Wearing a provocative scoop-necked dress, Violet smiled at the choir leader appreciatively.

Nobody else noticed the interchange between the choir director and one of his prize pupils—nobody but Betty Sherlin.

Reverend M. C. Daley, a fireplug of a man and a fireball of a preacher with a loud, gravel-throated voice, brought a powerful message that morning about the prodigal son. Preacher Daley believed in "full-body preaching." He didn't merely speak the Word; he flailed his arms, banged on the pulpit to emphasize his point, and even sometimes stomped his foot. The congregation responded with equal excitement and enthusiasm, occasionally shouting out "Praise the Lord!" or "Preach it, Brother!" or whatever came to mind. Some people stood up in the middle of the sermon. Every so often when someone really got "in the Spirit," they would run a quick lap around the inside of the sanctuary and then back to the front of the church. The more unusual expressions on the part of the parishioners sometimes frightened Eddie.

Preacher Daley railed against the sins of drinking and carousing and "whoremongering" in which the prodigal son engaged after demanding and receiving his portion of his father's inheritance while the father was still alive. "And after that boy had wasted all of his daddy's money on riotous living, he found himself in the pigpen of life!" Preacher Daley bellowed. "There he was, looking at the mush and sayin', 'Mmm-mmm, that stuff looks mighty good. But wait a minute! Even my daddy's servants have better food than that. I'm gonna get up and go back home and tell my daddy that I have sinned.'"

Reverend Daley looked right into Eddie's eyes as he preached about sin. Eddie squirmed. He felt the man of God was staring straight into his heart. Eddie always felt nervous in church. He feared that he might slide right into hell in the midst of every service. He assumed that he could never be clean enough—never quite good enough to satisfy God. To lessen his sense of conviction, he stared at the cross behind the choir loft and avoided looking at the preacher's face. But looking at the cross only heightened Eddie's sense of guilt.

Reverend Daley preached on, shedding his jacket somewhere in the middle of his message, walking down among the congregants, pointing his finger in various faces, and then finally returning to the pulpit to conclude his sermon. Pastor Daley didn't merely preach to impart information, he expected his listeners to respond.

"The choir will now sing hymn number 214, 'Just As I Am,'" he said. The preacher lowered his voice to a sonorous tone and implored: "If you've never come home to your heavenly Father, today might be your day. You come." He nodded toward the altar railing with a padded step at the front of the church, where several people seeking God were already kneeling to pray. "You may have been out there with the pigs. Your heavenly Father still loves you. Don't wait another moment. You ain't gonna get any cleaner on your own. While the choir sings, come and ask God to clean you up."

Eddie fidgeted as the congregation stood to sing.

Jim Sherlin was already in position, motioning the choir to stand as the organist played the well-known, evocative invitational hymn sung at the close of Billy Graham crusades. Several more members of the congregation made their way to the kneeling rail while the choir sang the first, second, and last verses.

The service concluded, and Eddie felt relieved to have survived another altar call without losing his composure. With all the thoughts and emotions he experienced these days, it was getting tougher each week to escape the searing eye of Reverend Daley. Worse yet, it was almost time for the annual revival, during which the congregation participated in at least a week of services geared toward the evangelism of unbelievers and the rededication of believers. Eddie knew his folks would require him to attend every evening. He shuddered as he thought about it.

Following the service, Reverend Daley and his wife greeted the members of the congregation as they made their way out of the church. While people stood in line to shake hands with the pastor or hug his wife, the members interacted among themselves.

"Wasn't it a wonderful service?" Francine Smithfield said to Betty Sherlin.

"Oh, yes, it was." Betty smiled at Francine. Betty smiled at several more parishioners as they inched along toward the pastor standing in the doorway.

"That was a fantastic song you all sang this morning," an elderly woman said to Jim.

"Thank you, Sister Miriam," Jim answered. "And didn't Sister Violet do well on the solo part?"

"She certainly did. That girl can sing like a birdie."

Standing next to Jim but turned slightly away from Sister Miriam's gaze, Betty Sherlin rolled her eyes. *Oh, yes, Violet is definitely some chickadee.*

The Sherlins greeted the preacher and his wife and then made their way toward their car. They were no sooner inside the vehicle with the doors closed before Betty's smile turned to a scowl.

"And why did you have to let her sing?" Betty spat, refusing to look at her husband.

"Wha . . . ?" Jim put the car in drive and headed out of the church's parking lot. "Who are you talking about?"

"You know perfectly well who I am talking about. Why did you have to give that slut a solo?"

"Betty! Watch your mouth. Not in front of the kids. And besides, she is not a . . . she's not that. She's had a rough time since her husband left her, that's all."

"She looked pretty smooth this morning. And it was plain to see that you couldn't keep your eyes off her. Have you been stopping in to visit her on your insurance route? I'm sure she would love to see you."

"I don't even know where she lives."

"And she can't even sing. If she didn't dress like a whore, nobody would even pay attention to her."

"Betty! I'm warning you."

Betty turned her head and stared out the window. "You could have given the solo to me. You know I can sing, buster."

"Yes, Betty, I know you can sing," Jim growled. "You are a great singer. You have no reason to be jealous. I wanted to give Violet a chance."

"I'm sure you did," she nearly shouted.

The verbal jousting continued all the way home, and once again Eddie was only too glad the ride was a quick one.

But not quick enough.

"Mama and Daddy, please don't fight," Delilah cried from the backseat. She and Debbie burst into tears. Bo, seated next to Delilah, stiffened and his face looked as though it had turned to stone.

Eddie felt a tear trickle down his face. He knew his mom and dad were good people, but their inconsistencies bothered him. He didn't understand how they could be so spiritual in church on Sunday and during Wednesday night Bible study and then be so mean to each other outside of church. He wished there was something he could do about it, some way he could draw them back together.

7

ANNA LIGON SAT AT HER KITCHEN TABLE late in the afternoon correcting some tests she had given to one of her classes at Union High School, the county-wide school for coloreds located in Gallatin. Anna became a schoolteacher after graduating from Tennessee Agricultural and Industrial University, later known simply as Tennessee State University, and earned a reputation as a tough but fair educator who loved her students. She recognized that getting an education was the only way her students could ever escape a life of poverty, servitude, and presumed insignificance. She possessed a passion for learning and drilled that attitude into her students as well as her own children.

Sheereeet!

Anna looked up from the test papers. She could recognize Tyree's signature whistle just about anywhere. Her youngest son had mastered the technique of placing two fingers in his mouth, contorting his tongue just right, and blowing to create the loudest and sharpest whistle Anna had ever heard.

Shereeet! Anna realized the whistle was coming from the direction of the whites-only park. That wasn't good. Anna stood up and stepped to the window to see if Tyree was anywhere in sight. Sure enough, Tyree was standing at the corner of their backyard fence that overlooked the whites-only playground. He paced back and forth, a serious expression on his face, as though he were standing watch at a bank robbery.

Because it was so late in the afternoon, few people were in the park. Anna noticed a single young white boy shooting baskets on the asphalt basketball court. That wasn't unusual; kids played at the park until dusk almost every evening. A group of white children and some men who might be their dads or coaches walked across the park behind where the white boy was practicing his foul shots. Tyree continued pacing near the fence, seemingly looking in every direction for something or somebody. As soon as the children and the adults were out of sight, Tyree let out another ear-piercing whistle.

Anna's mouth dropped open and she gasped when she saw Bill bounding out from behind a large tree growing inside the park. He had been hiding as the white folks passed by. As Bill joined the white boy on the whites-only basketball court, he waved to Tyree, who waved back. Anna shook her head and sighed. Bill knew better than to risk angering members of the white community by playing on their basketball court. But perhaps nobody would notice that one of the boys playing ball was black. With the sun going down, they couldn't play much longer, anyhow.

Anna was well aware of the local rules, stated and unstated, that colored and whites shouldn't mix. The Ku Klux Klan still had a strong influence in the area surrounding Pulaski, Tennessee, a mere one hundred miles down Interstate 65. Anna had been following the news about the racial tension only a few hundred miles to the south in Birmingham.

Yet because of her strong faith in God, she believed he was moving in the hearts and minds of people, transforming their attitudes about racial matters. She was aware that the times were changing, that a day was coming when whites and blacks would play together on the same playground. But with segregation still deeply entrenched in Gallatin, Anna also knew that day had not yet arrived in her hometown.

She peered out the window once more and saw Bill and the white boy playing together. She certainly didn't want Bill to be the catalyst for trouble, but she couldn't deny the sheer delight she saw on his face, even from a distance. She decided not to make a scene and allowed her son to continue playing on the whites-only court.

Maybe that's not such a bad idea.

On the asphalt court, Bill and Eddie were lost in their game, interrupted only by Tyree's shrill whistles when some white folks happened to walk by or through the park.

Bill carried on his usual imaginary play-by-play commentary as Eddie dribbled forward, looking for an opening. Then with Bill guarding him closely, he dribbled back to near the foul line. Keeping a hand lightly on Eddie's shirt all the while, Bill prattled on.

"Bob Cousy, star of the Boston Celtics, has the ball," Bill announced in his broadcaster voice. "There's only one man between Cousy and the bucket, one man between winning and losing. And that man is Willie Jones, the Detroit Pistons' main man. One man . . ." Bill continued his commentary as Eddie drove right by him on the left side.

Bill tried to recover by falling back quickly, but the move was awkward. Eddie was too fast and Bill was off balance. Bill desperately leaped into the air, attempting to block Eddie's shot, but Eddie had better position on him and barreled right through, his left shoulder slamming into Bill's upper body like a linebacker hitting the quarterback. Eddie's forward motion was enough to allow him to slip the ball under Bill's outstretched left arm and then up and into the bucket. Bill reeled backward and crashed to the asphalt. His elbows scraped along for several inches on the hard surface before his body slid to a stop.

Eddie retrieved the ball as it eased through the hoop and bounced off the pavement. He turned around and saw Bill lying on the ground, grabbing first one elbow then the other in obvious pain.

Bill looked at the thin smear of blood marking his hand where he had clutched his elbow. He was not happy. He scowled at Eddie. For a long moment, he and Eddie locked eyes and remained transfixed, staring at each other, both boys ready for a fight.

Eddie stood over Bill, looking down at him, poised to pounce. Then a subtle hint of a smile creased Eddie's face. He reached his hand out toward Bill. "Come on, man. You're not hurt."

Bill sat up and stared at Eddie's very white hand, noticing the light blond hair on his suntanned arm. He continued staring for several seconds, then suddenly grabbed Eddie's hand and allowed him to pull him off the ground. Bill hopped to his feet and, with both hands, brushed off his pants. He flinched a bit as his elbows bent. "Hey, that was charging. No points. My ball!"

"No way," Eddie fired back. "You were all over me, stumbling backward and flailing your arms like a drunk."

The boys became so immersed in their debate over the play they didn't notice the middle-aged white man who had pulled up in his car on the street near the south side of the park.

"Hey! What are you doin' in there, boy?" he railed, leaning out of the driver's side window. "Get yourself out of my park! Now!" The man jumped out of the car. He cursed at Bill while shaking his fist at him.

Stark terror struck Bill. His mouth went dry, his legs felt weak, and his heart pounded as he realized they had been found out. He feared the man might have a gun, and getting shot was not in his plans.

"Come on, Eddie! I gotta get outta here!" Bill was already running toward the chain-link fence.

Eddie grabbed the basketball and followed Bill. The two boys raced out the gate and scrambled up the hill toward Bill's house, with the man by the car still screaming at them.

"Whew, that was a close one!" Bill said.

The boys plopped down on the front porch steps.

"You're not kiddin'. That was scary," Tyree, who'd come from his post in the backyard, said.

"A fine sentry you were." Bill slapped Tyree on the back. "Good thing we weren't playin' in Birmingham or Montgomery. I'd be in jail by now. And I'm sure you'd come visit me, right?" He poked Tyree again, and the two brothers laughed.

Eddie joined in the laughter. "Yeah, we might not want to try that again anytime soon. No use taking chances, you see what I'm sayin'?"

"I agree," Bill said, his heartbeat finally returning to normal. "It's probably safer to play over at Cousin Ella Lee's house."

Hearing all the commotion on the front porch, Anna Ligon poked her head out the front door. "What's going on out here?"

"Oh, nuthin' much, Mama," Bill said. "We're just having a good laugh."

"Where have you been?" Anna tested the boys.

"Playin' ball over in the park," Bill said. "We're just hangin' around now."

"Hmm, playing basketball in the park. That is rather interesting." Anna regarded her older son. "And you aren't hanging anywhere." She corrected his English. "Are you going to introduce me to your friend?"

"Oh, sorry, Mama. This is Eddie," Bill said.

"Hello, ma'am," Eddie said. "How do you do?"

Ever the teacher, Anna smiled at Eddie but addressed her words to Bill. "And does Eddie have a last name?"

Bill drew a blank and stared at Eddie. "I don't know. Do you?"

"Eddie Sherlin, ma'am."

"That's it!" Bill slapped his knee. "Eddie Sherlin. I knew he had a last name!"

"It's very nice to meet you, Eddie." Anna extended her hand. Eddie returned the gesture, gently shaking Mrs. Ligon's hand without reservation.

"Sherlin? Are you Betty Sherlin's son?"

"Yes, ma'am."

Anna nodded. "Oh, I know your mother. She sold me a set of *World Book Encyclopedias* a while back. More than twenty volumes,

73

and I hear they're planning for even more. I'm still paying on those books every month." She smiled as she recalled the exorbitant purchase she had made as much to help Betty as her own three children's education. "How's your mom doing?"

"She's fine, Mrs. Ligon."

"Well, good. Please tell her I send my regards."

"Yes, ma'am," Eddie replied.

"Would you perspiring basketball players care for some lemonade? I just made a fresh batch."

"Oh, yes, Mama!" Tyree answered.

"Sure would," Bill said.

"Thank you, ma'am," Eddie chimed in.

"Okay, I'll have it for you in just a minute. Would you like to come inside?" Anna held open the door.

Bill and Tyree headed for the door, and Eddie started to follow then hesitated. "Er, I'd better not, ma'am," Eddie said. "If it is all the same to you, I'll just stay out here on the porch. Thank you, anyhow."

Bill and Tyree stopped short of the door. They turned back and eased toward the porch steps.

"Oh. Of course. Yes," Anna said, as though understanding had suddenly dawned on her.

Anna knew very well the attitudes with which Eddie had lived during his childhood, the same attitudes with which her three children grappled every day. It was unthinkable for a white person to step inside a black person's house. Anna understood that Eddie, just by playing basketball with Bill and sitting on her front porch at his young age, was already crossing lines many others refused to even consider. Anna understood all too well. And she appreciated Eddie's courage.

"I'll just bring some glasses and a tray out here on the porch, and you boys can enjoy your lemonade right here." She smiled at Eddie. "So nice to meet you, Eddie. Please feel free to come back any time."

"Thank you, Mrs. Ligon," Eddie said. "I'd be happy to do that."

To be sure, racial tension in Gallatin and Nashville's extended metropolitan area was relatively mild compared with that of Atlanta or Montgomery or Birmingham, to say nothing of the conditions coloreds endured in Mississippi. Throughout the South, they were expected to know and accept their place as an inferior race. Not only that, they were to show their appreciation to whites for allowing them to coexist. It was not a matter of debate. It had been that way for nearly two hundred years.

Beginning in 1866, Tennessee, like most Southern states, began developing an entire system of Jim Crow laws, named after a blackface minstrel character, which forced racial segregation. The system spawned the idea of "separate but equal" treatment for blacks, supposedly as a step forward in racial relations. In truth, separate but equal was heavy on the *separate* part and established a plethora of laws and unspoken rules to keep coloreds and whites who lived in the former Confederate states from interacting. The separate but equal principle was vapidly light on the *equal* aspect. Equal meant equally made in the image of God—though some Southern white Christians even wondered about that—but not necessarily equal before the law or in regard to getting an education or a decent job. Nor were coloreds and whites equal when it came to the way they were treated in public.

In October 1954, a young preacher named Martin Luther King Jr. arrived on the political scene when he became the pastor of Dexter Avenue Baptist Church in Montgomery, Alabama. King became enamored with the teachings of Indian civil rights leader Mohandas "Mahatma" Gandhi, who used nonviolent methods to confront British rule in India. Dr. King was convinced that in the struggle for civil rights for Negroes, peaceful protests could impact public attitudes and bring about positive change, but violence would only worsen conditions in the South.

By the early 1960s, the civil rights movement was gaining momentum, and Montgomery and Birmingham became flash points. Buses were torched, and numerous students were beaten by white mobs reacting against the protests. The backlash resulted in fire bombings, beatings, abusive "crowd control" with the use of high pressure water hoses, and even deaths.

In January 1963, Alabama inaugurated George Wallace as governor. During his inaugural speech, the openly segregationist delighted his audience with his adamant insistence, "Segregation now, segregation tomorrow, segregation forever!"

Then on April 12, Good Friday, Dr. King was arrested for violating an injunction forbidding public demonstrations in Birmingham. King knew about the injunction but marched anyway. He was thrown into solitary confinement for eight days, during which time he penned on pieces of newsprint and even toilet paper perhaps his best-known document: "Letter from Birmingham Jail." Ostensibly written as a response to eight clergymen in Birmingham who had written a letter published in the local newspaper urging King to slow down, contending he was disturbing the peace of Birmingham, King's real audience was the entire nation. Indeed, the letter fanned the flames on both sides of the segregation argument.

King was released from the Birmingham jail, and on August 28, 1963, he delivered his famous "I Have a Dream" speech in front of the Lincoln Memorial in Washington, DC. Three months later, President John F. Kennedy was assassinated in Dallas. Added to all of this chaos was the Cold War between the United States and the Soviet Union, the escalating war in Vietnam, and the growing antiwar protests on college campuses. Within the black community, while preachers such as Martin Luther King Jr. advocated nonviolent protests, Malcolm X, the former gangster turned radical Nation of Islam minister, stoked the fires of racism and violence, contending that "white people are devils" and the "demise of white America is imminent." The nation was seething with turmoil.

Amid the tumultuous bitterness on all sides of the racial debate, Anna Ligon realized that Bill and Eddie playing basketball together was no small matter.

8

SATURDAYS IN GALLATIN were always busy days. People from out of town came in to do their shopping or to frequent one of the local diners. This Saturday was particularly exciting because the Palace Theater was offering specially reduced prices on tickets to the matinee showing of *The Pink Panther*, starring Peter Sellers and David Niven. People who didn't ordinarily attend many movies because they had little money for such luxuries—folks like Eddie and his family, as well as Bill and his family—flocked to the Palace.

The Palace Theater, which opened in 1913 and was still in its original location on Franklin Street, was Tennessee's oldest silent movie theater. By the 1960s, the theater regularly showed popular features, although not always when the films initially released. Nobody in Gallatin seemed to mind. If they really wanted to see a new movie when it first came out, they could drive into Nashville. Few Gallatin residents did.

Eddie and Bo could barely contain their excitement as they covered the five-block walk up North Water Street toward the theater. The boys had talked their parents into going to the movie along with them—a rare treat for the family, especially on a Saturday, Jim Sherlin's insurance collection day. Delilah and Debbie struggled to keep up with the boys' fast pace, and Jim and Betty trailed even farther behind them.

Leading the pack, Eddie was about to take a shortcut by walking down Main Street, one block parallel to the theater. To his delight and surprise, Eddie saw his new friends, Bill and Tyree Ligon, along with their sister, Delores, and their mother, Anna, walking down Main Street, apparently heading toward the theater as well. Eddie started to cross over Main, hoping to intercept the Ligons, when Bo shouted, "Eddie!"

Eddie stopped in his tracks and looked back at his older brother. "What?"

"Get over here," Bo said sternly.

"Why? What's wrong?"

Bo nodded toward the opposite side of the street, where several colored shops were located. Eddie stood just a few steps away from walking on the colored side of the street rather than on the white side. Gallatin's main street was open for blacks to shop, but the white side of the street was off-limits to them.

Eddie raised a questioning eyebrow and was about to blurt, "So what?" but with their parents walking not far behind, Eddie quickly changed his mind, as well as his course. When the family caught up with Eddie, the Sherlins walked down the "correct" side of the street, almost parallel to the Ligon family.

Bill noticed Eddie, and the two boys exchanged glances, as though they shared a secret nobody else could imagine. Anna Ligon and Bo Sherlin, who knew something of Bill and Eddie's secret, both walked with their eyes straight ahead, but for different reasons. Anna did not wish to create an awkward situation for Eddie; Bo did not wish for his parents to discover that he had known about Eddie's playing basketball with a Negro and had done nothing to stop it.

When the two families neared the front entrance of the theater, Jim Sherlin gathered his brood around him below the vertical brightly lit PALACE sign in front of the ticket booth just outside the main entrance. A large crowd—all of them white—had already congregated outside the theater's entrance. So many moviegoers were gathered together that the sidewalk couldn't contain them all. People spilled out onto the street, conversing and laughing with those around them. Most seemed excited to see the matinee show.

The Sherlin siblings waited patiently as their father paid for their tickets. Together the family stepped through the front doors of the theater and made their way through the crowd in search of six seats together on the already packed main floor. Eddie spied a partially empty row and made a beeline for it, standing in the aisle in front of the row to ward off any potential seat hunters until the rest of the family made their way over and claimed their spots.

Meanwhile, the Ligons walked past the front entrance of the Palace and went around to the side of the theater, where several other colored families had congregated, waiting to purchase tickets for the show. Coloreds were not permitted to purchase their tickets in the same line as whites. Nor were coloreds allowed to enter the theater through the main entrance. While whites entered through the doors under the marquee, blacks were required to use the building's side entrance.

Anna Ligon and her family got in line and waited their turn to climb a long fire-escape sort of staircase on the side of the theater that led to the second-floor balcony entrance. No black person dared to sit on the main floor of the theater. In fact, to further define the boundaries between white and colored moviegoers, the entire balcony was enclosed with chicken wire.

At the top of the steps, a colored man named John "Pig-Eye" Rogan sat in a cubbyhole selling tickets. Once they had purchased their tickets, Anna and the kids stepped through the dimly lit doorway and handed the tickets to an old black man, who tore each ticket in half and returned a portion to each moviegoer. The smell of freshly made popcorn wafted through air, mostly rising from the customers on the main floor, but a few Negroes had also purchased popcorn, and the delectable aroma permeated the balcony.

Neither Bill's nor Eddie's family had extra money for a five-cent bag of popcorn.

Bill and Tyree quickly made their way to the front row of the balcony seats, while Anna and Delores followed. Bill leaned forward, poked his head through a hole in the chicken wire as far as he dared, and looked over the side of the balcony at the crowd of white folks seated below. He spotted Eddie in a row off to the right. Seated next to Eddie was Bo, their sisters, and the adult Sherlins on the end of the row. Just then, Eddie glanced up and caught Bill's eye. The two boys grinned but dared not wave.

The families settled in as the theater lights dimmed and an advertisement for Coca-Cola flickered on the large screen. Upstairs, off to the far side of the balcony where the chicken wire had long since been poked through by rambunctious kids, Bill spotted several colored boys tossing paper spitballs over the edge of the balcony railing onto the white audience below. Bill chuckled as he checked out the reaction of the victims. He would never misbehave like that. Besides being a well-mannered young man, Bill knew his mother would break his arm if she ever caught him tossing spitballs from the balcony. Several white kids below were looking up in the direction where the spitballs had originated. One big white boy stood up and shook his fist at someone upstairs. Bill shifted his gaze and stared straight ahead at the Coke advertisement.

Fortunately, a Looney Tunes cartoon feature lit the screen, capturing everyone's attention and diffusing what could have been a volatile situation. Bill settled back to enjoy the show. Oddly enough, *The Pink Panther* and the zany antics of Peter Sellers and the somber rebukes of David Niven resonated with both the coloreds and the whites in the Palace. The crowd laughed uproariously at Sellers and Niven, and when the film concluded, they all left the Palace with a lilt in their steps.

But a block away from the Palace, the moviegoers split off toward their respective sides of the street, whites on one side, coloreds on the other. That's the way it was in Gallatin, Tennessee, in 1963.

9

"HEY, BO, look at that Ferris wheel," Eddie said. "That's the highest one we've ever had here at the fair."

"Sure is. That's a beauty." Bo stepped back to admire the ride and stared upward, catching a glimpse of the top chair swinging in the air. "I can't wait to ride that thing."

Few activities brought the white people of Gallatin together as a community more than the Sumner County Fair, which was held annually on the east side of town during the last week of July or the first week of August. Although a few coloreds could be spotted on the grounds, mostly working in low-paying maintenance positions, Gallatin's Negroes were not welcome, so they had their own fair around Labor Day.

The Sumner County Colored Fair was considered one of the largest colored fairs in the United States. Negroes came from miles around—and some from several states away—to enjoy the fair, a sort of family homecoming and fall festival atmosphere. The popularity of the Colored Fair almost assuaged the pain of not being permitted to attend the white folks' fair—almost.

Like most county fairs in the 1960s, the Sumner County Fair was a family-friendly event, featuring agricultural exhibits and competitions, entertainment and music, carnival rides and lots of unhealthy food.

Bo and Eddie loved going to the fair and especially enjoyed the carnival rides set up literally overnight on the midway. But it took money to ride, so they'd go to the fair hoping to pick up some odd jobs and maybe earn enough spare change to afford a few rides on the Tilt-A-Whirl or the Ferris wheel. Because of his age, Eddie had a tough time finding a job, other than racking pool balls at the billiard hall downtown, and sometimes he made a few dollars running errands. Bo, however, was eminently employable, especially as far as the carnival employers were concerned.

"I hope I can find a job this year." Bo pointed at a large stuffed animal behind one of the carnival games. "I want to win one of those stuffed animals for my girlfriend."

Eddie rolled his eyes. Bo was barely fourteen years old, but he considered himself something of a ladies' man. He had been trying to impress Wanda Jean, a girl from school, so winning a stuffed animal for her might do the trick.

"I don't care about no girls," Eddie said. "I just want to earn enough money to buy some ride tickets."

"Yeah, you say that now," Bo said and laughed. "But pretty soon, some little honey is gonna capture your heart."

"Not me, Bo." Eddie smirked at his older brother. "I'm too busy playing ball to waste time messin' around with girls."

"We'll see!" Bo teased.

Bo and Eddie made the rounds, asking each of the carnival booth managers if they could work for them. "How old are you boys?" one carny barker said.

"I'm almost fifteen," Bo said, exaggerating. "And I'm strong. I can lift boxes or run errands, anything you need done. I want to earn some money so I can win a big stuffed animal to give to my girlfriend."

"Ha, is that right?" the friendly booth barker said. "Well, you're in luck, son. I happen to run the booth with the largest stuffed animals here at the fair. And I could use a bit of help. Matter of fact, I need to make a quick run over to Lebanon to get some more teddy bears. If you can come along and help me, I'll not only pay you a buck or two, but you can have a couple of stuffed animals too."

"Really? All right!" Bo was already dreaming of how his girlfriend might respond when he gave her such a marvelous present.

"Great. Name's Clarence Walker," the man said.

Bo studied the carny. He looked to be in his late forties, but the carnival was a tough life, so he may have been much younger.

The carnival barker glanced at Eddie. "Sorry, I can only use one of you, though."

"That would be me," Bo piped up. "I'm Bo. Bo Sherlin." Bo stuck out his hand as though he and the carny worker were signing a major league baseball contract.

Clarence smiled and shook Bo's hand. "Pleasure to meet ya, Bo. Welcome to the fair."

"Thank you, sir." Bo turned and looked at Eddie. "Don't stay out too late. Dad's working and won't be back for hours, and Mom is in Gatlinburg, so you're the man of the house."

"Okay, Bo." Eddie waved good-bye to his brother and headed off to see what he could discover at the fair. He knew what Bo meant. Their mom had won a trip from the encyclopedia company, so she was gone for the weekend. The girls were with some relatives, so Eddie was on his own. That was okay. He'd have fun checking out the fair.

Clarence and Bo piled into the carny's car and headed off to Lebanon, about thirty minutes away, on Tennessee Highway 109 over mostly rural roads. They arrived in Lebanon shortly before dark, and while Clarence paid for the stuffed animals, Bo loaded the boxes in the trunk and backseat of the car. "I don't think I can get another box in here," Bo called to Clarence. "We're crammed full, from the floorboards to the roof."

"That's good," Clarence said. "I'll be right with you."

The carnival barker and Bo headed back toward Gallatin. Clarence pressed the pedal to the floor, clearly wanting to get back to the fairgrounds while there was still an opportunity to make some money. Clarence began telling Bo some funny stories about carnival life, and they were talking and laughing as they rounded a curve and hit a straight stretch.

Clarence never saw the car that pulled out of a roadside beer joint and careened across the road on the wrong side. Bo saw it though. "Watch out, Clarence!"

Too late.

The three men in the car had been drinking heavily at the roadside bar. The driver pulled the car out of the bar's parking area and gunned the accelerator, veering into the oncoming lane just as Clarence rounded the curve and hit the straightaway.

Even inside the roadside bar, the crash of the enormous head-on collision stopped everyone's hearts. The bartender and patrons dropped everything, ran outside, and were horrified at the sight. Both cars were twisted into hideously contorted metal. The three men in the car driven by the drunk driver were all dead. Clarence was dead as well.

Bo screamed in pain. His face was covered in blood. Both of his legs were broken, as were both of his arms. Breathing was difficult, indicating serious internal injuries as well.

"Call an ambulance!" the bartender yelled.

"Don't bother; call a coroner," someone said. One of the women in the bar called the police instead, who relayed an emergency call to both the fire department and a paramedic crew.

Bo was barely breathing when the ambulance workers arrived. They strapped him onto a gurney and rushed him to a hospital in Gallatin, but he needed more care than they could provide, so they sent him to Vanderbilt Hospital in Nashville. "You can try to get him to Vanderbilt, but he ain't gonna make it," one of the paramedics said.

The Vanderbilt doctors did their best to save Bo's life, but few of them had any hopes for his survival.

Jim Sherlin was traveling his collection route when he heard on the radio about a bad accident between Gallatin and Lebanon. Of course, he had no idea his eldest son had been critically injured in the accident. Sometime later, he got the shocking phone call informing him that Bo was in the hospital. The police had found Bo's wallet, which contained identification.

Betty Sherlin raced back from Gatlinburg when she heard the news, and she and Jim set up a vigil at Vanderbilt Hospital. Members of their church rallied around them, praying for Bo's healing and recovery, as well as caring for Delilah and Debbie. Eddie was too young to be permitted in the Intensive Care Unit, so he spent most of his time on the playground during the day and stayed with relatives at night.

For thirteen days, Bo lay comatose. Betty and Jim and their friends at church kept praying. They refused to give up. On the fourteenth day, Bo slowly rallied. He was in awful shape, unable to move his arms and legs, but he was alive.

The church continued to undergird the family, and almost every day, someone brought them meals. Choir members offered to watch the girls so Betty could get to the grocery store or run other errands. Many members of the congregation sent cards and letters of encouragement. Almost all said, "We're praying for you." And the entire Sherlin family knew that the folks at the church were indeed concerned and praying for Bo's healing, as well as for Jim and Betty's strength.

For six months, Bo needed around-the-clock care. Because of the cast on his body, he couldn't get out of bed by himself, he couldn't feed himself, he couldn't do much of anything without help. When Bo first came home from the hospital, members of the Sherlins' church visited frequently, staying as long as necessary to give Betty and Jim a break, but gradually the number of helpers dwindled, and the family settled into a routine.

Almost as if to shield himself from the nightmare that had invaded his family, Eddie poured himself into sports—he played football, basketball, baseball, and he ran track. He spent any spare time he could find out back, shooting shot after shot at the makeshift backboard and goal that he and Bo had erected.

Jim and Betty felt bad that Bo could no longer play with Eddie. "Let's move his bed over by the window," Jim said. "That way Bo can at least look out the window and watch Eddie and his friends play."

"Good idea," Betty said. "That will give Bo something to do too." Day after day, Bo lay prostrate in his bed, forlornly staring out the window, watching Eddie shoot. Bo instinctively knew he was Eddie's idol when it came to sports—even though Eddie never told him so. But since Bo could no longer play because of his injuries, Eddie played for both of them.

Rather than causing the Sherlin family to question their faith in God, Bo's accident drew the family together. The tensions were still there, but they were able to turn their eyes from their own problems for a while and focus on Bo's needs, which made their small problems pale in comparison. In some ways, Bo's tragic accident was a blessing in disguise.

As he did most Saturday mornings, Eddie got up early and headed for the basketball courts at the park. His favorite court was his sanctuary—his carefree, idealistic world, a respite from all the stress at home—where he could remain oblivious to the rising conflicts in the outside world around him.

Dribbling his basketball as he ran toward the park, he stopped short when he noticed a pickup truck parked in front of the Ligons' house. It looked as though people were loading the truck with furniture and other household items.

Eddie bounced the ball into his arms and eased closer to Bill and Tyree's house. He watched as two older Negro men carried the Ligons' kitchen table out the door, off the porch, and then loaded it onto the truck. Anna Ligon followed, carrying a basketful of clothes, all neatly folded and stacked. Bill, Tyree, and Delores came out the door, all with sullen expressions, their arms filled with boxes.

By now Eddie was at the end of the park property and close to the Ligons' home. "Hey, Bill," he called out.

Clearly in a bad mood, Bill nodded to Eddie but made no move in his direction. Instead he went back inside the house without a word.

Tyree stopped. "Hi, Eddie," he said, barely above a whisper.

"Hey, Tyree," Eddie returned the greeting along with a nod.

Bill came out of the house, carrying another armload of boxes. He plopped the boxes on the tailgate of the truck and waited for one of the men to arrange them so they could make the most of the limited space.

Eddie boldly strode to where Bill was standing. "What's going on, Bill?"

"What's it look like?" Bill retorted angrily. "We're movin'."

"Movin'? Movin' where? Why?"

Bill saw the genuine concern on Eddie's face. "Across town," he said, his tone softening. "Mama's gonna work at Union High School full time, so we're moving over there to Blythe Street, by the Negro park. It's a nice park. Backboards are almost new. Got them new chain nets too. I can shoot all day if I want . . ."

"Great, but what about—"

"Come on, boys. Time to go." Anna carried a final box of kitchen utensils to her car that was parked in front of the pickup truck. She stuffed the box into the trunk and closed it.

Eddie looked at Bill plaintively. He couldn't believe his buddy was moving away. Although it was only across town, it was another world away from Morrison Street.

Bill shrugged. He was upset as well but was desperately trying not to show it, wiping away the tears that filled his eyes. Besides, there was nothing he could do about his mom's decision to move. "See ya around, Eddie," he said quietly.

"Yeah, I'll be looking for you," Eddie replied sadly. He watched as Mrs. Ligon slipped behind the wheel of the car and started the motor. Delores sat in the front passenger side, and Bill and Tyree got into the back. The pickup truck pulled out first and Mrs. Ligon followed. For a long moment, Eddie simply stood staring after the procession.

In the rear seat, Bill turned around and looked back at Eddie. When Eddie caught Bill's glance, it triggered something inside him. He continued watching for another moment or two as the car slowly moved up the street and turned the corner, heading toward the railroad tracks. Suddenly, against all logic, Eddie ran after the car, racing through a backyard and coming out on the same street as the Ligons' vehicle. Recognizing that he couldn't keep up with the car, Eddie stopped and waited as the car and truck approached the tracks.

He heard the baleful sound of an approaching train whistle moaning in the distance. A few seconds later, the red lights flashed and the railroad crossing barrier bar lowered behind the Ligons' car as Eddie watched his pal cross the tracks and drive away. Eddie continued peering after the Ligons until the train roared through, obscuring his view. A tear trickled down Eddie's face. By the time the train was gone, so were Bill and his family.

Eddie returned to the park, but he didn't feel much like playing. He used the ball for a seat and sat down on the sidelines, propping his elbows on his knees and holding his chin in his hands, watching some other boys play. For more than a half hour, he simply stared ahead as his thoughts raced. *I've lost my brother, and now I've lost my new friends. Although I'm close to my sisters, I feel alone in the world. I have nothing left but sports.*

Eddie stood, bounced the ball hard on the asphalt surface, moved onto the court, and took a shot.

Swish!

10

"LET'S GO! GET IN THE CAR!" Jim Sherlin called to his family members. "We gotta get to the church on time!" Jim glanced at his watch. It was nearing half past six, and the choir was scheduled to rehearse before the service began at seven thirty that evening. Jim had just gotten home from work and had barely been able to gobble down a quick bite of dinner. Eddie, Delilah, and Debbie had hurried to get their homework done as soon as they'd gotten home from school. Their dad was hurrying them along, encouraging them to get into the car and head to the special church service that night.

The start of the new school year always signaled time for revival services at the Assembly of God church in Gallatin. Many of the other denominational congregations in town held revivals around the same time of year. Something about the crisp September air and the beginning of harvest time for the farmers carried over to the church, creating an atmosphere of expectation. Many churches distributed flyers and hung large signs in front of their sanctuaries, announcing a time of spiritual renewal. Most hardened unbelievers ignored the notices, but revival was not merely a season of evangelism. It was also a time for the faithful to renew their commitments and for backsliders to return to their first love.

The Sherlins attended revival services anytime they were held at the church. Revival services had the flavor of an indoor camp meeting, so enthusiasm ran high. The congregation was accustomed to great gospel singing and strong preaching during revival time. Occasionally, the church brought in a famous guest singer for the week. And preachers! Oh, the marvelous preachers the Sherlins heard. Brother David Wilkerson, author of the bestselling book *The Cross and the Switchblade*, a powerful tale detailing Wilkerson's courageous evangelistic forays in the toughest sections of New York City and the subsequent conversion of gang member Nicky Cruz, was one of many outstanding speakers who had graced their pulpit. The congregation came with an attitude of great expectancy. Something big was likely to happen during revival time.

The Sherlin family—except for Bo, who remained at home with a neighbor because he was still immobile in a body cast—arrived at the church and parked, just as they did on Sunday mornings, in their normal space. Jim and Betty, as well as Delilah and Debbie hurried to the choir loft while Eddie slid into one of the front rows.

Soon the service began with lively congregational singing and testimonies. People all over the sanctuary stood and shared how God had blessed their lives after they had met Jesus. The choir sang a rousing version of an old favorite, "Victory in Jesus." Fortunately for Jim, they didn't need much rehearsal. Everyone knew the song and sang it with gusto.

Tonight's revival service did not feature a special speaker. Instead, Reverend Daley was preaching, so Eddie was uncomfortable already. Eddie got nervous every time Brother Daley preached. It always seemed as though the pastor was reading Eddie's thoughts, looking deep into his heart and mind and digging up his most personal secrets. Indeed, tonight as the preacher railed against sins of every sort, Eddie's mind quickly returned to the last time he and Bo stole cigarettes from the gas station a few weeks before Bo's accident.

Most of the adults in Eddie's extended family smoked cigarettes, so, not surprisingly, Bo took up the habit in his early teens. Eddie tried smoking, but it didn't appeal to him as much as it did to Bo, who was trying to establish a bad-boy James Dean image. Besides, since they had such little money, neither of them could afford cigarettes.

The boys went into the Red-A gas station, and Bo browsed, creating the appearance he was going to buy something. Meanwhile, Eddie watched until the gas station attendant went outside or was busy helping another customer. Eddie quickly reached across the counter and grabbed a pack of cigarettes from one of the open racks. He stashed the stolen cigarettes under his shirt and slowly ambled toward the front door, remaining as inconspicuous as possible. Occasionally, he snatched a piece of bubble gum or candy for himself.

Eddie always felt guilty after stealing. He tried to rationalize his thievery with the truth that their family was poor. He even thought that if he ever earned a few extra dollars helping local farmers harvest their tobacco, he'd come back and pay old Mr. Stockton, who owned the gas station. He might even confess his involvement in facilitating Bo's habit. Of course, he never did.

But that night as Brother Daley preached a fire-and-brimstone sermon, conviction fell heavily on Eddie. Although stealing wasn't Eddie's only sin, he could imagine himself dangling over the fires of hell, holding on by the length of a cigarette—a burning cigarette, at that.

Eddie's spiritual insecurity and the gnawing feeling that he could never be good enough for God, that he could never live up to the Bible's high standards, and his sense of guilt increased exponentially the longer Brother Daley preached. And that night, Brother Daley was on a roll! Perspiration streamed down his face as he passionately implored his people to "get right with God" and respond to God's call on their lives.

Eddie cringed when he said, "The Bible says very clearly that we've all sinned and fallen short of the glory of God. It's not how big your sins are or how many sins you have committed." Then he lowered his voice and said, "If you have ever sinned, you need a Savior."

Something deep within Eddie told him Brother Daley was telling the truth, so even though the message made him uncomfortable, he was grateful. *If I had a disease, I guess I'd want the doctor to tell me. Especially if he knew a cure.*

And Brother Daley was clear about the cure. "While we were yet sinners, Jesus Christ died for us. He paid the penalty for your sins and mine."

Eddie fidgeted in the pew.

"The wages of our sin is death, but the free gift of God is life, eternal life available through Jesus Christ. If you believe in your heart that God raised Jesus from the dead, and you confess with your mouth and are willing to turn your life over to Jesus and let him help you turn from your sin, then you *will* be saved!"

Eddie had heard similar sermons before, but for some reason tonight's message seared into his heart and mind in a fresh way. And for the first time, the message struck Eddie as good news rather than mere condemnation. Brother Daley no longer seemed so scary to Eddie but rather more like a loving father concerned for his children's safety.

"If you want to have a real relationship with Jesus, not just mere religion," Brother Daley said as he walked down from the pulpit area, "I am inviting you to come here to the front of the church and pray with us. You can place your trust in Jesus right now. Ask him to forgive you and give you a fresh, clean start in life."

The church musicians played "Just As I Am." Several people walked down the aisle to the front of the sanctuary. Some knelt at the altar rail, while others remained standing. "Oh, hallelujah!" Eddie heard someone shout. "Glory to God!" someone else said loudly.

Eddie's heart was pounding wildly. He knew what he had to do. Although he felt tears trickling down his face, his response to the gospel was not so much emotional as it was an act of Eddie's will. He decided that he wanted to trust Jesus. He stepped out of the pew in which he had been sitting, walked to the front of the church, and dropped to his knees.

Eddie didn't need anyone to help him pray. He had prayed for forgiveness hundreds of times in his young life, but he was grateful when Brother Dawson, a kindly older man with a gentle spirit, knelt down next to him and put an arm around his shoulder. With the music still playing in the background, members of the congregation singing softly, and Brother Daley continuing to encourage others to trust Jesus, it was almost hard for Eddie to hear Brother Dawson when he asked, "Eddie, why are you here?"

"I want to turn my life over to Jesus. I'm sorry for my sins. I don't want to live like that anymore."

"Well, Eddie, you know what the Bible says," Brother Dawson spoke softly as he turned to the back of his Bible. "'If we will confess our sins, he is faithful to forgive us of our sins, and to cleanse us of all unrighteousness.' Do you remember that, Eddie?"

Eddie nodded. "I stole a bunch of cigarettes," Eddie confessed to Brother Dawson. "I didn't smoke 'em, but I did steal them."

Brother Dawson nodded. "I understand, Eddie. You don't need to tell me; just tell it to the Lord."

"And I've had a bunch of lustful thoughts. And I've stolen candy."

"Uh-huh."

"And I've been using some bad language too. And there are some people I'm really starting to hate."

"Okay, Eddie. You don't need to confess your sins to me or to Brother Daley or to the church or anyone else. Only the Lord Jesus can really forgive you. Only he can satisfy your soul. Tell him all about it. Ask him to forgive you and to wash you clean. And then ask him to give you the power to live the way the Bible says and to help you love other people the way he loves them."

Eddie nodded at Brother Dawson and started to pray aloud, quietly but emphatically. The saintly gentleman next to Eddie closed his eyes and prayed along with him.

"Jesus, I am trusting you with my life from now on. I'm sorry I have sinned so much, but Brother Daley and Brother Dawson say you are willing to forgive me. So I'm asking you to do that." Eddie continued praying for several minutes. He didn't use fancy, religious language. He simply poured out his heart to God, asking for his forgiveness and help. "I'm trusting you, Jesus, to save me. Save me from hell, save me from sin, and even save me from my own selfishness."

Not until Eddie opened his eyes and looked around did he realize his parents were kneeling behind him, praying for him, as well as for themselves and for Bo and for the girls. Delilah and Debbie sat in the front row of the church. Tears of joy streamed down their faces.

Eddie slowly stood to his feet. "How do you feel?" Brother Dawson asked.

"I don't know how to describe it," Eddie replied honestly. "I just feel clean on the inside. Is that what it means to be born again?"

Brother Dawson laughed. "That's about as good of a definition as I've heard." He patted Eddie on the back. "Now let me give you a couple of tips that will help you stay on track with God. First, make sure you read some from the Bible every day. Understand?"

"Yes, sir," Eddie replied, drying the wet tears on his face.

"Second, talk to God, just like we are talking right now. That's what prayer is—talking with God. Got that?"

"Yes, sir."

"Third, tell someone what you have done here tonight, someone who knows you well and will be able to notice the changes that come about in your life."

"Okay."

"And fourth, make sure you get to church as often as possible. There's nothing magical about any of these things, but they will help you stay spiritually strong."

"Thank you, Brother Dawson."

"You're welcome, Eddie," the elderly man said. "I know you have never been a bad boy. But we both know that what you did here tonight was an important step for you."

"Yes, sir, that's right. But Brother Dawson . . ." Eddie shuffled and looked down at the carpet. "I've never felt that I was good enough for God, that I could ever live up to all the rules and regulations in the Bible."

"Ha! Me neither, Eddie." The old man slapped his knees. "But that's the best part of the Good News."

"The best part?"

"Yes, you don't have to be good enough. In fact, none of us are, or ever will be good enough for God on our own. But Jesus *is* good enough. When you trust him, you can go right into God's presence. The Bible says if you believe God raised Jesus from the dead and confess that with your mouth, you will be saved. You've done that tonight, Eddie. So you can be sure that from this night on, *you are saved*."

People around the room were beaming, their broad smiles lighting the room. Several were praying aloud, and others stood singing at the front of the church. Reverend Daley saw Eddie at the altar area and with one look at Eddie's countenance said, "Eddie Sherlin, you got saved here tonight!"

Eddie looked up at the preacher, smiled sheepishly, and nodded. "Yes, sir, I did."

11

"HEY, EDDIE! Show 'em how you can dunk the volleyball," Eddie's best friend, Buddy Bruce, called to him from the bleachers on the far side of the Gallatin High School gymnasium. Although Eddie was only in eighth grade and not even five foot eight, he could jump like he had built-in springboards in his legs.

Eddie smiled at Buddy, his gentle giant of a friend. Everyone in school was afraid of Buddy because of his stocky, muscular build. Everyone but Eddie. Eddie knew better. Inside Buddy's bulky bear of a body was a good, caring kid. But there was also the tough guy. Buddy became Eddie's protector, his bodyguard. If a bully threatened Eddie, Buddy whipped the daylights out of that guy.

Now that Eddie was playing basketball on the junior high team, he spent most of his spare time in the gymnasium, and Buddy was his biggest fan. One day, when Eddie was just fooling around playing a game of H-O-R-S-E, someone accidentally kicked a volleyball in his direction. Eddie caught the ball on the first bounce and in one or two steps, as though he were driving the lane to shoot a layup with a basketball, he palmed the volleyball and leaped toward the basketball rim. With room to spare, he slam-dunked the volleyball through the net. Watching from the bleachers, Buddy went nuts, yelling and cheering.

"Do it again!" Buddy yelled.

So Eddie did, dunking the volleyball as easily as he had the first time.

The other players in the gym hooted and hollered as though Eddie had just scored the winning bucket in the state championship game. "Whoa, Eddie! That is fantastic!" one of Eddie's teammates said. "How did you do that? How can you jump so high?"

"I don't know," Eddie responded. "I just saw the rim and jumped for it." He smiled sheepishly. "I wasn't tryin' to show off."

"Show off all you want!" another of Eddie's teammates gushed. "We don't mind."

Before long, word got out about the eighth grader at Gallatin who could dunk a volleyball. By the time Eddie completed junior high, although he grew a mere two inches, he was able to dunk a full-sized basketball.

When the varsity basketball coach, Jerry Vradenburg, saw Eddie dunk the ball, he was amazed. "Tell you what, Eddie. Why don't you do some layups before the varsity game tonight and warm up the crowd by showing them how you can dunk the ball."

"Really, Coach?" Eddie said. "You'd let me do that?"

"Sure thing. Even though slam-dunking is not permitted during regulation play, I think the home fans will love it." He smiled. "And I'll keep the referees busy down in the locker room while you entertain the crowd."

"Okay, Coach. I'll be glad to do it. It should be fun," Eddie said.

Tonight would be Eddie's first official experience as part of the famed Gallatin Green Wave. The unusual school nickname was initially applied to Gallatin athletes by William Bright Hunter, a popular Gallatin teacher and coach in the early 1930s. Coach Hunter was an avid fan of Tulane University in New Orleans—known as the original Green Wave. Absent any other label, Coach Hunter co-opted the tag and it stuck.

As the Gallatin Green Wave prepared to play the Springfield Yellow Jackets that evening, Eddie dressed in his junior high uniform and jogged onto the court. He stopped near the foul line. One of the team managers tossed Eddie a basketball. Eddie took several dribbles and then leaped toward the rim, soaring through the air, his feet nearly twenty-four inches off the floor, while balancing the basketball in his hands. He allowed his left hand to drop off the ball as his right hand dunked it through the net.

The crowd of Gallatin fans roared their approval. They had rarely seen tall players able to dunk the ball, much less a player Eddie's size. "Do it again!" someone called.

Eddie smiled toward the bleachers in the direction from which the voice had come. The manager bounced another ball to Eddie as he jogged around to the top of the key and continued on a hard-driving layup. Eddie, leaping into the air and grasping the ball with both hands, slam-dunked the ball through the net.

The crowd erupted in cheers and applause. Downstairs in the locker room, Coach Vradenburg smiled as he wrapped up his pre-game pep talk. "Okay, boys, let's go get 'em!" The varsity Green Wave players bounded out of the locker room, up the stairs, and onto the basketball court to the enthusiastic cheers of the home-team spectators.

Meanwhile, the Springfield team and fans, already demoralized by Eddie's performance, sat in a subdued hush. If Gallatin had an eighth grader who could dunk the ball, they didn't stand a chance.

Across town, over at Union High School, Bill Ligon had experienced a growth spurt. The brightest influence in Bill's life, other than his mom, was George Randolf Offitt, the Union High School bandleader. Unusually pale for a Negro, Mr. Offitt could pass for a white person outside of Gallatin but was committed to helping black children learn music, so he taught all his life at Union. Mr. Offitt followed in the footsteps of his father, a former band director at Union, and poured his effort into developing talented young musicians throughout the Union ranks. Since the elementary school was right down the street from the high school, Mr. Offitt went out of his way to start giving the students instrument lessons when they were young. He often allowed the sixth graders and other "more mature" elementary school students to perform with the high school band, keeping the students interested as they transitioned from elementary to junior high and into their final years in the Union school system.

Beginning in third grade, Bill had been accepted to play clarinet in Mr. Offitt's band. He played clarinet for three years and then moved to the trombone, which he played from sixth to eighth grade, despite the fact that the mouthpieces for woodwind and brass instruments were completely different. After eighth grade, football and basketball lured him away from the band.

The Union band—well-known in Gallatin and, indeed, most of middle Tennessee—was featured every year during the Gallatin Christmas parade. This performance was the closest any black musician ever felt to being truly accepted by the white people in town. But all too soon, the parade was over. The blacks and the whites were back to walking on separate sides of the street.

For Bill, the band represented freedom. That too could be credited to Mr. Offitt's dedication. The bandleader arranged for his band to perform in as many parades and concerts as possible, many of which required traveling to various parts of Tennessee and even to other states. The travel associated with the Union band made it one of the most attractive extracurricular activities available to students.

But troublemakers need not apply, because everyone knew Mr. Offitt, a World War II veteran, ran a tight ship. A kind, gentle man, Mr. Offitt was a living example of the biblical definition of meekness—power under control. He rarely had to raise his voice. Because of the respect band members had for Mr. Offitt, never once were any of his student musicians the cause of any racially motivated problems or even usual teenage mischief.

Always meticulously dressed, Mr. Offitt inspired his students to aspire to excellence in performance and in their personal lives. When the band traveled, he required the students to be neatly dressed, polite, and well-mannered to one another, and especially to white strangers with whom the band members came in contact.

Bill, of course, was a model student. He had to be whether or not he wanted to, because Anna's classroom, where she taught reading and writing, was located right across the hall from the principal's office. If Bill was called to the principal's office for any reason, Anna would know. And if Bill got a paddling from a teacher at school, Anna gave permission for the school principal to apply "the board of education to the seat of learning" again. Then he received another reminder when he got home. But Bill didn't need many paddlings. Between the church members watching out for and holding him accountable and Anna's fellow teachers keeping their eyes on him, Bill had little opportunity to get in trouble. He was also a good student and one of the more popular boys at Union Junior High.

Bill, no longer a skinny kid, had filled out physically and was growing taller every year. He loved football and played quarterback on the Union Junior High team. He had also developed into quite a basketball player, playing the forward position on the junior high squad.

During the summer, Bill earned $3 per day caddying at the Gallatin Country Club. He enjoyed being around some of the more affluent members of the community, including doctors, lawyers, and other professionals. These country club members not only opened his eyes to a broader world, but they also seemed to recognize Bill's potential.

One day, while standing on the fifth tee waiting for some slow players in front of his foursome, Marion Barlow, a leading businessman for whom Bill often caddied, tapped the ashes from his cigar against a ball washer. "Boy, you seem pretty sharp. What are you going to do after high school?"

"I'm hoping to continue my education, sir," Bill answered nonchalantly.

"You gonna play some ball too?"

"Oh, yes, sir. I certainly hope so."

"That's good." Barlow nodded. "Are you still gonna be available to caddy for me?"

"I hope so, sir."

"Good, that's real good." Barlow tapped another ash onto the ground. "You just keep your eyes off my wife, now, ya hear?"

"Of course, sir." Bill looked down at the ground and shuffled uneasily.

"I know you see her sunbathing at the swimming pool when we take the clubs back," Barlow said, "but I'd better never catch you giving her the eye. You understand me, boy?"

"I do, sir. I surely do."

What Bill did not say was that he had no interest in Barlow's white wife and couldn't care less where she was. Nor did Bill have any interest in Barlow's lily-white daughter, or any white girl, for that matter. He never understood why Barlow and his ilk always assumed all the black boys wanted a white girlfriend. Of course, he didn't say that to Mr. Barlow.

Caddying for Barlow, indeed! Bill thought.

Bill recognized the dichotomy between the way Negroes and whites were treated in Gallatin. His frustration with the status quo grew ever stronger as he advanced through junior high and prepared to enter high school. Bill, an avid reader, gravitated more and more toward the teachings of Malcolm X. He devoured the radical militant's materials, as well as those by civil rights activist Paul Robeson and other black leaders who advocated immediate change rather than gradual assimilation and acceptance of the blacks into American culture. Yet Bill himself realized that change was more likely to come slowly to Gallatin, if at all.

Bill perceived that although some people preferred pitting Malcolm X's brash rhetoric against Martin Luther King Jr.'s nonviolent actions, the two leaders weren't really all that far apart in their ultimate goals. Bill picked up on the changes in both leaders as Malcolm X became more disillusioned with the Nation of Islam's black militancy, while Martin Luther King Jr. was becoming increasingly impatient with conservative Christians' unwillingness to treat coloreds and whites equally.

All of that changed, of course, at a Memphis motel on April 4, 1968, when escaped convict James Earl Ray assassinated Dr. King. The gunman was a devout supporter of Alabama's Democrat governor George C. Wallace, a staunch segregationist.

King had barely been laid to rest before violence and disruptive demonstrations broke out across America, especially in the South—Memphis and Atlanta—but in many northern cities, as well—Chicago, Detroit, Philadelphia. Angry colored people rioted in most major cities, smashing windows and setting fire to buildings. Looting was rampant.

Ku Klux Klan crosses flared in response as far north as Akron, Ohio, where racially motivated riots and fires set downtown Akron ablaze. Police in Nashville and most of the towns surrounding the city, including Gallatin, imposed a dusk-to-dawn curfew.

Every evening, police in Nashville and Gallatin patrolled the neighborhoods as well as downtown, warning residents through squawking bullhorns, "Get off the streets. Get in your homes now, and don't come out until morning. Violators will be severely prosecuted." Nobody knew for sure what "severely prosecuted" might mean, but everyone assumed that anyone who was foolish enough to go out after curfew risked being shot on the spot. Liquor, gasoline, guns, and ammunition sales were all restricted or banned in town for several weeks following Dr. King's death.

Fear and anxiety gripped Gallatin. During the daylight hours, people of both races gathered in small clusters all over town, expressing their concerns. Pastors and other church leaders begged their parishioners to remain calm and refrain from violence. "Don't you even think about repaying evil with evil!" Bishop Lula Mae Swanson cautioned the small congregation at the Original Church of God one Sunday morning. "The Good Book says, 'Vengeance is mine, saith the Lord, and I will repay.' Don't you be overcome by evil but overcome evil with good."

Pastor Daley preached a similar message to the white congregation at the First Assembly of God church during an early service. "'Don't let the sun go down on your anger,'" he said, quoting the Bible. "And the Scripture says to let 'all bitterness and wrath and anger and clamor and slander and malice be put away from you.'"

"Folks, what's goin' on around our country and right outside these doors just isn't right." Brother Daley stepped out from behind the pulpit and into the aisle. He was nearly in tears as he implored his congregation. "Brothers and sisters, the Bible says, 'Be kind to one another, tender-hearted, forgiving each other, just as God in Christ also has forgiven you.' That's how we Christians are to live, and that's how we are to respond—not in hatred, but in love."

As the Sherlin family walked to their car after the service, Eddie was deeply disturbed. "Mama, why is it like this? Why is there so much trouble between whites and coloreds? What's so hard about being nice to one another?"

"Oh, I don't know, Eddie," Betty Sherlin said, as she wrapped her arm around his shoulder. "That's just the way things have always been around these parts. Some folks want to hang on to bitterness. But just because something has always been doesn't mean it has to remain that way. When I was a little girl, we never associated with coloreds. Now, I have some good friends who are colored, and I love 'em the same as I love white folk."

Betty thought of Anna Ligon, to whom she had sold some encyclopedias and with whom she had maintained a casual friendship. Although sometimes Betty expressed an attitude that colored people were inferior or even dangerous, as when she warned her kids to be careful in the colored part of town, her attitude had slowly started to change.

"Truth is," Betty said, "we know down inside that we're all equal, and if we have a loving and forgiving spirit in our hearts, we can all get along just fine. You know, Eddie, what they say is true: 'color is only skin deep.' Men may look at the outward appearance but God looks on the heart."

"I think you're right, Mom," Eddie said, as he thought of his friendship with Bill Ligon. He wondered how Bill's mom would answer the question. Or how Bill himself might respond. Eddie looked at his mom and smiled. For all her inconsistencies, Eddie knew that his mom loved God and loved people, regardless of their color. What more could he ask?

All over Gallatin, people were talking about the race riots they had seen on television or heard about on the radio. Whether outside Roscoe Robinson's barbershop for coloreds or across the street at Bob White's barbershop for whites or inside Joey's Place, the pool hall frequented by Negroes, or any of the local hangouts, the conversations were all intense.

"Why they burnin' up those cities and smashin' things downtown?" Roscoe asked a group of black men who had gathered at the barbershop. "And why we gotta be off the streets and in our homes after dark?"

"Everyone's angry," said Jeremiah Carter, a retired Union schoolteacher sitting in one of the chairs, scanning the newspaper and shaking his head. Mr. Carter was one of Roscoe's regulars who came into the barbershop every morning not to get a haircut but to talk. He and his opinions were highly regarded. "Dr. King provided hope to a lot of folks. Hope that maybe things would change around here. You know it's been almost fifteen years since Rosa Parks stood up to 'em in Montgomery."

"Who's Rosa Parks?" Willie Murphy, a young man in his early twenties asked.

Mr. Carter sighed and ran his hand through his hair, surprised at Willie's question. *Rosa Parks.* "Well, back in 1955, Rosa Parks was a forty-two-year-old seamstress who also worked as a secretary for the Montgomery branch of the National Association for the Advancement of Colored People."

Willie leaned closer, not wanting to miss a word.

Ever the educator, Mr. Carter spoke carefully but with great sadness. "Montgomery's buses had seats designated with a white section up front and a colored section in the rear. The bus drivers limited the number of seats available to Negroes any time the number of whites on the bus exceeded the number of coloreds. In other words, they'd take a seat from the Negro and give it to the white person."

"Nah," Willie said. "They wouldn't do that, would they?"

"Yes, they would." Several of the colored men in the shop nodded.

"Well, when a bus driver demanded that Mrs. Parks give up her seat in the black section on a crowded city bus so a white passenger could sit there, she refused. The driver called the police, who arrested her for violating the city's segregation laws."

"And they took her to jail for not giving up her seat on the bus?" Willie asked.

Jeremiah Carter nodded and looked to the ceiling for a few moments, as though he were reminiscing. "She was one courageous lady. Her simple action led to a campaign in which coloreds boycotted the city buses, refusing to ride until they were desegregated. Their protests lasted 381 days. A year after Ms. Parks said, 'No more,' a federal court declared Montgomery's bus segregation law as unconstitutional."

"So did things change?" Willie asked.

Jeremiah Carter raised the newspaper filled with reports of violence following the assassination of Martin Luther King Jr. and waved it toward Willie. "Not much, but we still got hope."

"I ain't got no hope," a young man told Roscoe as he stepped out of the barber's chair where he'd been sitting. "It won't be long till the streets are burnin' right here in Gallatin."

108

His words were prophetic. A few nights later, several Molotov cocktails were thrown into an empty building and a vacant house, and numerous windows of homes and businesses were broken near Union Elementary School. Firemen doused the flames, and the buildings suffered only minor damage. But later that same night, a large tobacco warehouse filled with equipment, straw, and dried crops on Red River Road was torched. The 144,000-square-foot structure was the largest tobacco warehouse in Gallatin, and the resulting inferno was enormous and could be seen for blocks.

Sirens screamed through the night. Firemen fought the flames but realized their efforts were futile. With no hope of saving the tobacco barn, they aimed their heavy four-inch hoses at the properties nearby in an attempt to prevent them from catching fire. A number of Gallatin's citizens stood outside their homes and watched as the warehouse burned to the ground. Other residents cowered in fear, worried sick that the entire town might be set on fire.

"Good God! What's happening here?" one man cried.

"Who would do something like this?" someone yelled as people ignored the curfew and ran door-to-door warning their neighbors about the fire.

"You know who," a gruff-voiced man answered. "Those darkies are out of control, and we'd better show 'em who's boss!"

Local police canvassed the area and quickly apprehended four Negroes, charging three of them with the crime and printing their names in the *Gallatin News Examiner*, the local newspaper. Although evidence was sketchy, the judge gave the men a choice: either join the army—in the midst of the Vietnam War—or go to jail. They chose the army. Most people in Gallatin thought the judge was being too easy on the troublemakers. The judge and the police felt they were being gracious.

The police sergeant who checked in the boys at the police station after their arrest put it this way, "Many people in town don't want the darkies indicted; they want them hung by the neck until they're dead."

12

THE MORNING SUN lit the kitchen as Betty prepared the usual breakfast of oatmeal and toast for her family. The family moved when Eddie completed the seventh grade and was now living in a more modern home at 128 Sunset Boulevard. The small house was located on the outskirts of town not far from where the colored fair was held each year. Like Bill Ligon, his counterpart at Union High, Eddie Sherlin, who was now a senior, was doing well in high school. He was the star quarterback on the football team, the highest-scoring player on the basketball team, and the most popular fellow at Gallatin High. Despite being bashful and uncomfortable speaking to crowds of people, Eddie easily won the election to become senior class president. Eddie covered his shyness by immersing himself in sports. Unlike Bill, Eddie was a poor student, but not because he lacked intelligence. He simply couldn't be bothered with schoolwork when he was preparing for an upcoming game. Yet Eddie somehow always received passing grades.

Bo had recovered from his accident, but he was confined to a wheelchair. He was Eddie's biggest fan, and with the help of Jim and Betty, he attended every game his brother played. Living out his dreams vicariously through Eddie had become Bo's life.

Two male voices chattered incessantly on the radio in Betty Sherlin's kitchen. "It's 8 a.m., and you are listening to Jesse and Al."

Betty stirred the bubbling pot of oatmeal as Delilah and Debbie, now sixteen and fourteen, respectively, sat at the kitchen table, cutting out newspaper articles about Eddie's sports accomplishments.

Jesse and Al enthusiastically babbled about the triumphant Gallatin High School basketball team. "And congratulations to the Gallatin High Green Wave hoopsters," Jesse said, "who took their perfect record of twelve wins and no losses into the divisional playoffs last night and emerged victorious, defeating the Hendersonville Commandos 58–39. Quite a definitive win, wouldn't you say, Al?"

"It certainly was, Jesse. The Green Wave looks hard to stop, especially when that Eddie Sherlin starts sinking shots from several feet outside the key."

Delilah smiled as she trimmed around a photo of Eddie featured in the sports section of the local newspaper. The photographer had caught Eddie in the midst of a jump shot, his feet off the hardwood by more than twelve inches, his body perfectly straight in the air, his hands in complete control of the basketball. Beneath the photo, which prominently showed the number 22 on his jersey, the headline read, GREEN WAVE WINS BIG!

Debbie watched excitedly as Delilah finished cutting out the picture and carefully pasted it in the family scrapbook.

The radio show hosts continued their enthusiastic banter. "Yes, sir, Al," Jesse jumped in, "and a win against the Springfield Yellow Jackets on Thursday night will put them smack-dab in the finals."

"And what about the performance of that All-State guard Eddie Sherlin? Twenty-nine points! What a shooter!"

"No kidding," Jesse agreed. "That boy just can't be stopped."

"He's sure something special," Al said.

Debbie couldn't take it anymore. She ran to the kitchen doorway and called upstairs. "Hurry up, Eddie! They're bragging on you on the morning radio show again!"

"Aw, that's okay," Eddie called back. "They're just yakking."

"Maybe so, but they're yakking about you!"

Eddie stepped into the kitchen, dressed and ready for school. He took his place at the table along with his sisters. Now a handsome young man, he'd remained humble and kind despite all the accolades heaped on him for his athletic ability. He still played football, basketball, and ran track. He loved baseball too, but Gallatin High didn't have a team. He even won a state tennis championship, even though he had never picked up a racket prior to entering the tournament. Sports and winning came naturally to Eddie.

Bo wheeled his wheelchair into the kitchen, a basketball resting in his lap. He tossed the ball to Eddie, nearly knocking over Eddie's bowl of oatmeal, but in a last-second grab, Eddie snatched the ball away from the table. Bo ignored Delilah and Debbie's effusive gushing over the newspaper clippings and looked directly at Eddie. "What's the name of that forward over at Springfield? He looks pretty quick."

"Knotts," Eddie responded between mouthfuls of oatmeal. "Yeah, he's quick all right. But I can keep up with him."

"Yeah, Knotts." Bo nodded. "He's the guy to worry about. You guys might want to break out of the one-three-one defense and go man-to-man for a while. That way Knotts will have someone on him all the time."

"Yep, good idea," Eddie said, knowing full well that Coach Vradenburg was not about to run a man-to-man defense against Springfield. But Eddie also knew how much Bo enjoyed playing coach, so he didn't contest his brother's suggestions.

Just then, Jim Sherlin entered the kitchen and made a beeline for the coffeepot. "Mornin', everyone." He poured his coffee and looked over at Eddie. "How's the knee?"

"Oh, not too bad, Dad. I just took a bad fall, that's all."

"Well, they should have called a technical foul on that Hendersonville boy who tripped you." Jim Sherlin waved his full cup of coffee

113

as he spoke. "He was way out of line on that one. I think his coach must have paid off the ref."

"They don't do that in high school basketball, Dad," Bo said. "But that kid did deserve to be ejected."

"Any pain in the knee?" Jim ignored Bo's comment and looked back to Eddie.

"Naw, Dad. Really, I'm fine," Eddie assured him.

"Okay, but if you feel anything different, be sure to let Coach Vradenburg know so he can rest ya," Jim suggested.

"Sure will, Dad."

"Ooh, look how nice this one came out," Debbie said, fawning over her work on the scrapbook. "Eddie, if they don't quit taking your picture so often, we're going to have to get more scrapbooks. I just got all your football pictures glued in, and I'm already out of space. And I need to start putting in the photos from your senior year in basketball!" Debbie thumbed through numerous pages in the scrapbook, all filled with pictures of Eddie's sports exploits.

"Time to go," Jim Sherlin reported to his family, even though nobody seemed to be listening.

"Me too," Betty said. "I have a list of contacts to visit today. I'll probably not be home till dinner."

The morning deejays continued in their irrepressible good humor. "Let's get this morning poppin' with the number-one song in the country," Al said.

"You betcha!" Jesse said. "Here are The Archies performing their hit song, 'Sugar, Sugar.'" The bouncy beat of bubblegum music filled the air, and as silly as it was, the song brought a smile to everyone's faces as the Sherlin family set out to begin their days. Debbie blew on the last photo she had pasted in the scrapbook and hummed along to the music. "It's going to be a great day!" she said aloud to herself.

13

SCHOOL BUSES DISGORGED the loads of students in front of
Gallatin High School, home to nearly fourteen hundred students,
almost all of whom were white. A few courageous Negro families
had braved the other families' attitudes, which ranged from indifference to contempt regarding the US Supreme Court's decision to
integrate public schools. Each year since the Court's decision, two
or three more Negroes asked for and received permission to attend
Gallatin High. But the numbers were minuscule.

Inside the school, looking out his office window, high school principal Dan Herron ran his hand over his short, closely cropped hair.
Now in his midfifties, Principal Herron possessed a stoic, military-like
presence and exuded sternness and professionalism in all his deal-
ings with faculty and students alike—and sometimes even at home
with his wife and children. A strict disciplinarian, Herron served
as an infantry officer during the Korean War. He signed on with
Gallatin High School in 1963 and was a no-nonsense principal. He
was probably one of the best men Gallatin could have in his position
during the tumultuous years of desegregation, and especially following the assassination of Dr. Martin Luther King Jr. Schools around
the country experienced racial strife almost daily. Fights between

115

blacks and whites, a growing gang presence in (and out of) schools, and the tension within the general population made it difficult to navigate the new policies being enforced by the federal government.

Principal Herron, a bright man with a great heart who was known for his personal integrity, possessed a genuine concern for every one of his students, regardless of their race, status, or family background. He knew the Negro students were coming to Gallatin High. The courts had already decided that. And as much as the Klan and some other outspoken critics in Gallatin kicked up dust and complained, their expressions would not thwart the integration process. Right now the school had only four or five colored students, but he knew the buses would soon be filled with them. The potential for problems and discontent was mammoth.

From his window, Principal Herron spotted Eddie Sherlin bounding up the sidewalk. Eddie walked to school every day, or, more accurately, most days he ran to school, either playing catch with a football or dribbling a basketball.

Principal Herron nodded to his vice principal, Bob Marlin, who walked into the office. "I'd take ten Eddie Sherlins any day," the principal said. "The boy minds his manners." He watched Eddie until he entered the school grounds and got lost in the crowd.

Once inside the school, Eddie proceeded down a hallway packed with students who were opening lockers, getting out books, and preparing for the day. Everyone seemed to know Eddie, or at least thought they did. All students knew his name even if they knew little of his personality or the motivation behind his excellent athletic career at Gallatin. Few of his fellow students ever would have dreamed that the popular Sherlin was haunted by insecurity and shyness, especially around females, who flocked to him wherever he went. Fewer yet knew that Eddie's determination to win at sports was fueled by his desire to play for his older brother, Bo, who remained wheelchair-bound.

"Hey, Eddie." Someone patted him on the back. "Nice game the other night. Man, you were shootin' the eyes out of the basket."

"Thanks," Eddie answered quietly. "The other guys on the team did a great job."

"We're goin' all the way this year, Eddie," another kid declared. "Thanks to you!"

"I appreciate that," Eddie said sincerely as he approached an intersection in the hallway that was clogged with students. Girls he didn't even know rubbed shoulders with him as he attempted to move through the crowded hallway. Eddie had his head down momentarily when the flow of students suddenly halted. He didn't stop and bumped right into a pretty girl he recognized as a leader in the junior class. "Oh, I'm so sorry," Eddie said.

The young woman whirled around and opened her mouth as though she were about to scold whoever had bumped into her. When she saw it was Eddie, she flashed a big smile and faced him squarely. She stood close to him in the crowded hallway. "Oh, that's okay, Eddie," she said. "I didn't know it was you. What's going on?"

"Oh, er, ah, nothing's going on." Eddie tried in vain to get his tongue to cooperate with his brain. "I'm really sorry for bumping into you."

The pretty girl smiled at Eddie again. "I didn't mind a bit, Eddie. I hope you bump into me again sometime."

"Er, yeah. I'll try to be more careful."

The pretty girl raised her eyebrows, tossed her hair with her hand, and veered off in a different direction.

"Smooth move." Eddie heard the familiar voice behind him: Buddy. "That girl likes you, can't you tell?"

"Oh, hey, Buddy." Eddie lifted his head in a nod. "Whatcha doin'?"

"Gettin' you through this crowd, that's what I'm doing." Buddy raised his hands and shouted, "Okay folks, give the man some room." He waved his arms in front of himself and Eddie as though doing the breaststroke. "Make some room, I said," Buddy barked. Buddy pushed aside a kid who was too slow in responding. The young man shrank back without a word. Nobody at Gallatin High dared mess with Buddy. He was one of the roughest guys on the football team. His reputation as a fighter was well known, and his self-appointed role as Eddie's main man, best friend, and bodyguard was also common knowledge among Gallatin students and local Green Wave fans.

"Buddy, you really don't have to do that, ya know," Eddie said.

Buddy ignored the comment and surged forward into the mass of humanity. The crowd of students parted like the Red Sea, and Eddie made his way up the hall on clear, dry ground and with little interference. Buddy shoved another boy out of the way, but mostly he simply glared at the students and they moved off to the side, making way for him and Eddie to pass. Other students called out greetings to Eddie as they moved through the hall. A few even said hello to Buddy.

Finally, they reached Eddie's locker, and Buddy stood guard as Eddie reached up and pulled out a notebook and several textbooks. Buddy laughed when he saw Eddie loading up on academic materials. "Ha, what are you going to do with them? Are you planning on using them for a stepladder or something?"

"Hey, I study . . ." Eddie feigned a hurt expression. "Sometimes."

"Yeah, right. About as much as I do, probably less."

"Definitely less."

"How's your knee doing?"

"Not bad." Eddie instinctively rubbed the spot on his knee that had slammed onto the floor during the last game.

"You took a bad tumble," Buddy said. "When that guy tripped you, I was ready to come out of the stands and deck him!"

"Oh, no, Buddy. Don't do that. We'd both get thrown out of the game," Eddie said and laughed.

"Well, that was a dirty move he pulled."

"Yeah, I know. But you know what they say: the guy who swings back is the one the referee always sees."

"The whole gym saw that kid trip you. Everyone but the ref saw it."

"Well, it worked out okay. I didn't get hurt, and we won the game."

"Yeah, but we could have lost the season had you gone down and stayed down. Did you ice your knee yesterday?"

"Sure did. For a couple of hours. The swelling—"

Dewey Daniels, another Gallatin student, poked his nose in between Eddie and Buddy. "Hey, Eddie, great game the other night."

"Ah, thanks."

"Man, you had a hot hand in the second half, and that one shot you made from the top of the key—"

"Hey!" Buddy bellowed. "Dewey! Can't you see that Eddie and I are talking? We are engaging in an important, high-level conversation with crucial ramifications."

Eddie smiled but said nothing. He always loved it when Buddy tried to talk above his raisin'. Sometimes Buddy misused real words, sometimes he made up his own smart-sounding words, and sometimes, like now, he just took on that academic tone that was almost as foreign to Buddy as French class was to Eddie.

"I . . . er, I . . ." Dewey stammered. "I just wanted to say it was a great—"

Buddy waved his hand in a chopping motion that cut off Dewey's words midsentence. "Are you a moron or what? Can't you see that we are talking?"

"Well, I, er . . . well, yeah, I guess, I mean—"

"CAN'T. YOU. SEE?" Buddy roared at Dewey.

"Yeah, sure. Sorry, Buddy. Sorry, Eddie."

"It's too late for sorry," Buddy said, balling his fist. "Sorry is okay the first time, but after two or three times, 'sorry' just ain't enough." Buddy smacked his fist against his hand.

Dewey backed away several feet.

"Hey, hey, take it easy," Eddie said to Buddy. "It's okay. We're all friends here, remember?" He turned to Dewey. "I appreciate your comments. Thanks, Dewey." Eddie turned back to Buddy. "Calm down, Buddy. You're going to get us both in trouble one of these days."

"Ahem!"

Eddie, Buddy, and Dewey turned toward the gravelly sound of a man clearing his throat. There, planted in the middle of the corridor, was the imposing figure of Principal Herron. Hands on hips, he stared at the three boys as other students flowed by him in both directions, careful not to bump into him or draw his attention their way.

"Time for class, boys," he said matter-of-factly.

"Yes, sir. Good morning, sir," Dewey said as he hurried around the principal's left side. Buddy hugged the side of the hall as he and Eddie walked by Principal Herron on his right side. "Keep it down, Buddy," the principal grunted.

"Yes, sir. Sure will."

"Nice game." Principal Herron turned slightly and looked at Eddie as he passed by, close to the principal.

"Thank you, sir." Eddie nodded toward Principal Herron.

"What do you have there?" The principal pointed to a hall pass Eddie had in his hand. Eddie dutifully presented the pass to Principal Herron.

The principal read the pass and scowled. He was not fond of his student athletes skipping study hall, but the pass had been legitimately signed by one of Eddie's teachers. "Hmmph," Principal Herron grunted, handing the pass back to Eddie. "Make sure you keep up with your studies, Eddie."

"Yes, sir. I sure will."

Rather than heading to first-period study hall—a highly valued gift for most students who liked to do last-minute cramming before tests—Eddie journeyed toward the gym to practice shooting foul shots. For the star basketball player, school was a breeze.

14

"BILL! TYREE! DELORES! Come on, let's get moving," Anna Ligon called upstairs to her three children. "No dawdling, now. We must be on time for school."

"We're coming, Mom," Tyree said. "What's the rush?"

"I'll tell you what the rush is. You kids need to set the example for the other students. If the teacher's kids aren't on time for school, why should anyone else bother? Now, get the lead out of your shoes, and let's get going!"

"Yes, Mama," Tyree said.

Bill had been listening to the radio as he gazed into the bathroom mirror, struggling to get his growing Afro haircut to look uniform all the way around his head. "I'm comin', Ty. Be right there."

The voice of Johnny Rocket, the suave deejay at WLAC-AM radio in Nashville, caught Bill's attention. "It's Johnny R. here at WLAC, playing the real stuff, all the R&B hits from the past and the present. Here's one you may recognize from Marvin Gaye." The deejay began spinning Gaye's Motown hit "I Heard It through the Grapevine" quietly behind his voice.

"Marvin had a number-one hit with this song. But did you know that a full year before Marvin Gaye recorded 'Grapevine,' Gladys

Knight and the Pips put out the song, and it went all the way to the top of *Billboard*'s R&B charts, landing at number one? That's right, Gladys Knight and the Pips had the original hit on this song in 1967, and then Marvin came along and made it a hit again a year later. This is Johnny Rocket tellin' ya the truth. I won't lead ya astray. Keep your ear right here." The deejay then brought up the sound on the Marvin Gaye version of the song.

Bill fluffed his hair in disgust one more time. It was simply too short to rival the Afro styles he'd seen in some magazines, but he liked the look he was developing.

All three Ligon children loaded into Anna's station wagon and rode the short distance to Union High School, where Anna now taught home economics as well as language arts.

Union High School opened in 1922. It was built largely with Rosenwald funds and matching dollars put up by Julius Rosenwald, the white son of a German-Jewish immigrant. He was a clothier by trade who rose to become the president and part-owner of Sears, Roebuck, and Company. When approached by Booker T. Washington about helping to build schools for Negroes in rural America, Rosenwald agreed to assist.

The "new" part of the building in which Anna taught and all the Ligon children attended classes opened in 1951. Hardly any improvements or upgrades had been made to the building in the nearly two decades Anna had been teaching at Union, but the school remained a vital part of community life.

Indeed, for most black people living in Gallatin during the 1960s, life revolved around two main focal points—church and school. They were the two safest places to congregate. Consequently, Union High hosted activities all the time. Music and athletic programs dominated the schedule. A rehearsal, a recital, a dance, a play—something was always happening at the school.

Union's budget, however, barely covered basic necessities and didn't allow for luxuries. That exasperated many of the school's teachers, especially Frank Brinkley, who complained to bandleader George Offitt one day. "It's maddening that most of the books we use at Union are hand-me-downs from Gallatin High. If a book was discontinued at the white school, why is it still regarded as 'good enough' to be used at the Negro school?"

Mr. Offitt nodded in agreement. "I know what you're talkin' about. We see the same pattern all the way from senior high to elementary school. A fifth grader at Union might be given the same book to use that a white third grader had used a few years earlier across town in Gallatin's public schools." The bandleader shook his head. "The same is true when I try to get some band instruments for our students. Once the white children have nearly destroyed them, the school district passes them on to us. Don't get me wrong. I appreciate any instruments we can get for our kids. But it would be nice to get some new instruments once in a while, rather than the old beat-up ones."

"Well, I'm not as gracious as you, George. The last time one of those condescending Gallatin teachers came over with their out-of-date books and their broken-down equipment, I packed it all up and hauled it right back over there."

"Ha! You're a bold one, Frank. But the truth is, it's the same in every department here at Union—hand-me-downs and discarded equipment. Even our football uniforms and equipment came from somewhere else. At the beginning of the season, I saw our Union players and coaches painting football helmets that had been cast off by the Green Wave. I'm amazed Mr. Malone can keep such a good attitude about it all."

Mr. John Malone, the school principal at Union High, took his job seriously. A soft-spoken, intelligent, and insightful man, "Professor Malone," as many of his students and faculty members called him, was proactive about preventing problems before they happened. He gathered the student body together on the bleachers in the gymnasium daily and stood on the gym floor to make his announcements. "Good morning, ladies and gentlemen," he began in a sonorous voice.

"Welcome to Union High School, where everybody is somebody important." He paused and swept his gaze over the students' eager faces. "That includes you," he said, pointing to a young woman. "And that includes you," he said, looking up at a young man on the top row of bleachers. "You all have tremendous potential, and it is our goal, as your teachers and administrators, to help you discover it."

Mr. Malone ran through the perfunctory school announcements and then concluded by saying, "Now let's pray and ask God's blessing on our day."

The students and faculty respectfully bowed their heads as the principal prayed. Mr. Malone closed his eyes. "Heavenly Father, we thank you for your many blessings. What a privilege it is for us to come to school today. We ask your help in taking advantage of this new opportunity to learn. Open our hearts and minds. Let us discover not merely more information, but let us see your mighty hand in biology, in history, in mathematics, in art, in every sphere of life. Bless our teachers and our students today. Give us a good day at Union High, a day after which each of us can hear you speaking to our hearts, 'Well done.'" After a concluding "amen," Principal Malone dismissed the students to begin their classes.

Although Union was not a religious school, either Mr. Malone or his assistant, Mr. Stewart, always began each day with some sort of group prayer. A few who were new to Union traditions sometimes snickered or yawned during the prayers but were quickly reprimanded by those who had been around awhile. Mr. Malone was a deacon in his church and Mr. Stewart was an ordained minister, so they set a spiritual tone for the entire student body. Teachers taught not only information but also values, especially concepts of truth and right and wrong as determined by a biblical code rather than personal whims. To enhance the sense of family and close community at Union, the administration and faculty felt it was important to meet regularly, so they held an assembly every Monday morning and Friday afternoon. Both students and faculty were expected to attend.

Union boasted only about 250 students, and Bill Ligon was known by almost all of them, especially after leading the Union Devils to success in football and basketball. At six feet two inches, Bill was the tallest student in the school.

At the close of his sophomore year, Bill's coach, Ed Martin, stopped him in the gym one day. "Bill, I want you to work on your hook shot over the summer. I need you to play center next year."

"But I'm happy as a forward," Bill protested mildly.

"I know, but we need you at center," Coach Martin said. "Besides, I want to build the offense around you and run all our plays off you as the center."

The change proved to be a wise move, and Union's basketball team turned into a powerhouse during Bill's junior and senior years, even though only four schools allowed the all-black team to compete against them, playing both home and away games. Other schools either refused to play at Union or did not want the Negro players from Union to play on their "white" courts. Some schools allowed the team on the court but not in the locker rooms or showers. Bill and his teammates dressed on the bus or in a classroom, went in and played the game, and then got back on the bus without being able to clean up afterward. The odds were definitely against them, but everyone at Union knew their team could hold its own against anyone.

Bill moved through the halls of Union High with the ease of a man who knew where he wanted to go and how to get there. In his heart, his dreams reached far beyond Gallatin. Bill recognized that most Negroes who remained in Gallatin found only farm work, picking tobacco or hauling hay, or other grunt work. Most Americans living in northern or western states could not fathom the ferocity of the racial tension and hatred that existed in the South, so at first they welcomed the influx of low-paid workers. For the Negroes, even a low-paying job was better than no job at all. Consequently, the Great Migration spurred millions of black people to move northward in search of manufacturing jobs in Indianapolis, Chicago, Detroit, and other northern cities. Many who left Gallatin in search of work never returned.

"You gotta get out of here," Mr. Jones, one of Bill's teachers told him. "Gallatin has nothing for you. If you stay here, your future is sure to be bleak. So when you leave Union, I hope I never see you back here again."

"Where should I go?" Bill asked.

"Anywhere," Jones replied. "Anywhere but here."

But for now, in his senior year at Union, Bill was a superstar. At eighteen years old, Bill was handsome, articulate, well-mannered, and athletic; he seemed to have everything going for him.

"Hey, nice game the other night, Bill," a fellow student called out as he made his way to class.

"Thanks, man," Bill replied. "They were tough, but we took 'em down."

Bill cradled a stack of books under his arm. On top of his textbooks was a copy of *Malcolm X Speaks*, a collection of speeches by the Negro leader. Many of Bill's fellow students had no idea who Malcolm X was or why his speeches should be of any interest to them. In Gallatin, radical concepts about racial issues, such as those espoused by Malcolm X, were not welcome. But Bill was intrigued by Malcolm X's ideas.

He turned to put some books in his locker, and as he did, Martha, one of the prettiest girls in the senior class, eased up next to him. She batted her eyelashes flirtatiously and cooed, "Nice game, William."

"Hello, Martha," Bill replied, attempting to pretend not to be interested. But it was difficult for any healthy young man at Union High not to notice Martha.

"Do you have any plans for after the game on Friday night?"

"Just a hot shower and a cold drink."

"And what about Charlene? She seems to think you belong to her."

Bill held his arms out wide. "I've got no strings on me," he said and smiled as he closed his locker door.

"Mmm, we'll see about that, won't we?" Martha smiled back at Bill as she sauntered down the hallway.

"Hey, Bill!" Joe Malone, the principal's son and one of Bill's best friends, shoved the local newspaper toward him. "Have you seen the paper and what those guys are sayin'?"

Bill glanced at the newspaper but didn't take it. "I've got better things to read, Joe. You ought to try reading something other than the sports page." Bill started down the hall toward his class.

"Oh, yeah? Well, look at this," Joe groused as he fell in step with Bill. He opened the paper so Bill had to see it. "Look there. Right on the front page of the paper. GREEN WAVE ROLLS ON. And check this out." Joe read the subtitle above the article. "'Sherlin Leads Green Wave to Victory.' And they got a picture in the paper too. A big one. Why doesn't the newspaper ever put in a picture of you, Bill? Or one of our guys? Nope. Only white guys get their pictures in the paper. Green Wave on the front page. And where are the Union Devils? I'll tell ya where. We're on the bottom of page 6. No picture—nothin'. Barely a mention of the game details. Just a small byline: 'Union Advances to Semifinals.' I'm tellin' ya, Bill, it ain't fair. It just ain't fair."

Bill kept walking but nodded his head, indicating his agreement with Joe. Like most of the guys on the Union team, he longed for the day when he might see his picture in the local newspaper. White kids who scored ten points and sometimes less were photographed, but even a star at Union never saw his image in the paper. Neither did any of his teammates.

"Don't they understand?" Joe went on. "All we want is to see our pictures in the newspaper once in a while too." He jerked the newspaper open wide. "We're in the same city, the same sport, same division, and we have the same undefeated record as Gallatin. So why do they get page 1 and we get page 6?"

Bill raised his eyebrows. "Typical. No use worrying about it, Joe. Do I want to see my picture in the paper? You bet I do! But they aren't going to show a Negro on the front page of the paper, or page 6 either. That's just typical of the South."

"Well, it ain't gonna be so typical when we whip their butts," Joe said with a huff.

"Yeah, I agree."

"Bill!"

Bill stopped and turned around, recognizing the voice of his basketball coach, Ed Martin, a large man in his midforties who could still hold his own on a basketball court.

"Hey, Coach."

"Got a minute?"

"Sure, what's up?" Bill asked.

"We have a problem. They're telling me that Roy Jackson is on the verge of being ineligible for the rest of the season."

"What?" Joe piped in. "They've already disqualified Shooter and Doug. They can't take our team captain too."

"They can and they will if Roy doesn't do something to help himself," Coach Martin said matter-of-factly.

Joe shook his head. "No way! We can't make it to the finals without our main man."

Coach Martin nodded. "I agree, Joe. That's why I need you guys to help me."

"What can we do?" Bill asked.

Coach Martin shrugged his shoulders. "Roy is slacking off doing his homework. Says it doesn't matter because he's not going to graduate anyhow. He's been skipping classes. Mr. Malone says that if he doesn't finish his assignments and pass the math test, he will not be allowed to play. I've already talked with Roy, and he seems resigned to mediocrity. But maybe if you boys put some pressure on him too, he will come to his senses."

"I'll talk to him, Coach," Bill said. "Roy's been having a tough time lately. Maybe we can get him some help. A tutor or something."

"A tutor is a good idea," Coach Martin said, "but Roy is no dummy. He can do the work. He just has to want it for himself."

"We'll see what we can do, Coach," Bill said.

"Thanks, guys. It's not just the finals I'm worried about. This is Roy's life he's messing up. I appreciate your nudging him in the right direction."

"You got it, Coach," Bill said as the class bell rang. Bill and Joe waved at Coach Martin and stepped inside their classroom just as the bell's tone faded.

After school that day, Bill borrowed the Plymouth station wagon from his mom while she attended a teachers' meeting. Bill and Joe drove the short distance out of town to a large tobacco farm owned by an elderly white couple, Patrick Bonner and his wife. They drove slowly down a narrow dirt road between row after row of tobacco plants, when Bill spotted Mr. Bonner sitting on his tractor, taking a break. Bill stopped the car on the dirt road and waved. "Hello, Mr. Bonner."

"Why, hello there, boys. Good game last Friday night." The old man turned off the tractor's engine.

"Thank you, sir," Bill and Joe replied almost simultaneously. They smiled at each other.

"Are you looking for Roy?"

"Yes, sir. We are," Bill responded.

"I believe he is up at his place. Seems like I saw him there a little while earlier."

"Thanks, Mr. Bonner." Bill waved his hand out the window.

The old man put his fingers to his hat and nodded; he fired up the tractor again as the boys headed up to the simple wooden farmhouse built to accommodate the help on Mr. Bonner's property. In the distance behind the house sat a much larger white house high on a hill. That was the Bonners' home.

Joe knocked on the farmhouse door, while Bill stood behind him, waiting. No answer.

"Try again," Bill said. Joe rapped harder on the door.

"Yeah?" a voice called from inside. "What do you want?"

"Hey, Roy!" Bill answered. "Open up. It's Joe and Bill."

The boys heard shuffling inside the house. Nearly a minute went by before the door swung open, revealing Roy, a tall, muscular Negro around eighteen years old. He stood aside, dressed in farm coveralls, shirtless and shoeless. "Come on in," he groused. "Maybe you can help me with this television antenna. I can't get this thing to work, no matter which way I twist it." Roy gave the cheap wire antenna a sharp jerk, and the television screen momentarily cleared and then returned to static.

Bill was not amused. "What are you doin' here, Roy?"

"What's it look like I'm doing," Roy shot back in his usual sarcastic tone. "I'm watchin' TV."

"You ain't watchin' nothin'." Bill walked over to the television and turned it off. "Why weren't you in school?"

"Didn't feel like it. But a better question is, what are you guys doing here?"

"We came to talk," Joe said.

"Talk?" Roy looked first at Joe then to Bill. "About what? And why here? You guys can talk to me anytime after practice."

"Don't you care about the rest of our games?" Bill said.

Roy shot Bill a dirty look. "Sure, I do. You know I've never missed a game."

"Well, you're about to," Joe fired back.

"No way," Roy spat out.

"Joe's telling you the truth, Roy," Bill said. "Pop Malone is going to suspend you if you don't bring up your grades—and fast—especially in math. There's a test coming up, and if you don't pass it, we're sunk."

"Well, I guess he's gonna have to suspend me," Roy said.

"Roy! What's wrong with you?" Joe yelled, standing almost nose to nose with Roy, his body tense and looking like he was about to punch him. "Don't you care about the team?"

Bill calmed down Joe with a strong look. "Cool it, Joe. We have enough problems."

"Of course, I care about the team," Roy said, "but you guys both know I don't have a snowball's chance of passing that math test."

"What's the problem?" Bill asked. "Math ain't that tough."

"Maybe not for you," said Roy. "Besides, I ain't got no problem. I've already received my acceptance letter from Fisk University. The coach said I'll probably be able to start my freshman year. Good ol' Mr. Bonner is footin' the bill for me to go to school, so I don't have to worry about getting a scholarship like you guys. Not that I could, anyhow. But you get my point. I'm all set. I don't need no more school."

"You need to graduate," Bill said icily.

"I'm not like you guys," Roy snapped.

"What are you talkin' about?" Joe retorted.

"You know what I'm talking about," Roy said. "I don't have teachers for parents." He nodded toward Joe. "You, Mr. Principal's son." Roy gave Bill a long look. "And you, Mr. Ivy League, Princeton-bound hotshot. Studying doesn't come easily to me, so why do it?"

"Because you need to finish what you started, that's why," Bill said. "Not to mention that the rest of us are counting on you."

"Ha! You're sounding more like my grandpa every day, Bill." Roy's eyes flashed. "I have to take his guff day and night, and now you're on my back too. Well, you two and Grandpa can all go stuff it."

As Roy continued to spew a litany of insults, an elderly man quietly stepped into the room behind him, unbeknownst to Roy. Bill and Joe recognized Roy's grandfather.

"Ahem!" Joe exaggerated his throat clearing.

Bill held his hands palms out and waved slowly at Roy.

Roy continued his rant. He had already gone too far, but he wasn't done yet. He pierced Bill with a look. "From now on, I'm doing things my way. Not your way, or Grandpa's broken-down, sharecroppin' way, or Joe's way. I don't have to please anyone but myself. From now on, I'm doing things the Roy Jackson way. D'ya hear me? The Roy Ja—" Roy turned his head slightly and spotted his grandfather. Roy towered over the short, stocky seventy-year-old, but the senior Jackson clearly was a man who commanded respect. Roy gulped hard.

"Oh, Grandpa! Sorry. I didn't mean . . . I mean, I didn't . . ."

Grandpa Jackson didn't flinch. He gave Roy a narrow-eyed stare, looked him right in the eyes, and said, "You *will* pass that test, my boy."

15

ACROSS TOWN AT GALLATIN HIGH, the Green Wave basketball team was scrimmaging at the far end of the gym. Everyone on the team except Eddie, that is. Eddie was at the opposite end of the court, shooting long set shots outside the key, shots that would one day, due to a rule change, be awarded three points instead of two. But for Eddie, they were just normal, everyday basketball shots.

Coach Vradenburg, a tall, good-natured fellow with a flattop haircut, complete with the greased front edge that stood straight up, was rebounding and returning the ball to Eddie after each shot. "Pretty shot," he said. "Nice."

Swish! Eddie popped a long shot, nearly a thirty-five-footer.

"Sweet!" Coach Vradenburg called. "I wouldn't try that one very often, but it's nice to know that it is in your range."

"I used to hit shots like that all day when I played in my backyard," Eddie said. "When the tree limbs didn't block the arc," he added, smiling.

Coach Vradenburg nodded. "Well, if you can arc the ball over those tree limbs, you can certainly get it over the head of a six-foot-four-inch center. And I really can't think of too many in the county who are even that tall. Maybe we'll meet a few big guys when we get to the state finals."

Eddie nodded and swished another shot.

On the sidelines, the cheerleaders completed their routine with a flurry of precision kicks and jumps and a human pyramid, punctuated by a bevy of smiles.

The smile on the face of Missy Hamilton, the team captain, quickly faded as she took her position in front of the other girls to address her squad. An attractive, perfectly proportioned seventeen-year-old going on twenty-six, Missy was the stereotypical, prissy "Southern belle in training." Even while cheering and performing vigorous jumps and kicks, Missy's perfectly coiffed hair never seemed to move, her eye makeup never smudged or smeared. Missy was Miss Perfect. At least in her own mind.

"Okay, that's it for today, ladies," she said. "Wonderful work. We are really looking quite good. There are, of course, a few things we need to work on to be ready for the upcoming tournament games, but we can fix those easily enough. Same deal tomorrow. Please get here on time, so we can all get started together. That's it."

The cheerleaders' post-practice meeting broke up, and the girls began moving toward the gym doors leading to the women's locker room. Missy caught Betty Ann by the arm and walked alongside her. Betty Ann was an adorably cute but slightly pudgy young woman, and Missy never stifled an opportunity to remind her.

"Betty Ann, stay off the chocolate. If that pimple on your forehead gets any bigger, we're going to give it a name."

The girls walking nearby laughed aloud at Missy's caustic comment, but Betty Ann, a year younger than most of the others and sensitive about her body, quickly covered her face, which had already flushed a deep shade of red.

"And what are you laughing about, Mary Jo?" Missy said. "Your maid must be using extra lard and flour in whatever she's been cooking." Missy playfully slapped Mary Jo on her butt. "If that behind of yours gets any bigger, you are going to qualify for the Union squad!"

The group of very white cheerleaders giggled at Missy's racial quip.

Mary Jo did a flirtatious sort of bump-and-grind move and stuck out her tongue at Missy. "You're just jealous, Missy Hamilton. Tell the truth. You got all your stuff up front." Mary Jo pushed out her chest in Missy's direction. "And you're just mad that you don't have any motion in your caboose." Mary Jo sidled along in front of Missy, purposely exaggerating her hip movements.

"Yeah, and you are out of your mind," Missy said. She let Mary Jo move on ahead as she slipped up closer to Betty Ann. "Buy some Clearasil, girl," Missy added quietly.

"Okay, Missy," Betty Ann said barely above a whisper. "I will."

The cheerleaders sauntered by the bleachers where Eddie was sitting with a towel draped over his shoulders, his gaze focused on the scrimmage action on the court. Eddie knew that shooting was his primary role on the team, but almost like an additional coach, he studied his teammates, looking for new ways they could take advantage of their strengths while exploiting the weaknesses of the opposition. His coaches welcomed his input and trusted his ideas. Most of all, they appreciated his example to the other players.

"Stay underneath, Alton!" Eddie stood up and called to his teammates. "Don't let them draw you too far outside, Tim. You're lettin' our belly wide open!"

He was so focused on the action on the court that he barely noticed the attractive group of cheerleaders. But they noticed him and his strong, toned body, his shorts and basketball shirt revealing the ripples on his bare muscles. Every cheerleader flashed Eddie her best smile as she passed by, whether or not he noticed.

"Hey, Eddie," Mary Jo said. "Hi, Eddie!" the others echoed.

Eddie nodded at the girls but continued staring right through them, his eyes glued to the action on the court.

Missy approached Eddie. She flashed him her perfect smile and tilted her head slightly. Her flirtation was flagrantly obvious, but it had an effect on him, nonetheless. He stepped down from the bleachers to face her.

"Hi, Eddie," she said in her best sultry voice.

"Hello, Missy."

"Where did you go after the game the other night? We missed you at the party, mister." Missy smiled.

Eddie looked down at the hardwood. "Oh, I had some things to do."

"Like shooting baskets in the gym after everyone else went home?" Missy asked.

It was Eddie's turn to smile. "Maybe . . ." He cocked an eyebrow.

Missy shook her head. "You are something else, Eddie Sherlin. You aren't human. If you aren't playing basketball, you are watching or thinking about basketball. You probably dream about basketball too, don't you?"

"Well, as a matter of fact—"

"Don't you ever think of anything else, young man?" Missy struck a sexy pose, tilting her head slightly to the left and placing her index finger on her lower lip as she stepped closer to Eddie, her body nearly touching his.

"Oh, I think 'bout other things." Eddie waggled his eyebrows playfully.

Missy slapped his shoulder. "Yeah, sure. I'll believe it when I see it." Missy placed her hands on her hips. "Speaking of seeing you, I *will* be seeing you at my birthday party, won't I?"

"Of course. I'll be there." He wrinkled his nose. "When is it again?"

"On my birthday, Eddie."

"Oh, yeah. I knew that."

"And you will be coming. Do you promise?"

Eddie glanced around to see if anyone watching them could hear him. Standing nearby, Maureen, one of Missy's friends and a fellow cheerleader, saw him but turned away. "Yes. Sure. I promise," Eddie said warmly.

"That's my baby," Missy said. "Oh, and one more thing."

"What's that?"

"I don't want you to buy me a birthday gift."

"It's your birthday," Eddie protested.

"I know. I know. But I also know you have been practicing night and day and haven't had time to earn any extra money."

"Yeah—"

"And your folks work real hard for every penny, so I don't want you borrowing any money from them." Eddie stared at Missy in disbelief.

She patted his arm. "Don't worry. We'll have plenty of time for you to buy me expensive gifts after you are a rich and famous basketball player." She smiled condescendingly. "Or baseball player . . . or whatever ball you're tossing around when the time comes." Missy puckered her lips and blew Eddie a kiss. "See you later." She waved as she sauntered away. "Come on, Maureen."

Maureen fell into step behind Missy, pausing long enough to lean in close to Eddie as she passed him. "Don't be a fool," she whispered. "She wants a present. And it had better be a good one." Maureen swept away from Eddie, chasing after Missy.

Eddie watched both young women sashay out the door. He scratched his head in confusion.

The bell shrilled, signaling the dismissal of classes and sending a flood of students swirling into the hallways. A trio of senior boys—Scott, Terry, and Neil—gathered around Terry's locker, in no hurry to get to class. "Your daddy is going to whip your stupid butt," Neil warned Scott. "Looks like you flunked another test, didn't ya?" Neil pointed at the large forty-nine written in bright red ink on Scott's paper.

"Oh, let the moron alone," Terry said. "Can't you see you are hurting his feelings? You know how sensitive he is."

"Aw, shut up," Scott said.

Terry laughed at his own weak joke and was about to punch his buddy in the arm when he stopped short. He frowned at the sight in the hallway a few yards away.

Walking in his direction were two of Gallatin High's black students—Leah Rogan and Jepthah Swank, both bright and articulate, both new since the push for integration in the county. Jepthah was slight of build and bookish in nature, a feature exacerbated by the large black-framed glasses with Coke-bottle lenses he wore. Petite and classy, Leah carried herself with dignity and sophistication. She was always dressed in a sweater, blouse, and skirt combination.

As the two newcomers walked by, Terry turned to Scott and spoke loudly enough for everyone in the hall to hear. "I bet even Jepthah there did better on his test than you did, Scott."

"Is that right, Scott?" Neil added. "Did you let colored do better than you, Scottie boy?"

"I said shut your mouth," Scott retorted.

Terry jerked on Scott's arm, pulling him down the hallway behind Leah and Jepthah, with Neil trailing right behind them. "How 'bout it, Jepthah?" Terry said the name as if it were a dirty word. "What did you get on your test? Come on, darkie. Don't be bashful. You can tell us."

Leah said nothing. She touched Jepthah's arm and the two of them kept walking. Jepthah tucked his books close to him and eased his body closer to the lockers alongside the hall.

The first day Leah had ridden the school bus, several white girls had refused to allow her to sit down and spat on her, dotting her dark black hair with saliva. Both Leah and Jepthah learned quickly that the best way to avoid foolish conflicts and unnecessary confrontations at Gallatin High was to keep moving.

That's what they attempted to do, but Terry and Neil were relentless, squeezing in between them, pushing Leah aside and sandwiching Jepthah between the two of them.

"Come on, boy." Terry nudged Jepthah. "What'd ya get? I really want to know."

Jepthah looked at Terry squarely for the first time. "Ninety-five."

"Ninety-five!" Terry bellowed. "You boys hear that? This darkie scored ninety-five out of a hundred." Terry looked at Scott. "Man, what did you have, Scottie? Forty-something? Wow, he got almost double what you scored. How's somethin' like that happen?"

"Yeah! How does that work?" Neil chided. "How does a white man do half as well as a colored man?" Neil shoved Scott against the lockers. "Maybe you should take the test twice, Scott, so you can do as good as this darkie." Terry and Neil laughed uproariously. Scott bristled.

"Hey, Jepthah," Terry taunted. "Are you and Scottie related?"

Leah and Jepthah attempted to move farther down the hall, trying to ignore their tormentors, even though they were encircled by the boys' derisive laughter. "Maybe you should get this darkie to take the test for you, Scottie." Terry pointed toward Leah and laughed.

Suddenly the laughter died.

Terry and Neil looked up almost at the same instant, recoiling at the large, imposing presence of Principal Dan Herron standing in the center of the hall. Mr. Herron nailed Terry, Neil, and Scott with a glower. He turned briefly to check on Leah and Jepthah. Evidently discerning that they were physically unhurt, he waved his hand at them. "Move on. Get on to your classes."

Terry started to move past the principal, but he raised his hand to Terry's chest. "Not you." He glared at Neil and Scott, who had stopped in their tracks. "You two get to class. I don't want any more trouble from either one of you. Do you understand?"

Neil and Scott lowered their heads and hurried away. Terry tried to smile. "We're just havin' a little fun, Mr. Herron."

"Go to my office," the principal ordered. "Now. Wait for me there."

"Yes, sir."

Principal Herron shook his head as he watched Terry shuffle down the hall toward the administrative offices. It was going to be a long afternoon.

The commotion in the Gallatin High School parking lot captured the attention of everybody inside the building, as well as onlookers outside. A large number of cars converged on the visitor parking spaces, and what looked to be about forty Negroes, mostly women, stepped out of the cars and headed toward the school's majestic front entryway. Someone inside the building yelled, "Watch out, it's a protest march sponsored by the National Association for the Advancement of Colored People!"

"No, it's not," someone else said. "It's that Southern Christian Leadership group."

Actually, they were teachers and staff members from Union High School, all there to attend another of what were intended to be frequent meetings that would, hopefully, make the integration process smoother in Gallatin.

Complicating matters enormously, however, was the decision of the local school boards to completely close down Union High School after the conclusion of the 1970 school year. The Union students, faculty, and staff would be merged into the Gallatin High School program. That was the general plan, but everyone affected by the change had lots of questions.

The administrators of the schools scheduled a series of discussions with local, county, state, and federal government officials. The meetings were intended to help explain how the transition could be

140

made peacefully and most efficiently. A number of similar community confabs already had been held in local churches and civic buildings. Most of the meetings had started out calmly enough but quickly turned vitriolic when parents realized that both coloreds and whites would be closely interacting, which included not only being seated next to one another in classes but also eating in the same cafeteria, using the same restrooms, and even drinking from common water fountains. This afternoon's meeting was the first between the people whose lives were going to be affected daily by the merger—the teachers, administrators, and other staff members of both schools.

Because attendance by the coaches was mandatory, basketball practice wrapped up early, so Eddie packed his gym bag and headed out the front door. He had no sooner gotten off school property before a car pulled up the street and stopped along the curb closest to him. A man in the car waved. "Hi, Eddie! How ya doin'?"

He immediately recognized Mr. Long, a slightly balding man in his midfifties who owned a local sporting goods store. "Oh, hi, Mr. Long. I'm fine. Good to see you today." Mr. Long had been extraordinarily kind to Eddie over the years. He gave Eddie more sports equipment than he ever sold to him. Whether he needed a new baseball bat or glove, or a new pair of running shoes, Mr. Long always set a price he could afford—even if that price was zero. When Eddie didn't have enough money to order his Green Waves letterman jacket, Mr. Long said, "Eddie, don't worry about paying me. I'll order the jacket for you, and if you can pay for it, great. If not, that's okay too." As it turned out, when the jacket arrived, Mr. Long gave it to Eddie for free.

Mr. Long turned off the car and stepped out, pulling his Sansabelt trousers up over his ever-growing potbelly. The store owner shook Eddie's hand. "What's going on at the school today?" he asked as he closed the car door.

"I don't know for sure," Eddie replied, "but I think it is one of those integration meetings. All the teachers and coaches are required to attend, so we got out of practice early."

"I guess they're never going to let that desegregation thing go, are they?" Mr. Long shrugged. "Well, I'm glad I bumped into you. I have something to show you."

"To show *me*?"

"Yep. You alone?" He glanced first one way, then the other. "Loo-kee here what I just got in the store." Mr. Long retrieved a shoebox from his car and slowly, almost reverently, lifted the lid.

Eddie was intrigued. He watched intently as Mr. Long peeled back the tissue paper in the shoebox. "Look at these. Direct from the factory to my store—the latest Converse All Stars. But these babies aren't made of canvas. They're made of leather!"

Eddie gazed at the shoes in amazement. He had been wearing Converse All Stars with green shoelaces for some time, just like members of the Boston Celtics and other pro teams. Some of the superstars were even switching over to Converse high-tops, although that trend hadn't hit Gallatin yet. But not even Eddie had ever seen leather Converses.

"Wow, Mr. Long! These shoes are fantastic!" He caressed the shoes as though he were examining a priceless treasure. "Oh, man, they're nice."

"Look at that padding, Eddie," Mr. Long pointed out. "Just like the professionals wear. Same thing."

"Really?"

"Yep, and they are all yours."

Eddie's eyes widened. "For me? Mr. Long, are you kidding?"

"Ha! No, I'm not kidding at all. I special ordered them for you, Eddie. Nobody else in the state has a pair of shoes like these. Only you."

"My goodness, Mr. Long. I don't know how I can ever thank you."

"No thanks necessary. Wear 'em and enjoy 'em. It's the least I can do for the cause. Do you think you boys can take Springfield in the District Twenty semifinals?"

Eddie stroked the fine leather on the Converse All Stars. "Well, Springfield is pretty tough, but I think if we get our offense working well, we have a good shot at beating 'em."

"I sure hope so. Win one for Gallatin High. Of course, every time you win, I win too. My business booms. All the kids want the same sort of wristbands that Eddie Sherlin is wearing."

"But they're the same white wristbands that everyone else is wearing."

"That doesn't matter." Mr. Long laughed. "It only matters that you are wearing them. I can't wait to see how many parents want to order leather Converse All Stars for their kids if you guys beat Springfield. Er . . . I should say, *when* you boys beat Springfield."

"We'll sure do our best, Mr. Long. Thanks again for the shoes!" Suddenly, loud profanity drew their attention to the front of the school. Some white adults were standing outside the school, taunting some black teachers who had arrived for the meeting.

Mr. Long said something under his breath that Eddie couldn't hear. "Sir?"

"I don't understand why they're still kicking that dead horse."

Mr. Long shook his head. "We have a good town here. Coloreds and whites all get along just fine. Everyone is happy with things the way they are. Why stir things up? I don't know why those politicians in Washington can't simply let well enough alone."

Eddie gave a slight, noncommittal shrug.

Mr. Long patted Eddie's shoulder. "See ya at the game, Eddie." He got into his car, waved once more, and headed back toward his whites-only store.

16

INSIDE THE SCHOOL, tension was building as the teachers and administrators entered the auditorium and gravitated toward seats occupied by people of their own color. Principal Herron's distinguished wife, Susan Herron, who also taught biology at Gallatin High, welcomed each person—black and white—as they filed into the room.

A sophisticated and traditional Southern woman, Susan struggled with embracing integration. Accepting it did not come easily to her, but as a Christian she recognized the moral rightness of racial equality, as well as desegregation's inevitability, especially now that the federal government was involved. She felt it was her duty to set the example for the other faculty and staff at Gallatin High, so she went out of her way to welcome each person from Union.

"Oh, so good to see you!" Susan said to a black woman. The woman smiled weakly and shook hands with Mrs. Herron. "Pleased to meet you," Susan gushed to a male teacher from Union, extending her hand awkwardly. He stared at her hand momentarily, shook it briefly, and then quickly moved on to find a seat. He wasn't purposely trying to be rude. This was new territory for everyone.

At the front of the auditorium, sitting behind a bank of tables on the floor level rather than on the stage, Mr. Larry Aire, the sixty-year-old white superintendent of schools, and Donald Pepper, a thirty-ish black official with the Tennessee Racial Equality Commission, shuffled their notes, fidgeted nervously, and took repeated sips of water as they waited for everyone to arrive. Mary Wertheimer, a white volunteer social worker in her midfifties, adjusted a microphone in front of the tables. Gallatin's congenial mayor, Bill Knapp, stood along the side of the room, greeting and glad-handing with his constituents.

Union principal, John Malone, entered the back of the auditorium and looked first for his Gallatin counterpart, Dan Herron. Spotting Herron across the room, Malone smiled and waved. Herron, not a demonstrative sort of fellow, nodded curtly but cordially. The two principals took their places behind the tables at the front of the room.

Susan Herron spotted Anna Ligon and made her way over to her before the meeting began. "Anna, so good to finally meet you," the principal's wife said. "I've heard so much about you over the years. Your reputation at Union is an example for all of us."

"Thank you very much," Anna said. "It's nice to meet you as well. I'm looking forward to working with you."

"Oh, yes," Susan said. "I'm sure we will get along fabulously." About that time, Union's Coach Martin entered the room and waved to Gallatin's Coach Vradenburg as they both took their seats. Like most of the others, the coaches found spots with people whose skin color matched their own. More than a hundred men and women were now gathered in the auditorium, with about two-thirds of the crowd white and one-third colored.

Superintendent Aire called the meeting to order. "All right," he said loudly. "If we can all be seated, we'll get started and try not to keep you too long. Thank you for being here. I say this from the bottom of my heart: it is truly good to see each of you."

The superintendent paused momentarily and looked at Mayor Knapp. "We're also delighted that the good mayor of our city could be with us this afternoon. As you know, he is a busy man, so he cannot stay long, but let's thank him for dropping by to greet us." Aire led a round of weak applause.

Mayor Knapp waved and smiled as though he were running for office again—which in his mind he probably was. The mayor stood behind the microphone at the front of the auditorium. "It's so good to see all of you today. Good luck with what you are doing here." He paused momentarily as though he weren't quite sure exactly what the group was indeed hoping to accomplish and then quickly moved on. "We'll see you all at the spring fair. Oh, and wasn't the Christmas parade just sensational? You know that Union's band was really a special feature this year."

A pall dropped over the crowd like a heavy wet blanket as the educators realized they had most likely witnessed the last performance ever of the Union band in the Gallatin Christmas parade. Thanks to desegregation, there would be no more Union High School by next Christmas. The mayor stammered, trying to put a good spin on his gaffe. Finally, he simply waved good-bye and hurriedly exited the auditorium, a smattering of applause in his wake.

Superintendent Aire picked up the pace. "I'd like to thank Principal Malone and Principal Herron for helping to organize this event. And, of course, thank you all for choosing to attend. Although you didn't have an option, I'm sure if you didn't want to be here, you could have found some excuse. But I'm glad you didn't.

"As you know, this is another of several meetings that we hope will aid the integration of the Sumner County school district. We don't expect any problems; however, we don't expect everything to come off without a hitch either. So as we make this transition, we will hope for the best and prepare for the worst.

"Before we get too far down the road, I'd like to introduce to you Mr. Donald Pepper from Birmingham, who represents the federal Department of Health, Education, and Welfare and is working under the authority of the HEW's Director of Civil Rights, Leon

Panetta. Mr. Pepper has been assisting us as part of the Tennessee Racial Equality Commission. We're glad to have him with us. Mr. Pepper."

Dressed in a stylish, well-tailored suit, white shirt, and tie, the young Negro stood and walked to the lectern. Poised and confident, he spoke with assurance. "Thank you, Superintendent Aire. Good afternoon to all. First, I want to congratulate both schools, Union and Gallatin, on their undefeated basketball seasons as they head into the district and state tournaments."

Regardless of their skin color, almost everyone in Gallatin took their school sports seriously. Basketball was basketball, and both of the victorious teams belonged to their hometown. So Pepper had no problem getting a response from the audience.

Smart move, Principal Herron thought.

But then Donald Pepper lost the audience's enthusiasm, displaying for all to see and hear that he was not a Gallatin native. "And just think what kind of team you all will have next year with the best of both schools playing together," he declared.

Only a few people in the room applauded his comment. Coach Martin suddenly found his shoes terribly interesting, and the Gallatin coaches stared straight ahead into space. Some of the white teachers were less than enthusiastic about the possibility of a winning Gallatin team comprised of both black and white players.

Pepper hastily moved on. "Yes, well, then, before we begin the seminar section of our meeting, let's open the floor for any questions or comments you may have. Don't be bashful." Pepper scanned the audience for a brave soul who dared to ask a question. Silence. He adjusted his tie and shifted at the lectern. "No questions? Surely, there's something on your mind."

Finally, a white teacher put up her hand.

"Yes, over here." He pointed to the woman.

The nattily dressed middle-aged woman stood. "I just wish to say, on behalf of the Gallatin faculty, we are looking forward to all the folks over at Union coming here to Gallatin High and being part of the Green Wave family."

Her comment was met with scattered applause, especially from the white members of the audience. Anna Ligon applauded politely, but several of her Union colleagues were not so quick to join in. One Union teacher called out, "So we're keeping the same name? Is it going to be Gallatin High? And the Green Wave? What about our nickname, the Devils?"

Another teacher from Union added an even bolder statement. "I didn't think this was about being invited to someone's house. I thought we were going to be building a new house together."

Several of the Union teachers nodded in approval.

Donald Pepper attempted to pull in the reins before he lost complete control of the meeting. "If I may clarify," he began. "We made the decision to close down Union next year for practical purposes and to integrate here at Gallatin. With the new annex we are putting up, there will be plenty of room for all the students, so centralizing in a modern structure such as this is the right way to go. As far as the name of the school and all that, well . . ." He took a deep breath, but before he had opportunity to say another word, another black teacher popped up.

"So this annex you mentioned? Is that where the colored students will go?" Visions of mobile home–style trailers parked around the school and serving as temporary classrooms likely filled most of the audience members' minds.

"Oh, no," Pepper said unconvincingly. "*All* the facilities—all the classrooms and the teachers will be integrated. All students, white or colored, will have the same books and the same supplies."

Another Union teacher raised his hand.

"Yes, sir?"

"That's good news about the supplies. My name is Frank Brinkley. I'm a biology teacher. See, every few years, folks from Gallatin High bring over the used and discarded books and the old microscopes and all. That's what we would get for *supplies*." The way Brinkley drew out the word made it obvious that the supplies were insufficient. "And despite our poor, inefficient tools, Union High School has graduated students who have gone on to be doctors, lawyers, and teachers. Last year, when I saw the box of outdated books and broken beakers from Gallatin, I finally got fed up and told them what to do with all their ol' junk."

A few Negroes in the room laughed.

But Brinkley waved everyone quiet. "No, I was wrong. And I got called on the carpet for my comments. So I went over and talked to the superintendent and told him how I felt about Union always getting Gallatin High's castoffs. I explained that it offended me—not that I wasn't appreciative—but it frustrated me that we couldn't do better than that. It insulted me that they'd bring those leftovers to us and dump 'em on us and expect us to teach with that stuff. So I'm glad to hear you say we won't have that problem anymore."

A female teacher from Union turned around in her seat to address Brinkley. "See, as for me, Frank, I don't care so much about the facilities or the supplies. Sure, I know that we have to make do with secondhand things, but that doesn't bother me. Because I know that at Union, if a student has a problem, he or she is going to be noticed. It is not just that student's problem; it is my problem too. That's one of the best things we have going for us at Union. We give our kids personal attention and instruction. Will our kids have that over here?"

Several black people frowned and shook their heads, while several white people nodded.

The Union teacher continued. "Some of our kids ride the bus for an hour to get to school. When they come in, they are hungry; these kids need food and lunch every day. Some of them need coats and other clothing. At Union, we teachers notice our students. We notice how the kids are dressed or if a student needs eyeglasses to see the chalkboard. We correct their posture and keep an eye on who is socializing with whom."

A white male teacher stood. "So why can't you do that same thing here? You will still be seeing and counseling the same students. You'll just be doing it in this building rather than in the old school across town."

"So we will be integrating the schools but segregating the counseling? Is that what you're sayin'?" a colored man spoke up. "Coloreds watchin' out for coloreds; whites watchin' for whites. That doesn't sound like desegregation to me."

"Hold on, everyone," Donald Pepper shouted into the microphone, holding his hands up like a traffic cop. The room got quiet. "Hold on!" he repeated. "Let's have only one person speak at a time so we can all hear and consider what is being said. Okay, who's next?" He spotted a white teacher who had raised his hand.

The man in his midforties stood. "I, for one, can understand what the folks from Union are saying. They're looking out for their own kids, just like we look after ours. That makes sense to me. What doesn't make sense is this: If they don't want this integration program, then why in the world are we doing it?"

"That's right!" several white teachers chimed in, along with several Negro teachers. "If nobody wants this change, why are we doin' it?"

A Negro teacher stood to his feet. "Sir? Mr. Pepper, sir. We have a good school at Union, and we have a good school at Gallatin. Why can't the government just let us alone? This desegregation mandate is going to ruin our schools."

Pepper shifted uneasily in his seat and scribbled something on a notepad.

The Negro teacher continued. "Did you look at yourself in the mirror this morning, Mr. Pepper?"

Pepper looked up at the man and blinked.

"If you did, you saw a Negro man. Sir, you are one of *us*. Why are you trying to be one of *them*?" He pointed to the white teachers around him.

Pepper bristled at the teacher's remark. "I'm not one of you or them. Frankly, sir, I am not here to worry about your schools. I'm here for one reason only: desegregation. I'm here to deal with segregation and to see that it ceases within this school system."

Another female white teacher spoke up loudly from her seat, without being recognized by Mr. Pepper. "Personally, I thought the Freedom of Choice policy we instituted in the early sixties worked pretty well. If Negroes want to attend Gallatin High, they can, but they don't have to. If white parents want their kids to go to Union, they can do that too. We have a number of Negroes at Gallatin, and we're doing fine. What's wrong with that arrangement?"

Susan Herron had been holding her tongue, but she refused to remain silent any longer. To imply that the Freedom of Choice policy the school district had implemented was working was beyond the pale, as far as she was concerned. Susan stood to her feet and faced the crowd. "We've had thirteen Negro students attend Gallatin High in five years since the Freedom of Choice policy was enacted. Thirteen. And almost half of those students came this year. Meanwhile, no white students have chosen to go to Union. None. Not one. While the current attitudes may not be entrenched forever, we are fooling ourselves if we think the Negroes and the whites have actually *decided* they want to attend school together. They have not."

A Negro teacher broached the question likely on the minds of most Union faculty members. "Who is going to decide, and on what criteria, which of our teachers will still have jobs? When our schools merge, Gallatin will have a couple hundred more students, but I'm sure the school board will not want to duplicate classes. Most of our teachers have been at Union for ten or twenty years. Some even more. We don't have a large turnover of faculty members, so many of our teachers, while highly experienced, are not spring chickens. This is no time for them to be going out looking for new jobs, especially when the one school where they have been welcome is closing. And what about our coaches? Will Coach Martin be the basketball coach of the Green Wave now? Or will he merely be an assistant? We have to face these kinds of issues at every position."

A white teacher sprang to her feet. "This is not fair. I am picking up on a lot of hostility from the Nigras—"

Susan Herron put her hands over her face. She wanted to scream. *Oh, no! Did that woman actually just say that?*

She had. And Susan wasn't the only person in the room who picked up on it.

"The *Nigras?*" a colored man spoke out of turn. "Wait. Did you say, 'the Nigras'? Are you not an English teacher at Gallatin? I'm a history teacher at Union. If I can learn to say *Caucasian,* surely you are intelligent enough to pronounce *Negro* correctly. That's the kind of thing—"

Anna Ligon covered her mouth with her hand, as though she could somehow silence what she was hearing. "This is not making things better," she whispered aloud.

Several teachers, both coloreds and whites, leapt to their feet, wanting the floor. Mr. Pepper waved his arms emphatically, trying to calm everyone. But no one paid him any attention.

"Yes, and what about history? Whose history are we going to teach? White history or black history, or some amalgamation?"

"This is an insult," a stylishly dressed, sophisticated-looking white woman clutching an Etienne Aigner handbag declared. "When I invite someone into my home, I want that person to feel welcome, but I don't tolerate that person disrespecting everything I have established."

"Are the darkies going to shower with the Gallatin students after physical education classes?" a custodial staff member wanted to know.

Recognizing that all semblance of order had disappeared, Donald Pepper stood up and placed his hands on the table in front of him. Without even bothering to use the microphone at the podium, Pepper yelled, "That's enough!" He raised his fist and slammed it down on the table. A metallic *bang!* echoed in the building.

The noise startled the crowd and got their attention. "Everyone, please calm down!" Pepper implored. "And sit down!" He glared at several dissenters who had stood and were yelling at one another.

Slowly, the schoolteachers and administrators regained their composure.

Pepper shook his head, obviously irritated. "And we are supposed to be the best of those who understand the need for integration and how it should work," he said as much to himself as to his colleagues.

He moved to the lectern and adjusted the microphone, speaking softly at first and then increasing in volume and intensity. "I will hear no more talk about going backward. This is one of the last school districts in America to desegregate. It is time to start doing things right.

"You folks in Gallatin have been dragging your feet for far too long—ever since the *Brown v. Board of Education* court decision in 1954. Ladies and gentlemen, desegregation is the law of the land, whether or not you like it. If Gallatin fails—if you fail to make this work—your schools will be either put in receivership and administrated by the federal government or shut down completely. Am I making myself perfectly clear?"

Pepper waited for a response. Blank faces stared back at him. The silence in the room was his only indication that the audience had understood his strong words. He took that as a plus.

"Good. Now we will move on. Most of you know Mrs. Wertheimer from the state social services office. She will now address how we can most sensitively communicate these transitions to our students."

Expressions of disgust and a few slight smiles flitted across the faces in the auditorium. The outbursts had shown them that they hadn't figured things out themselves.

As Mrs. Wertheimer stood to begin, Principal Malone caught the eye of Principal Herron and motioned for him to meet in the hallway. The two principals stepped outside the auditorium, where Herron guided Malone into a nearby unoccupied classroom. Herron closed the door and each of the two men momentarily sized up the other in light of what they had just experienced.

"Have a seat," Principal Herron offered his counterpart. "What are your first impressions?"

Malone shook his head sadly. "Dan, I believe what we just saw and heard was the tip of the iceberg. There are a whole lot of cold, slippery, precarious crevasses lying just below the surface. We are going to have to step carefully. I'm not sure we are ready for all of this."

Herron nodded. "Well, we knew it was coming. Frankly, I'm not surprised. It is difficult to legislate good conduct." The stern military man sighed. "At least we have the rest of the school year and over the summer to ease into things, and to help get ready and organized."

"Maybe not," Principal Malone replied.

Principal Herron looked at him quizzically. "Really? What do you mean?"

Malone rubbed his chin pensively. "Are your boys going to beat Springfield in the district semifinals on Wednesday evening?"

"Well, I hope so. We beat them handily during regular season play. But what does that—oh, no." Concern rippled across Herron's strong face. "I see where you are headed. And Union is most likely going to beat Westmoreland . . . oh my. Union has never played Gallatin. The Negro school pitted against the Caucasian school that the Negro school is being forced by law to merge with. Nothing like this has happened before in these parts."

Principal Malone nodded. "I hate to say it, but I have been living in denial too."

"How so?"

"I've been trying to ignore the obvious. Or at least put it out of mind for the past few weeks." Malone took a deep breath and stood, slowly pacing the room.

Herron watched Malone pace in silence.

"But it is happening," Malone finally said quietly.

"Yes, it is," Herron agreed. "And tonight's display has lit a fire under the pressure cooker and placed it on the front burner."

"That's for sure."

"And there's not a thing in the world we can do to change things."

"No, sir," Principal Malone said. "The championship will be on the line, with both the white community and the colored community wanting to show what they're made of . . ."

Herron let out a low, soft whistle.

Principal Malone finished his statement. "This will be the first time they play . . . and the last."

17

BILL PULLED OUT A COCA-COLA from the refrigerator. "Bill, honey," Anna Ligon said, looking up from a stack of test papers on the kitchen table. "Would you please take my car and go pick up Tyree? It's almost time for him to get off work."

"Sure thing, Mama. Is it okay if I pick up Joe Malone and Roy Jackson and take them with me?"

"Yes, that's fine. Just don't be late for Tyree."

"I'll be on time, Mama." Bill retrieved the car keys from the rack hanging on the wall by the door. "Be back soon," he called over his shoulder. Bill loved driving the family station wagon, even if it was only a short drive over to the Oakes Drive-In, where Tyree worked. It also happened to be his favorite hangout. He picked up Joe and Roy and headed over to the Drive-In, or as Ty referred to it: "One of the most happenin' places in Gallatin."

Bill eased the car into the parking area, being careful to park straight ahead, facing the windows so he could see inside the glass-fronted, classic drive-in restaurant that featured great burgers and ice cream, as well as plenty of Southern fried favorites. Although it was a weeknight, the place was buzzing with activity. Music from radio station WLAC in Nashville blared from a cheap sound system inside the restaurant with a few broken-down speakers mounted outside under the eaves of the restaurant. A half dozen cute, young Negro waitresses and waiters raced between the cooking area inside and the cars outside, where they took orders or attached trays loaded with food to customers' car doors or windows.

On the other side of the lot, several Negro teenage boys leaned against old cars, while a group of young black teens talked and laughed at the outdoor picnic tables. A few other colored boys hung out their car windows, calling back and forth to the kids at the tables. At one table sat a group of Vietnam veterans, back from the war but still fighting it in their minds every day and night. One of the vets was missing a leg and leaning heavily on crutches. A few dating couples sat together in cars, eating or simply talking. There were no white folks at the Oakes Drive-In. This was a Negro teen hangout in Gallatin. Whites had their own ice cream stand, Dari Delite, on the other side of town.

A car with three pretty teenage girls was parked next to Bill's. A cute girl with a short bob and a stunning smile sat in the passenger's seat with the window open. She spotted Bill. "Hi, boys," she called dreamily to Bill, Joe, and Roy.

"Hey." Bill and Joe waved nonchalantly.

"Did you guys come to make a date to take us to the movies on Friday night?"

Bill smiled. "I don't think so."

"There's a double feature at the Palace Theater for only a dollar," the cute girl added.

"That's nice," Bill said. "I haven't been to the Palace in a long time. Are they still making the coloreds sit upstairs in the balcony?"

"Well, yeah, I guess so. I've never tried to sit downstairs," the girl replied. "But it's more fun in the balcony anyhow."

"Not for me," Bill said.

"Okay, but you don't know what you're missin'," the cute girl tried one last time.

"Yeah, I do," Bill answered.

The girls waved as they drove off, and Bill settled back in the driver's seat to wait for Tyree's shift to be done. He pulled out a copy of the book he was reading, *Black Reconstruction in America* by W. E. B. Du Bois, a Harvard-educated Negro journalist who was instrumental in the founding of the National Association for the Advancement of Colored People.

Joe sat in the front passenger seat, patting his hands on the dashboard to the beat of the music playing on the outdoor speakers. In the backseat, Roy Jackson worked on his math homework—not that he was happy about that for a second, but Bill had insisted.

"Hi, Bill!" called Kim, one of the most popular waitresses at Oakes. She finished serving a customer and stopped in front of Bill's car window. "Anything you'd like?" she asked.

"No, thanks, Kim. I'm just waiting on Tyree to finish up." He nodded toward his brother, who was delivering a meal and some drinks at another car.

"Okay, just let me know if you need something," Kim said cheerily. "How about you, Joe?"

"Nah, I just ate supper a while ago. Thanks, Kim."

"And how 'bout the genius in the backseat there?" Kim chirped. Roy grunted.

"Don't mind him," Bill said with a grin. "He's fine. Unless you've got a secret formula that will help him learn how to do equations."

Kim gave Bill a funny look, then waved good-bye.

Roy muttered something under his breath and slapped down his math homework on the car seat. "There, I'm done with that."

"Let's see." Bill turned around and picked up Roy's homework. "You ain't done, Roy!" He laughed. "There are three pages in that assignment. You've only done one so far. Check it out."

"Whaaa? What are you talking about?" Roy grabbed the papers out of Bill's hand and read the instructions. Bill was right. Flustered and irritated, Roy said, "What good are all these equations? Doesn't help me figure out how much money I can spend or how much I need to save to buy a car. What good is it?"

Bill flashed a sly smile. "The good of it is if you don't do it and you don't graduate, you get a one-way ticket to Southeast Asia, where you can join that new fraternity known as Mekong Delta. I hear their initiation program is pretty tough."

"Yeah, and if you're lucky enough to dodge all the bullets while you're there," Joe added as he nodded toward the vets sitting at the picnic table, "you get a front row seat at the world-famous Oakes Drive-In, right there with James and the boys." Joe paused long enough to watch one of the vets pass around a small bottle of liquor. The guys at the table were only a few years older than Joe, Roy, or Bill, but they looked much older. They appeared worn and haggard, having experienced life far beyond their years.

"And every night for the rest of your life, Roy," Joe continued, "you can come out here and swap horror stories. Or, if you still have your arms and your legs, you might be able to get a minimum-wage job over at the shoe factory."

"Or if you are messed up in the head," Bill added sadly, "like Bernie there, maybe you can get a disability check from the government and sit around the park all day, looking at birds—"

"Oh, all right, I hear ya." Roy pouted a moment. "Gimme that book. I'll get the assignment done."

"I thought you'd see the light," Bill quipped.

———————————

Across town and equipped with a better stereo system and a full repertoire of Elvis Presley albums, the white counterpart to the Oakes Drive-In, known simply as the Dari Delite, was also hoppin'. The shop was located just off the main drag, so cars whizzed by in a constant stream, many of which were driven by teenage and young-adult drivers wanting to show off their cars and strut their stuff. The Dari

Delite was the most popular hangout in town for the white kids. It also boasted the best burgers and malts for miles around, so when they could put up with the loud Elvis music, even white adults stopped by. But the clientele was mostly teenagers flirting with other teenagers.

Bo Sherlin sat in his wheelchair, holding court as he often did at the Dari Delite. His dad had dropped him off earlier in the evening, helping him get situated in the wheelchair near a favorite table where some of his friends usually congregated. "I'll have Eddie pick you up after practice later tonight," Jim Sherlin told his son.

"Thanks, Dad. I'll see you later," he added, although he knew he probably wouldn't—especially if some of his older buddies bought some beer. But Bo didn't go to the Dari Delite to get drunk. Mostly he went so he could brag about Eddie.

"Do you remember that game a couple weeks ago when Eddie scored about twenty points by halftime?" Bo asked a couple of his post–high school buddies. "The team was behind by ten points, but Eddie saw one of the cheerleaders crying and worrying about losing. So he told me later, 'Bo, I just could not stand to see that pretty girl so upset, so I knew I had to do something extra special.' Eddie went out and scored fifty-five points that night!"

The dropouts slapped their knees. "That's plumb amazin', Bo!" one of them said.

Many of Bo's stories about Eddie came with a good measure of exaggeration, but Eddie's athletic abilities were so widely known, even some of Bo's most outlandish tales of Eddie's exploits were not out of the realm of possibility.

"Yep!" Bo said. "Broke the state scoring record, and the Green Wave won by twenty points!"

The dropouts surrounding Bo stomped their feet and cheered as though they were on the bleachers at Gallatin High. Jim Scanlin, the manager of the Dari Delite, walked over to the table and scowled at them. "Can you guys keep it down a little? You're scaring off some of our best customers and aggravating others."

"Oh, yeah, sure," Bo said much too loudly. "We'll cool it a bit. Sorry, boss. I forgot for a second that I am Bo Sherlin not Eddie. If Eddie were in here, he could hoot and holler till the cows came home and nobody would care." Bo paused and eyed the dropouts. "Because . . . we all know why, don't we?"

"Sure do," one dolt said.

"We do?" another asked.

"Of course nobody would care," Bo boomed, "because he is Eddie Sherlin, superstar of Gallatin High!"

"Okay, Bo," the manager said. "But I'd appreciate it if you could tone it down a little."

"Of course!" Bo nearly yelled.

The manager shook his head. *No use causing more of a spectacle.* Everyone knew that Bo had been impossible to control since the accident. And everyone felt awful about Bo's inability to play sports or do the things other guys his age took for granted. Most people, the manager included, cut Bo some slack for as long as they could. But there were times . . .

Just then, in his peripheral vision, Mr. Scanlin saw Eddie's car pull in to the parking lot. Eddie got out of the car and spotted Bo inside the restaurant before making his way to the entrance. Mr. Scanlin slipped away from Bo and his buddies and stepped outside to intercept Eddie.

"Evenin'," Mr. Scanlin said casually.

"Good evening."

Mr. Scanlin looked back toward the inside of the restaurant where Bo and his friends were still causing a ruckus. "He's not doing so well tonight."

"Oh, no. I'm sorry. Did they break anything?"

"No, just making a lot of noise. New folks who come inside aren't used to Bo and his buddies, so they don't understand why I don't throw them out."

"I'm so sorry—"

162

"No, I'm the one who is sorry, Eddie. I wish there was something I could do—or something anyone could do."

"Well, thanks for not calling the cops on him. That's something right there."

"I wouldn't do that to poor old Bo," Mr. Scanlin said, shaking his head sadly. He and Eddie both looked inside at Bo, who was even more animated than earlier. "I used to see all of Bo's games when he played Little League—back, you know—before the accident. He could really play ball."

Eddie pursed his lips, as though reminiscing about his early years playing ball with Bo. "Yes, he could," he said slowly. "I'd better go get him. Thanks again."

"No problem, Eddie. Anytime."

Eddie and Mr. Scanlin walked inside the Dari Delite together. Customers immediately recognized Eddie and waved to him. Several called out to him, saying, "Hey, Eddie!" "Good to see ya!" "You gonna whip those Springfield fellers?"

He responded as best he could, but his eyes were fixed on Bo.

"Hey! There he is!" Bo hollered when he saw Eddie. "Why, there's number 22 himself, ladies and gentlemen. Playing guard for the Green Wave and averaging thirty-three points per game . . . from the great state of Tennessee, it's Gallatin's own . . ." Bo paused and raised his eyes toward the ceiling, as he yelled at the top of his lungs, "Eddie! Eddie Sherlin!"

A few of Bo's dropout buddies applauded Bo's outburst; others looked on in shock, while still others turned their heads away, almost as though they were embarrassed for Eddie.

Eddie stepped over to Bo and gently placed his hand on his brother's shoulder while still exerting a firm pressure. "Thanks, Bo. Thanks for those kind words." He patted Bo's shoulder and then grasped his arm. "Did you get enough to eat? All finished?" Eddie knew that Bo probably hadn't eaten a thing, but he continued on. "Okay, great. Let's go. Come on, pal. Time to go home."

"Home? No way," Bo said. "I still have a bunch of stories to tell the boys, here. I promised I'd tell the folks about how we fell in love with the game of basketball. You remember that, Eddie? How we dragged that huge pallet for several miles to build a backboard."

"Yeah, Bo. I remember. Maybe some other time." Eddie reached for Bo's wheelchair to diplomatically get him out of the Dari Delite without further disruptions.

Bo ignored Eddie and continued speaking loudly, as though doing a speech for all the other customers. "We went to Vandy when we were just kids—Dad and Eddie and me—to see our uncle play. We'd never been to a real gymnasium before. We'd never been to downtown Nashville. But me and Dad and Eddie . . . walking into that place, you know, it is so enormous in there. I never saw anything like it. And the cheerleaders! Oh my . . . those cheerleaders in their tight little outfits . . . and the crowd and the noise . . . and the sound of the ball going through the hoops—*swish! Swish!* Right, Eddie?" Bo looked up at his brother standing nearby. "Eddie loves that sound. Oooh, and the popcorn smell? That did it. We both decided, right there on the spot. We're gonna *play*—" Bo stopped and slammed his fist on the table so hard that the violent vibration sent a ketchup bottle careening off the table and shattering on the floor.

"All right, Bo. Let's go!" Eddie grabbed the handles of Bo's wheelchair and turned him around, wheeling him toward the door. Eddie looked at Mr. Scanlin and nodded toward the mess of glass and ketchup on the floor and mouthed, "I'll pay you for that."

The manager waved his hands and shook his head, communicating, "Don't worry about it."

Bo tried to rise up out of his wheelchair as they neared the door. "I'm not done!" he yelled. "I'm not finished."

"We'll finish later, Bo," Eddie said, still aiming toward the door.

"These people want to hear me!"

"Some other time, Bo."

164

Bo angrily attempted to jerk his wheelchair out of Eddie's grasp. Eddie was too strong for that, but the chair banged into another table, sending the silverware and more condiments onto the floor.

It was now Eddie's turn to get mad. He whipped his brother's wheelchair around 180 degrees on the spot and pulled Bo out the door backward, with Bo still screaming. "I get to have some fun too, you know. I'm Bo Sherlin, after all." Bo was still hollering as the door shut behind him.

Eddie wheeled the chair over to the car and then manipulated Bo into the front seat. He folded the wheelchair and placed it in the trunk. After climbing into the driver's side, he slammed the door shut. For several seconds, Eddie leaned his head on the steering wheel, not starting the car, not saying a word to Bo. Finally, he sat up, sighed heavily, and turned the ignition key. The two Sherlin brothers rode in silence most of the way home, with Eddie staring straight ahead at the highway and Bo leaning his head against the passenger's side window. Just before Eddie turned the car down the road toward their house, Bo raised his head.

"Eddie."

"Yeah, Bo."

"I'm sorry."

"For what?"

Bo turned and looked at his brother in the dark. He was the same in the dark as he was under the bright lights. Tears filled Bo's eyes and trickled down his face.

Eddie reached over and grabbed Bo's forearm. Bo couldn't see them, but Eddie's eyes had welled with tears too.

18

THE AFTERNOON of Missy Hamilton's birthday party, Anna Ligon hurried home from teaching at Union High School to change clothes and iron the white, heavily starched blouse and dark-colored skirt she would wear to the party. Not that she had been invited. No, nary a chance of a colored person being a guest at a party thrown by one of the most affluent white families in the South. But Anna's friend Naomi had called the day before to ask a favor.

"Miss Anna, I'm working the birthday party at the Hamiltons' on Friday night, and I am a bit shorthanded. They have their own butlers and maids, but they've also hired Mr. Cox and our team to help with the serving duties, making sure everyone's drinks are filled, picking up empty glasses, washing dishes, emptying the garbage, and the likes."

"That sounds like a lot of work, Naomi," Anna said.

"It certainly is. And we could use a few extra hands. Would you be willing to help me out? Mr. Cox pays real good, and you can even eat dinner at the party—there will be gobs of food—and you will probably be home before midnight."

"Well, I don't know. That is a school day, and I will have already worked a lot this week."

"Oh, please, Miss Anna. I'd be most grateful. And I know Mr. Cox would be most appreciative as well."

"Well, okay. I'll be glad to help you. What time do I need to be there?"

Now that Friday afternoon had come, between finishing her responsibilities at Union and rushing home to get ready, Anna was wondering if she had made a mistake. But Naomi was a good friend, and the extra money might cover a few expenses necessary for Bill's graduation.

Bill and his friend and teammate Roy Jackson were already there when Anna arrived home. She greeted the boys and quickly set about putting up her ironing board. Bill was reading *The Militant*, a newspaper focused on racial equality issues, while he watched over Roy, who was struggling through his math assignments.

Anna hurried around the house getting her "serving clothes" ready. "Bill, honey, I'm going to have to leave in a few minutes. I'm working tonight, helping Naomi. Delores can get you boys something to eat."

"Oh, that's okay, Mom," Bill said. "Roy and I are going to the Drive-In later on . . . after he finishes his math homework," Bill emphasized.

Roy looked up and shrugged. Anna smiled. She was glad Roy was trying, whether or not he got to play basketball. She busied herself ironing her clothes for the party. Just about the time Anna put a firm crease in the sleeve of the white blouse, she heard a loud knock at the front door.

Seeing his opportunity to escape his taskmaster of a tutor, Roy bounded to his feet. "I'll get it, Mrs. Ligon."

Bill didn't even look up from his newspaper. "Sit down." Roy sighed and bent over his math assignment again.

"I'll get it, Ma," Bill called. He gave Roy a steadying glance before going over to the door and opening it.

Bill recognized the tall, lean frame of Robert Klein, head basketball coach at Austin Peay State University, located in Clarksville, about an hour north of Nashville.

Bill turned and looked behind him. "Keep at it, Roy. I'll be right back." He stepped outside, meeting Robert Klein on the porch. "Hello, Mr. Klein. How are you?"

"Hi, Bill. How's it goin'? How's my favorite center?"

Bill smiled at Mr. Klein's smooth pitch. "Oh, I'm all right."

"Are you boys ready for the big game? Semifinals, that's hot stuff."

"We're ready. I know they're tough, but we're gonna put up a good fight."

"I know you will. Bill, I heard you went up to Princeton recently. How'd that go? Personal escort by Bill Bradley. That's impressive. The man could shoot a set shot, that's for sure. Now he's playing for the Knicks and talking a lot about politics. But a good fellow."

"Yeah, Princeton was great," Bill said. "Not sure I'd want to be there in the wintertime. It was cold in the late summer when I visited. Plus, basketball isn't all that important to them. You know they don't scholarship their athletes directly. You gotta get into the school academically before they'll take a look at you on the court."

"Well, you being a Merit Scholar should take care of that," Mr. Klein said.

"Yeah, they were nice to me. Made me feel real welcome."

"We'd make you feel real welcome at Austin Peay, Bill. I know we can't compete with the major universities you are looking at, but you could be a standout star at Austin Peay, and who knows where you might go from there. I know you are a Detroit Pistons fan, and I could easily see you getting a tryout with them."

"Thank you, Mr. Klein. I appreciate that," Bill said sincerely.

"I know there's not much we can offer you compared to the big boys, but you could go to school for free. Wouldn't cost your mama a red dime."

"Yes, sir, that is an advantage—"

"And I tell you, Bill. You'd be the biggest star to ever hit our school. We don't get many top nationally ranked recruits up in Clarksville. We're not exactly Los Angeles or Chicago or New York. But I'd hate to see you get caught up in the crowd at one of those big schools when you could be Mr. Everything right here at home. And your mom and your brother and sister could drive up occasionally to see you play."

"I know, I know, Mr. Klein . . . and I appreciate your generosity—"

"We have a strong basketball program, Bill."

"Yes, sir. You do have a good program, Mr. Klein. I've seen your team play, and you're a great coach. No doubt. And I'm grateful for your interest in me." Bill paused and took a deep breath. "But I have to be honest with you. Going to college in another small town after growing up in Gallatin just doesn't have much appeal to me. Don't get me wrong. Clarksville is a nice place. We stopped there a couple of times on the way to visit my aunt. And I have to tell ya, compared to Gallatin, Clarksville is downright progressive!"

Both Mr. Klein and Bill laughed, since both rural communities were anything but progressive. Indeed, Gallatin's recalcitrance in the face of government-mandated integration was widely known.

Bill continued. "We know things are supposed to be changin' around about these parts, but these little towns . . . it's gonna take a while. Right now they don't seem as if they are ever going to change, you follow me? And frankly, Mr. Klein, I can't imagine what it would take to ever stimulate real change around here regarding racial matters."

"I understand, Bill. But keep us on your list. We're interested. Very interested."

"I sure do thank you, Mr. Klein. But in all honesty, if basketball can get me out of these small-town attitudes, I want to get as far away from them as possible."

Bill shook hands with Mr. Klein and walked back inside the house.

Anna had finished ironing her blouse and was in the other room changing clothes. Roy looked up from the math assignment with which he was struggling. "What was that all about?" Roy asked.

"Nuthin'," Bill said. "Nuthin' at all."

19

EDDIE WALKED INTO DON SAVAGE'S pawn shop and over to the glass cabinets containing gold chains. He peered through the glass panes at the various diamonds and other precious gems in the display. *Wow!* He had never seen so many pretty, sparkling things in one place.

"Are you looking for something special, son?" the elderly Savage asked. He'd recognized Eddie as soon as he entered the store. Don had been in the pawn business for more than forty-five years. He'd sold diamonds, guns, guitars—lots of guitars—fancy ink pens, and plenty of gold bracelets and necklaces, but he still got a kick out of the young people who came into his shop looking for just the right gift for their high school sweethearts. It wasn't always easy—especially on the kids' limited budgets—but Don did his best, and most of the time he was able to help them find something special within their price ranges.

"Yes, sir," Eddie answered. "I am." He held up his class ring so Don could see it. "I'm looking for a nice chain so my girlfriend can wear my ring around her neck."

Don's eyes lit up. "Oh, she must be a special lady."

"Yeah, she kinda is."

"Well, then, I have just the piece you will want." Don slid an array of ultrathin twenty-four-carat gold chains out of his display case. "How about this one, right here?" the old gentleman asked.

"Wow, Mr. Savage. That is beautiful. I'm not sure I can afford it though."

"Oh, I'm pretty sure you can," Don said. "How much money do you have?"

"Ten dollars."

"Well, this is your lucky day, Eddie. This lovely chain here will make a mighty fine necklace when you run it through your class ring, and it so happens that it requires only a ten-dollar down payment. You can pay me the rest when you get it." Don smiled at Eddie. "Just make sure you beat Springfield or the price doubles!"

"Oh, wow. Okay, Mr. Savage," Eddie said, passing ten one-dollar bills across the counter. "How much did you say the gold chain costs?"

"We'll figure that out later, Eddie. You take good care of that girl of yours."

"Yes, sir! I will."

"And keep your eye on that left forward from Springfield. That kid is a fast one."

"Yes, sir. I sure will. Thank you, Mr. Savage." Eddie hurried out the door with a wave. *People in Gallatin are so nice to me*, he thought.

Later that day, Eddie stopped by Bob White's barbershop. He wanted his hair short for the upcoming play-off games and also to look his best at Missy's party. He was getting genuinely excited about attending the party, even though the thought of being at her house with all those people seemed rather daunting. He much preferred mingling in smaller groups rather than in large groups like he'd find at the sort of parties Missy's family threw.

After the barber had worked on Eddie's hair for a while, he turned Eddie around to face the mirror and get his opinion.

"How's that looking to you, Eddie?" the barber asked.

"Just a little more off the top, Mr. White. I don't want any hair in my eyes this week."

"No danger of that," Mr. White responded as he trimmed Eddie's already short hair above his forehead. Just as the barber's scissors moved precariously around Eddie's ears, the shop door opened, and a teenage girl leaned in and snapped a Polaroid photo of Eddie sitting in the barber's chair.

"Delilah!" Eddie called out in surprise. "What in the world are you doing?"

"Just working on my business plan," Eddie's sister said. "Hurry, Debbie, don't let that hair go to waste." Catlike, Debbie slipped into the barbershop and got down on her hands and knees. Crawling around the floor, she swept up the hair clippings below Eddie's chair and deposited them into a plastic bag. "Oooh, this piece should sell easily," she said, holding up a longer strand of Eddie's hair.

"Oh, come on," Eddie moaned. "You are taking this too far."

"We'll see!" Debbie beamed. "You don't realize how popular you are, Eddie. But we do. We hear the girls talking about you at school all the time."

"Oh my!" Eddie looked to Mr. White for help.

The barber shrugged and grinned. "What are you going to do, Eddie? When you've got it, you've got it."

"Thanks a lot, Mr. White."

Eddie hurried home and dug around in his closet until he found his best dress pants. He hadn't worn them for several years and the waist still fit him perfectly, but he had grown several inches, so the slacks now looked like the high-water pants Huckleberry Finn might have worn to go fishing. *Well, that will never do*, Eddie thought. "Mom!"

He took the trousers to Betty and explained the problem. "And you are going to wear these to a party tonight? At the Hamiltons' *home*?" Betty asked. "Let's see what we can do. Get up on that kitchen chair, and I'll try to let out the seam on the cuffs."

"Thanks, Mom," Eddie said, hopping onto the chair. He felt a bit silly standing there wearing a T-shirt and too-short dress pants, but hopefully his mom could save the day. He didn't have the time or money to buy a new pair of pants. And he knew better than to ask his mom or dad for any cash.

"Oh, dear," Betty said. She seemed upset. "This won't work."

Eddie looked down at his mother, who was bent over, tugging at the fabric, trying to pull it down far enough to cover his ankles.

"At least you could have given me some warning!" she huffed.

"Sorry, Mom."

Just then, Jim Sherlin came in from work, looking tired and frazzled, but he seemed amused at the sight that greeted him in the kitchen. "What's going on?"

"Oh, nothing much. Your son is going to a party at the Hamiltons' home tonight, and his dress pants are three sizes too small." Betty tried in vain to smooth out the extra crease at the bottom of Eddie's dress pants. "I'll iron them while you shower," she said. She looked up at Jim. "He'll need to wear your sports jacket. Sounds like it is a formal party."

Jim cocked his head when he saw Eddie's ankles. He looked up at Eddie and then back down to the pants legs, smiled hopelessly, and shook his head. "That looks ridiculous."

"It's the best I could do," Betty said apologetically. "He just now told me about the party. Can you please just get the jacket?"

"I guess so," Jim said.

"Okay, now take these off so I can press the cuff," Betty instructed. Eddie slipped out of the pants and hurried to his room in his T-shirt, underwear, and socks, carrying his tennis shoes in one hand. His room was tiny, but he had still found space on the

174

dresser to display some of his trophies. Several pictures of Eddie in his football and basketball uniforms decorated the walls, and one very special photo of him and Bo out back at the old house, after they had been shooting baskets, was prominently displayed on the dresser.

Eddie tossed the shoes under the bed and then hustled down the short hall to the bathroom. He pitched his remaining clothes into the hamper and hopped into the shower, lathering up with the rough lye soap his mom made. After a quick shower, he grabbed a towel. Still drying off, Eddie hurried back to his room to get dressed. Just as he opened the door and stepped inside, he heard a chorus of girls screaming. Startled, Eddie looked up, still holding his towel around his body.

Outside his bedroom window, Delilah, Debbie, and several other freshman and sophomore girls were jumping up and down, giggling and squealing with delight. Eddie, realizing the girls were staring and laughing at him, let out a yell. "Debbie! Delilah!" He clutched the towel to his naked body. "Mommmm!"

Eddie reached for the window shade in an attempt to close it but pulled too hard, sending the entire blind crashing to the floor. The girls outside the window looked on, first in shock, and then in absolute glee as Eddie fumbled around the room, trying to cover himself and get out of view.

Delilah's businesswoman instincts kicked in. Immediately, she produced a small plastic bag with a lock of Eddie's recently shorn hair. "This hair, only a few hours ago, was on the head of superstar Eddie Sherlin," she announced. "Girls, this is a rare treasure, worth a lot of money, but since you are now some of Eddie's most intimate fans, I'm willing to give you a special deal . . ."

Eddie was rescued by his mother who delivered his freshly pressed pants. He knew that even wearing his best clothes, he'd still be one of the most poorly attired people at the party, but Missy wanted him there. That's all that mattered to him. So he got dressed in what he

had on hand. He even found time to wrap Missy's birthday present in pretty giftwrapping left over from Delilah's birthday, and he
painstakingly attempted to piece together the shiny, slightly used
paper in a pretty pattern.

Ready to go, he bounded into the living room. "Mom, Dad, can
one of you give me a ride over to the party? Or can I take the car?"

"Hey, not bad," Jim said, admiring Betty's work on the trousers.
"Eddie, you look pretty sharp."

"Yes, you do," Betty said, slipping over to give Eddie a kiss on the
cheek. "You look very handsome, son."

"Thanks, Mom. Can you give me a ride?"

"Go ahead and take the car," Betty said. "We're not going anywhere tonight." She looked over at Jim, slumped on the couch in
front of the television.

Eddie gratefully picked up the keys to the family car—a two-
toned, four-door Buick LeSabre—and drove the old vehicle toward
the Hamiltons'.

After a short drive out of town, Eddie pulled the clunker up the
Hamiltons' long red-gravel driveway, passing white painted fences
enclosing lush green fields where sleek, well-groomed horses grazed.
With the sun setting over the hillside behind the Hamilton home
prominently positioned at the back of the plantation, the scene
looked as though it could have come straight out of *Gone with
the Wind*. He parked the car in the grass and walked the remaining
distance to the enormous Southern colonial-style mansion, replete
with a huge front porch and tall white columns.

Eddie made his way up the wide steps leading to the ornate entrance. An elderly Negro butler with a neatly trimmed mustache
and dressed in a white tuxedo jacket, bow tie, black dress pants, and
shiny black shoes greeted Eddie at the door. Eddie couldn't help but
notice that the help was dressed better than he was.

"Good evening, sir," the butler said kindly but formally. "May I
help you?"

Eddie reached inside his jacket pocket and pulled out the invitation to Missy's party. "Howdy," Eddie said, smiling. "I've got this." He waved the invitation so the butler could see it.

"Yes, sir. Thank you, sir. Welcome." The butler stepped aside so Eddie could pass. He opened the door and Eddie eased into the foyer. The scene in front of him was unlike anything he had ever experienced. An enormous crystal chandelier hung from the high rotunda-style ceiling. Huge paintings rested on the walls and Persian rugs were located strategically on the hardwood floors. The scent of flowers filled the house. Eddie gawked in amazement. Although he and Missy were considered a couple at school, he had never visited her home. He was overwhelmed.

A crowd of formally dressed men and women, mostly adults but a few high school and college-aged young people, engaged in chit-chat in the foyer and front rooms of the house. Many of the men sported tuxedoes; the women wore formal gowns or cocktail dresses. Eddie stepped into the living room, where an even larger crowd was laughing and talking. A number of people were also dancing to the sounds of "Tennessee Waltz" played by a string quintet.

Eddie tugged awkwardly at his collar, then fiddled with the waistband of his dress pants, trying to make sure the pant legs were indeed long enough. He walked past several sophisticated Southern belles, none of whom paid any attention to him. A middle-aged Negro waitress carrying a tray filled with glasses of champagne stopped beside him, waiting for him to make his selection. Eddie wasn't sure what was in the glasses, but he noticed the smell of alcohol. "Do you have any Cokes?" he asked.

"Yes, suh," she said. "I will get you one. Right away, suh."

"Oh, there's no rush," Eddie said. "Just whenever you have time. I'll be here for a while."

The waitress looked at Eddie oddly. "Yes, suh."

Then Eddie noticed Missy, dressed in her Southern-belle best, conversing with a group of well-dressed, college-aged friends. She slowly weaved her way through the flock of her admirers, moving in his direction.

"Hey, Missy!" Eddie called out, waving his hand high and then quickly pulling down his arm, embarrassed. Missy spotted him and rushed over. She gave Eddie a formal hug and held out her hand, intending for Eddie to kiss it. Eddie misunderstood her gesture and shook Missy's hand instead.

"It's about time, Eddie Sherlin," she said with a breathy Southern drawl. "I was beginning to think you were going to let me down."

"Oh . . . no," Eddie said. "Had a little problem with my suit." Missy looked him up and down, from head to toe. She moved close to him—so close he could smell the sweet fragrance of her perfume—and straightened his tie. "Well, now, you look fine to me." She smiled flirtatiously. "Look at you . . . all dressed up and proper. Ain't you just the cutest thing?" She tugged on his coat sleeve and then clutched his hand. "Come on. Let's go in the other room. My brother is home from college for a few days. He came in special for my birthday. I want you to meet him and some of his friends."

Missy pulled Eddie into another room, which was also filled with people. Feeling bashful and unsure of himself, Eddie stumbled along behind her, trying not to step on her dainty white shoes. Missy drew him over to a group of white, college-aged men, all dressed in Southern Ivy-League blazers and white or beige slacks. A group of admiring young debutantes, also white, hung on the college boys' every word.

Missy tapped the shoulder of a tall, immaculately dressed college man who was entertaining a fawning group of young men and women. "Charles, this is Eddie, the fella I've been telling you about. Eddie, this is Chuckie, my older brother."

"Hello, Edward," Charles said. "It's a pleasure."

Eddie extended his hand, but Charles ignored him, continuing on with his speech to his rapt admirers. "I told Daddy that my degree from Duke law school was not going to impress anyone in New York City, but he, of course, insisted . . ."

Embarrassed, Eddie pulled his hand away, looking around to see who saw the rebuff and pretending he had never really intended to shake hands with Charles. He stood to the side, squirming. The rich-kid conversations bored him. The banal banter was all about academics, law and medical schools, banking and finance. Charles's friends eyed Eddie condescendingly and disinterestedly, as though pitying him. A member of Charles's group gave Eddie's outfit the once-over and smirked, with mocking disapproval apparent on his face.

Eddie noticed the man's arrogant stare and averted his eyes. Another of Charles's friends flirted with Missy right in front of Eddie, filling his comments with the sort of sexual innuendo that must have been common and accepted on his Ivy League campus.

Eddie blanched in shock when he heard the cad's comments and then bristled with anger. He was about to have a word with him, when he noticed Missy was basking in the attention, eating up every word, laughing at his off-color jokes, touching his arm, and flirting right back with him. Still, that was no way to speak to a lady, and Eddie stepped forward to let the collegian know it.

But just then, Missy's father, Charles Hamilton Sr., a distinguished-looking man in his early fifties, dressed in a white suit with a red pocket handkerchief, swept into the room with several of his rich male friends. "There's my birthday girl," he said loudly. The crowd of young men around Missy immediately stepped back in the presence of her father, not so much out of respect, but so he might notice them.

Without greeting Eddie, Mr. Hamilton continued his conversation with the men accompanying him. "Yes, sir, this boy hit a shot almost from half-court," he nodded toward Eddie, as though he were a mannequin propped up in front of him. "He makes those thirty-footers look as easy as a layup," Mr. Hamilton continued, raving about him. "Isn't that right, Eddie?" Hamilton asked, catching Eddie off guard.

The men surrounding Missy's father laughed. Eddie shrugged awkwardly. He didn't know what to say, so he tried to smile, but he could feel the blood flushing his face.

It didn't matter. Mr. Hamilton clearly did not expect him to speak. In fact, he was already rambling on, talking about Eddie as though he were a racehorse he was considering for purchase. "Yes, boys, that kid right there—what is he, five-ten, five-eleven?—he can jump higher than any man his size I have ever seen. The boy can dunk a basketball! He's something special, all right. He's got a pair of colored legs on him. If I didn't know better, I'd wonder if he doesn't have some black blood running through his veins."

Eddie stepped back from the conversation, nearly bumping into a Negro waitress serving appetizers behind him. As soon as he saw her, Eddie not only felt embarrassed, he felt sorry for her, hoping she hadn't heard Mr. Hamilton's insensitive remarks. If the woman had heard his comments, she had given no outward indication, but Eddie detected hurt in her eyes. He took another step away from Mr. Hamilton.

"Yes, sir, five-foot-ten, and the boy can dunk that ball. Amazing—"

"Daddy!" Missy broke in. "You're embarrassing Eddie with all those grandiose comments. He's much more than a basketball player, you know."

"Nonsense!" Hamilton railed. "We're mighty proud of your basketball abilities, Eddie."

"Thank you, sir," Eddie muttered, but Hamilton wasn't listening. One of his friends jumped into the conversation.

"Where are you going to play college ball, son?" the friend asked.

"I've already signed with the University of Tennessee. Mr. Bill Battles, a fine Christian gentleman, recruited me to play football, basketball, and baseball."

"You got scholarship offers in all three sports?"

"Yes, sir," Eddie said, sheepishly.

"That's unheard of! How are you going to play three sports at the college level?"

"I'm not sure, sir. First, I've got to get my grades up."

"Ha, you don't need grades when you can play ball the way you can, son. Don't you worry none about those grades. You just take good care of yourself and stay in shape."

"Yes, sir. I'll sure try to do that."

"Where did your folks go to school?" another of Hamilton's friends asked.

"Well, they went to high school, but they never had a chance to go to college. They've had to work real hard and all," Eddie said.

Hamilton's friend nodded condescendingly. "Of course they have."

Missy's father boomed, "U. T. thinks they have Eddie signed, sealed, and delivered, but we're getting this boy over to Duke. Come this time next year, he's gonna be a Blue Devil. Right, Eddie?"

"Well, I'm committed at Tennessee—"

"Oh, that's no problem. U. T. is so big they won't even know you're gone."

"Well, I . . ."

Again, Hamilton wasn't listening. He was already immersed in another conversation with his fellow bloated egos, each bandying bombastic statements to impress his peers. Eddie slipped farther behind Missy and tried to stand out of the way.

As the party went on, Eddie followed behind Missy like a loyal puppy. She relished the attention lavished on her by the college boys, and she seemed quite impressed with their sophisticated conversational skills, so after a while, Eddie simply sat down on a couch and watched the spectacle. In addition to all the puffery, Eddie particularly noticed the way the white guests treated the Negro waiters and waitresses. Or, more accurately, how they did *not* treat them, often not even acknowledging them as human beings but simply as hired help, expecting them to serve and clean up after the guests, without a word of thanks or appreciation. It didn't seem right to Eddie.

While Missy flitted from guest to guest, Eddie amused himself by taking a few popped champagne corks from a tray and tossing them into a large, empty wine glass someone had left on a coffee table. "Swish!" Eddie said with a laugh every time he sank another cork. When he had loaded the wine glass full, he retrieved the corks and began shooting all over again.

At one point, he went into the bathroom, and when he came out, Missy was gone. Eddie walked down a hallway, sidestepping a waiter who was hurrying past him with a tray loaded with empty drink glasses on his way to the kitchen. When Eddie's eyes followed the waiter into the kitchen, he spotted the familiar face of a woman washing dishes at the sink. He looked more closely, peering down the dimly lit hallway.

Sure enough, he recognized the woman. It was Anna Ligon, Bill's mother. She was dressed in a maid's uniform, busy helping with the party. Eddie stepped into the kitchen as Anna sprayed a large pan with hot water, the spray dousing her apron as well.

"Mrs. Ligon?"

"Yes?" Anna turned toward Eddie.

"Do you remember me?"

Anna squinted in Eddie's direction.

"I'm Eddie. Eddie Sherlin."

"Oh my goodness, Eddie! I didn't recognize you!" Anna hadn't seen Eddie in years, except for the occasional photo in the newspaper that Bill or Tyree pointed out to her. She knew he was a star athlete at Gallatin because, although the boys didn't really follow him specifically, they were always looking in the newspaper, hoping to see a picture of themselves. But they couldn't help but notice Eddie and occasionally would remind Anna of when they had all played together in the park adjoining their home.

Anna dried her hands on a dish towel and stepped over to give Eddie a quick hug. "It is so good to see you," she said. "Honey, look at you! All grown up now." She looked Eddie up and down, not at all put off by his outfit. "You are quite the handsome gentleman these days."

182

Eddie looked down bashfully. "Thank you, Mrs. Ligon. I'm feelin' a little out of place here." Eddie made a sweeping motion with his hands.

"Oh, don't worry about that," Anna said.

Eddie quickly changed the subject. "How are Bill and Tyree doin'?"

"They are just fine. Like you, all grown up already. That Bill keeps growin' like a weed. I can't hardly keep him in clothes that fit. He's over six foot three inches tall now."

"I know," Eddie said. "I saw him play against White House. He was blocking shots all night. I didn't get a chance to talk with him, though, after the game. You know how they whisk everyone out of the gym so fast."

"Yes, I do," Anna said wistfully. Of course, they didn't whisk away the white players, only the Negroes. But she knew that wasn't Eddie's fault. "Oh, I heard about your brother's awful accident a few years ago. I'm sure sorry about that. How is he doing these days?"

"He's doing okay. Not good, but okay. It's hard to understand why those bad things happen sometimes. I haven't figured it out yet."

Anna nodded. "I know what you mean. The Lord allows us to go through some difficulties in life. But he always sees us through."

Eddie smiled at Mrs. Ligon's great attitude. He admired her faith. "Yeah, he sure does."

"And how is your mother, Eddie? Is she still selling encyclopedias?"

"Yes, ma'am. She's still at it. Not as often now, since Bo got hurt, but she's still selling."

"I expect that I still owe a fortune or two before I ever get outta debt on that deal." Anna laughed. "But the boys and Delores have used the books all through school, so it was a good investment."

"Yes, ma'am. It sure helped me too." Both Anna and Eddie chuckled.

"The time certainly has flown by," Anna said. "It seems like yesterday when you boys were out playin' ball over at the park and at Cousin Ella Lee's."

"Yep. Sure does."

"Funny how things work in this town," Anna said. "You move five miles away and you'd think you moved all the way to the moon."

Eddie nodded, recalling how he had rarely seen Bill since both of their families had moved away from the old neighborhood.

"But Bill kept up with you in the newspapers. He was always sayin', 'Hey, Mom, look what Eddie did. Broke this record. Broke that record.' I think in his own way, Bill is proud of you."

Eddie was genuinely surprised and happy that Bill hadn't forgotten about him and had kept track of him throughout their high school careers.

"That's really nice, Mrs. Ligon. I saw the scores, but I didn't see much else from Bill's games." They both knew the paper simply didn't cover Union the same way it covered the white schools in the area.

"Oh, that's all right. Bill understands that," Anna said. "I'd better get back to work now, but it certainly is good to see you, Eddie."

"Work? Huh? Oh . . . yeah. It sure is good to see you too. Please give my best to Bill, and tell him I hope to see him one of these days real soon." Eddie glanced back toward the main part of the house. "I guess I'd better go find my date," he said with a laugh.

"Have fun," Anna said.

"You too, Mrs. Ligon . . . er, ah, well, you know what I mean."

"Yes, Eddie," she said with a warm smile. "I do."

"Before I go, let me help you with those." Eddie nodded toward the large stack of dishes still sitting aside the sink.

"Oh, no, Eddie. That wouldn't be good."

Eddie motioned back toward the living room. "They won't even know I'm gone, ya see what I'm sayin?"

Out in the living room, several Negro waiters wheeled a large birthday cake through the crowd of festive onlookers, many of whom had drunk too much alcohol. Mrs. Hamilton, an attractive

184

and stylish woman, stood along with Mr. Hamilton. "Let's sing 'Happy Birthday' to our marvelous daughter, Missy!" Mrs. Hamilton began singing and the group joined her. Missy stood in the center of the room, her hands at her sides, beaming in one direction and then another as the well-wishers sang to her. She dipped down in a slight curtsy and then leaned low to blow out the candles on the cake, to the applause of the crowd. Missy acknowledged the smiles and approving nods of everyone around her, noting especially the exuberance of the college boys. She flashed a broad smile to them as the Negro waitresses moved in to begin cutting the cake. But when Missy looked around, she couldn't spot Eddie in the crowd.

She searched for him through several rooms, accepting hugs and birthday wishes as she went, but she still didn't see him. Almost on a whim, she leaned into the kitchen. To her surprise, she saw Eddie sitting at the kitchen table drying dishes and laughing with one of the help. Missy's eyes widened and her mouth formed an O.

"Eddie!" she shrieked as though she had seen a ghost.

"Oh, hi, Missy. How's the party going?"

Missy looked at Eddie quizzically. "I'm going to open my presents now. Don't you want to join us?"

"Oh, yeah. Sure. Okay, I'll be right there." Eddie looked at Anna. "So long, Mrs. Ligon."

"Good-bye, Eddie. And thanks again for your assistance. You've saved me a great deal of time and work."

"My pleasure, ma'am." Eddie waved and hustled over to Missy, who was standing, arms across her chest, obviously not happy.

"You missed them singing 'Happy Birthday' to me."

"Sorry about that."

"And what are you doing out here in the kitchen with *the help?*" she said loudly enough for Anna to hear, before she closed the kitchen door behind them and pulled Eddie toward the living room.

"Ah, there's our princess!" Charles Hamilton Sr. said. "Let's gather around."

For the next forty-five minutes, Missy sat in the middle of the room and opened expensive birthday gifts given to her by the attendees. She moved from one gift to another, barely acknowledging the givers, always looking for the next present, which her mother quickly handed to her. When the last present was unwrapped, Mr. Hamilton put his arm around Missy's shoulder. "And there is one more. Let's count it down everyone! Ten, nine . . . eight . . ." As the crowd joined in the countdown, Mr. Hamilton placed a blindfold over Missy's eyes and led her to the French doors at the back of the living room. He opened the doors that led to the backyard and swimming pool area.

Mr. Hamilton and Missy stepped outside, followed by the crowd. ". . . three . . . two . . . one!" The crowd cheered in approval. Mr. Hamilton removed the blindfold from his daughter's eyes. Missy blinked and then saw what all the fuss was about. Sitting out on the back lawn was a brand-new red Corvette convertible.

Missy forgot Eddie was even there. She rushed out with the crowd to admire her birthday present, opening the driver's side door and slipping inside the convertible, her hands caressing the steering wheel and luxurious leather seats and turning the radio on full blast.

Standing in the doorway, Eddie watched Missy as the college boys surrounded her, all gushing over her new car. Eddie looked down at the tiny present in his hands that he had wrapped in used birthday paper. He palmed the gift and inconspicuously slid it back into his pocket, then headed for the front door.

Late that night, Anna Ligon, weary from a long day at school and then serving at the party, entered her home and tossed her sweater on a chair. She was physically exhausted, but she couldn't repress a smile when she saw Roy Jackson asleep on the couch, his school books and notepaper spread out on the floor.

Maybe there's hope, after all, she thought.

Anna peeked into the boys' bedroom. Tyree was asleep, but Bill was still awake, reading a book in his bed.

He looked up at his mom. "How'd it go?"

"Oh, fine. Did you boys eat?"

"We had some chicken over at the Drive-In."

"Okay. Don't stay up reading too late. Good night, Bill."

"Yeah, 'night, Mom."

Anna moved to go to her room but turned back toward Bill. "Oh, guess who I saw this evening at the big party over at the Hamiltons'?"

Bill shrugged. "Could be anybody, I guess. Anybody white, that is."

Anna ignored Bill's caustic remark. "Eddie. I had a nice conversation with Eddie Sherlin."

"Eddie?" Bill raised his eyebrows, suddenly interested.

"Yes, Eddie. And he said to say hello to you."

"You talked to Eddie Sherlin at the Hamiltons' hoity-toity party?"

Anna smiled. "Yes, I did."

"Really? Where? Where did you see him?"

"I was doing dishes in the kitchen when he came in. We had a delightful conversation. We talked for quite a while, actually. He's still a kind, sweet boy. He said to wish you luck in the semifinals. I thought that was nice of him."

"Yeah, real nice," Bill said sarcastically.

"Bill! I don't appreciate your tone."

"Mom, I don't care about that high school stuff anymore. As far as I'm concerned, I'm outta here, already."

Anna sighed. "What are you talking about, Bill Ligon? You still have several months of high school remaining. And, yes, you've had some good scholarship offers, but if you don't finish well, those can disappear."

"Ain't nothing gonna disappear but me. A few months from now, I'll be at Princeton or Vanderbilt. I just don't understand why you want to lower yourself to be a servant at a party for a bunch of white folks. Haven't you heard that slavery ended a long time ago? Don't you know that half the crackers there are lookin' down at you, and the other half of them are sending nasty letters to Vanderbilt because they're mad that a colored kid can get in but their kids can't?"

Anna's eyes flashed with anger. "Don't you use that sort of language around me, young man. And what are you so angry about, Bill?"

"I'll tell you what bugs me. It bugs me that you are lowering yourself. Why are you working as a maid? You ain't no maid; you're a schoolteacher. I know we can always use some extra money, but we get by okay without you allowing them to turn you into slave labor."

"It has nothing to do with money, Bill. Certainly, we need the money, with you graduating this year and Tyree and Delores coming along right behind you. But my working the Hamilton party was not for the money. Naomi needed the help. Like I told you, it was a big party."

"Well, if Naomi needed help, she should have hired herself some other maids, not a respected teacher who has a good brain and plenty of skills."

"Now, you listen to me, William Ligon." Anna stepped into the room and stood over Bill's bed, her hands on her hips. "You may have the right to be angry about the way things are in this town. We know there is still a long way to go before the races achieve real equality. But deep down, everybody is the same—white or colored. It is how we treat one another that matters. So while you may have the right to be angry at the status quo, you do not have the right to hate anyone. And you will never have the right to be disrespectful or mean to me. Not in this house. And not toward my friends, such as Naomi. Do you hear me? Do you understand me, William?"

"Yes, ma'am." Bill, having been properly chastised, put down his book and shrank lower below the sheets. Anna twirled on her heel and left the room. Bill glanced over at Tyree, who had been pretending to be asleep.

Tyree opened his eyes and smiled. "I guess Mom told you, big brother."

"Aw, shut up and go back to sleep," Bill responded. Tyree chuckled and turned over.

Bill stewed in what he knew to be the truth of his mom's rebuke.

20

THE DAY OF THE SEMIFINALS, Gallatin was buzzing. Jesse and Al held court on WHIN, and they could barely contain their enthusiasm. "The division semifinals in high school basketball feature two—count 'em!—two Gallatin teams playing tonight in Springfield," Jesse exuded. "It is unheard of that two teams from the same town should be so prominent in the playoffs, but here we are!"

"Yes, indeed, Jesse," Al jumped in. "The Green Wave should have it relatively easy against Springfield, since they defeated them earlier in the season by nineteen points, but that might just inspire the Springfield boys to get some revenge. It is sure to be a great game!"

"That's right, Al. And Union could have their hands full with Westmoreland, as well, simply because they don't have any idea what to expect. The Devils haven't played against them in the regular season."

"Ha, you mean, Westmoreland *wouldn't* play them," Al said. "That's more like it. Nobody wants to play Union on their home court. A couple of those fellows in the front court at Union could probably start for most major colleges."

About that same time, in Gallatin High School, Eddie was taking a history test. He was completely unprepared, since he hadn't studied for the test and had read no more than a few assignments.

Most of Eddie's teachers made allowances for him, even if he didn't do the work in their classes.

Even on test day, the teacher administering the test was excessively gracious. As Eddie attempted to answer the multiple-choice questions, the teacher gazed over his shoulder. "Now, Eddie, you know that isn't right," the teacher whispered when he saw Eddie's answer.

Eddie moved his pencil to the next multiple-choice selection, stopping momentarily until he noticed the teacher shaking his head slightly. He skipped that answer and moved on to the final two of four choices. The teacher walked on, knowing that now Eddie had a fifty-fifty chance of getting the answer correct.

Over at Union, Bill and Roy were concentrating deeply, immersed in their math test. Roy looked confused about several answers, but to Bill, a National Merit Scholar, the test was a breeze. He easily worked down the page, finishing well ahead of Roy. Bill glanced over at Roy, who was still poring over the test paper. With nothing left to do, Bill leaned back and stretched, letting his mind roam to the semifinals game against Westmoreland.

On the radio, Al and Jesse were still bantering. "I have a question for you, Jesse."

"Okay, Al. Fire away."

"Gallatin and Union are both in the semifinals."

"That's right."

"So what if both Gallatin and Union win their games? You know Union has always wanted to play Gallatin. They've had a few informal scrimmages over the years, but they've never competed in a regulation game against each other. This could set up one of the biggest athletic contests in sports history in this part of the country."

The dividing lin

Eddie, age 11

Bill, age 11

courtesy Eddie Sherlin

Eddie, shooting hoops.

Ligon siblings. From left
Delores's friend, Delores,

Anna Ligon

Sherlin family

Betty Sherlin

Union High School team

Dist. 2ᵈ Runner-up

Bill, senior year

Eddie, senior year

Gallatin High School team

Dan Herron

John V. Malone

GALLATIN SENIOR HIGH SCHO
ALL TIME RECORDS
BOYS   GIRl

EDDIE SHERLIN 1970	1766	MOST POINTS CAREER	LEILA JONE
EDDIE SHERLIN 1970	923	MOST POINTS SEASON	LEILA JON
EDDIE SHERLIN 1970	55	MOST POINTS SINGLE GAME	LEILA JONE 1972-197
EDDIE SHERLIN 1970	31.48	BEST POINT AVERAGE SEASON	KIM GRIZ 197

Gallatin High School records

Gallatin High School

Union High School historical marker

Eddie

Bill

"Whew, oh, Nellie!" Jesse blurted. "This could be the biggest thing to hit Gallatin since the Underground Railroad!"

In the Gallatin High School administrative office, Principal Herron sat stiffly, staring across his desk at Terry Poster and his father, Reginald, a man in his midfifties, whom the principal knew to be involved in Ku Klux Klan meetings out near Lock Four Road on Old Hickory Lake. Rumor had it that the senior Poster had participated in several KKK cross burnings in attempts to intimidate the local Negro population. Slumped in his chair, Terry's father was making it clear through his body language that he felt greatly inconvenienced by the mandatory meeting with the principal.

Principal Herron, however, was determined to address the issues posed by Terry's repeated racial slurs and his harassment of Negroes, the most recent involving Jepthah Swank and Leah Rogan. The principal began kindly but firmly with Terry's father.

"Thank you for coming in today, Mr. Poster. I don't like pulling you away from your workplace, but I thought it was important for us to speak face-to-face."

Poster didn't say anything in regard to the principal's comments. His son, Terry, smirked as though implying that no matter what Herron said, it was going in one ear and out the other.

Ignoring the tone the Posters set, Principal Herron pushed on with his own comments. "Recently, I witnessed another incident in which your son, Terry, was harassing some Negro students here at Gallatin High School. We do not tolerate such conduct."

Principal Herron leaned forward. "Mr. Poster, this is your and Terry's second warning. If we have to address this issue again, Terry will be suspended from school for at least a week. If your son commits any additional infractions, he will be expelled from our school for good. Any questions?"

Reginald Poster stared back at Principal Herron without saying a word. Following his father's example, Terry maintained his snarly smirk, clearly indicating to the principal that this meeting was useless.

After a long few moments of holding the principal's gaze, Terry's father finally spoke. "That it?"

Principal Herron scowled. "Yes, that's it."

Poster glared at the principal, got up, and walked toward the door without uttering another word. Terry sneered, clearly proud of the way his dad had put the principal in his place.

"Oh, one more thing," Principal Herron said, just as Poster reached for the doorknob. The principal looked at Terry. "Thank you, Terry, you can go. My secretary will issue a hall pass for you to return to your class."

Terry didn't move. Instead, he looked to his dad for instructions. The older Poster nodded toward the door, and Terry made a hasty exit, though not before putting a hand on his dad's arm. "See ya later, Dad." Then turning so Herron could clearly see and hear him, Terry said, "I'll meet ya down by Lock Four later this evening." The boy flashed a devious grin and went out the door.

Principal Herron caught Terry's intent but ignored it. Instead, he turned to Terry's father. "Have you ever been in the military, Mr. Poster?"

"No," Poster snarled.

"I didn't think so." Herron paused momentarily, and looked directly at Poster. "I was a colonel. In the infantry. Sometimes orders came down from the top, and we may not have liked them. Might not have even agreed with them. But that didn't matter. We carried them out. Why? Because that's what the legal authorities governing our actions demanded."

Mr. Herron paused again and glared hard at Poster. "Frankly, Mr. Poster, I don't care what you think or what you like. You may have certain political opinions contrary to mine. I don't care. Who you like and who you don't? Not my concern. What you and your

194

racist friends do outside of this school is cowardly and abhorrently offensive to me, but your actions and those of your son are outside my jurisdiction once you are off this school property." Herron leaned farther forward.

"But here at Gallatin High, I am in charge. I am a man under authority, and I have been given my orders by my superiors, which I plan to carry out—without incident. Now, I would advise you to talk with your son, because if he so much as looks sideways at one of the colored students in our school, I am going to hold you personally responsible."

Poster said nothing but continued staring coldly at Herron. After a moment, Principal Herron turned his gaze toward some papers on his desk in front of him. Then he looked up at Poster. "Dismissed," he said firmly.

Poster's anger flared. He clenched his fists and stormed out of the office, slamming the door behind him.

Principal Herron watched through his office window, spotting Terry standing outside, an idiotic smile on his face. Terry's father grabbed him by the shoulder and led him out the hallway a few steps away, then stopped suddenly. He turned to Terry and slapped him viciously across his face. Poster marched out of the school and down the sidewalk, leaving his son rubbing his face. The imprint of his father's hand on Terry's skin turned red immediately, although it was difficult to tell because Terry's face was also red with embarrassment. He glared back toward Principal Herron's office, when he made eye contact with the principal. It was apparent he had witnessed the slap. "You'll get yours," Terry mouthed before turning and walking away.

About that same time, over at Union High School, stress of a different sort was mounting. Joe Malone looked through the window of a classroom door and saw the math teacher grading a paper at her desk. Sitting alone at a student desk in the middle of the class-room was Roy Jackson. A worried look flashed across Joe's face as he noticed Roy's despondent expression. Roy slumped further in his seat as he awaited his grade.

Bill sat reading a book on the stairs out in the hallway while Joe kept him apprised of what was happening in the classroom. Joe shook his head. This did not look good. If Roy didn't pass this test, then he would not play in that night's semifinals game against Westmoreland. The team needed Roy on the court.

Bill looked up at Joe. "What's goin' on?"

"Nuthin' at all," Joe said. "He's just sittin' there, lookin' mad. Wait. Wait a second." Joe pressed his face against the glass. "We got some action."

Bill bounded to his feet and joined Joe at the window. They spotted Roy walking toward the teacher's desk. The teacher seemed expressionless as she handed Roy his paper. He looked down at it, equally emotionless. He said something Bill and Joe couldn't make out and then turned and walked toward the door, the guys outside still unable to interpret his expression.

Roy opened the door, nearly bumping right into Bill and Joe. He looked up, slightly surprised, then broke into a broad smile. "I passed!"

Roy held up his paper so his friends could see it. A bright red D+ was scrawled at the top of the test paper. Joe exhaled in relief, and Bill shook his head. Roy hadn't passed by much, but he hadn't failed. Bill took that as a good sign.

Somewhere in the distance, the Union band was playing the James Brown hit "I Feel Good."

21

SPECTATORS POURED into the Springfield High School gymnasium as soon as the doors opened, each person excited to witness the 1970 District Twenty semifinals, as Gallatin faced off against Springfield and Union battled Westmoreland High. Cars and buses from all four schools crowded the parking lot as people hurried inside to grab the best seats. Union, whose fans sat together in a cluster on the far side of the bleachers, was the only Negro school.

WHIN was broadcasting the games, and Jesse and Al were seated at half-court behind a table, along with the scorekeepers. "Good evening, everyone," Jesse said, staying close to the microphone so he could be heard over the din. "Welcome to the Sumner County high school divisional semifinal basketball games. Tonight, you can hear both games right here on your hometown radio station, so don't touch that dial. I'm Jesse—"

"And I'm Al, and we have a couple of humdingers for you tonight, with Eddie Sherlin and the undefeated Gallatin Green Wave against the twice-beaten Springfield High School Yellow Jackets. But Springfield has home-court advantage, so who knows what might happen."

In the background, Eddie and his teammates were going through their pregame warm-up, doing layup drills with perfect precision on one side of the court, while the Springfield players, dressed in their bright black-and-gold warm-up outfits, tried to ignore the Green Wave and concentrate on their own routines. It wasn't working.

Al continued with his pregame commentary. "And then the night-cap pits Westmoreland High—with only one loss—against the mighty Devils of Union High School, also from Gallatin. It is really unusual having two teams from the same town in the semifinals, but here we are. What a night it is going to be!"

Since Union had never before played Gallatin, Coach Martin permitted Bill, Joe, Roy, and the other Union players to sit up in the stands during the first half of the Gallatin-Springfield matchup. Bill kept a close eye on Eddie as he went through his pregame routine and then practiced long set shots and jumpers.

Bill leaned in to Roy. "Whew, Eddie is like a machine on those long shots from outside the key."

"We can't worry about that," Roy said. "If we play them, we just have to protect the inside."

"Yeah, I guess you're right," Bill said as he glanced around the now-packed gymnasium. Bill recognized a number of the faces in the crowd. He rolled his eyes when he saw Mayor Knapp and the white mayors from the other towns posing for the obligatory pregame handshake photo. He also saw the Sherlin family seated together. Jim and Betty sat on the end of the bleachers, with Bo in his wheelchair on the floor, and Debbie and Delilah perched behind him. Bill located his mom and his sister, Delores, with Tyree sitting nearby with some friends in the Negro cluster, right behind the Union cheerleaders.

Missy and the Green Wave cheerleaders assembled on the sidelines in front of the Gallatin fans. Charles Hamilton Sr. and his wife munched on popcorn in the stands, along with several of their overdressed friends.

Across the court, Principal Herron stood rigidly in front of the door to the boys' locker room, paying careful attention to everything going on around him. His eyes scanned the crowd looking for potential troublemakers. Union's Principal Malone sat comfortably with his family on the third row of bleachers in the Negro section. Bill couldn't help but notice big, boisterous Buddy Bruce standing in the first row of Gallatin seats, facing the crowd and leading a rousing cheer for Eddie. The piercing sound of the gymnasium buzzer broke Bill out of his reverie.

The referee tossed up the opening jump ball at midcourt, and Alton Rourke, Gallatin's tall center, tipped it to Eddie, who ripped down court, stopped in front of one of the Yellow Jackets' defenders, and fired a long jump shot from about twenty-five feet away. *Swish!* Gallatin scored first.

The Green Wave defense did its job, forcing Springfield to take several unwise shots before turning over the ball without even scoring. Meanwhile, Eddie hit for three more quick buckets, and the Green Wave rolled onward.

Springfield's quick guards raced back and forth across the court, trying desperately to keep up with the powerful Gallatin offense, but once out in front, they were difficult to catch. At one point near the end of the first half, one of the Springfield forwards was dribbling the ball up court, just across the center line. Eddie swooped in for a steal, tapping the ball away from the forward and picking up the bounce, and then with almost supernatural spring in his legs, he took it all the way in for an unopposed easy two-pointer.

The crowd went wild. Even the Westmoreland and Union spectators grudgingly acknowledged Eddie's incredible athleticism.

"Absolutely amazing!" Al unabashedly cheered into the WHIN microphone, momentarily forgetting all sense of neutrality in his broadcasting. "Eddie Sherlin was flying through the air for that bucket!"

When the Springfield coach called a time-out to slow down the Gallatin offense, Missy and her Green Wave cheerleaders strutted onto middle court, evoking a strong response from the already fired-up Gallatin crowd.

Eddie and his teammates didn't need much encouraging. By half-time, the lighted scoreboards high on the walls at each end of the gym read: Gallatin 28, Springfield 17. The Yellow Jackets jogged off the court with their heads hanging low, while the Green Wave remained confident.

The second half produced more of the same, with the coaches yelling instructions, the fans cheering, and Eddie and the Green Wave putting on a show. Perspiration soaked their uniforms as the teams gathered on the sidelines during a time-out. The cheerleaders continued to work the crowd into a frenzy. It was high school basketball at its best.

The Yellow Jackets—continuously trailing behind Gallatin—grew desperate, taking more chances and fouling more frequently, as they lunged for the ball or fought for rebounds. At one point, the Springfield center purposely shoved Eddie. Eddie lost his footing and tumbled to the court, skidding several feet across the hardwood.

Bo, angry about the obvious infraction, shook his fists and strained in vain to get up out of his wheelchair. Buddy Bruce leaped to his feet and started down off the bleachers, ready to deck the guy who had shoved Eddie. It took four of Buddy's friends to restrain him from jumping over the people in the first few rows and racing onto the court.

In his peripheral vision, while still on the floor, Eddie noticed the commotion Buddy was causing in the bleachers. He quickly bounced to his feet and waved Buddy back, motioning for him to sit down.

Eddie sank the foul shot then backpedaled down the court.

Springfield scored, and Alton brought the ball out to Eddie, who passed to Tim and then cut behind the man defending him. Tim saw Eddie's move and fed him the ball on a high pass around midcourt. Eddie pulled down the ball and dribbled full tilt toward the top of the key. He faked to the left and cut back to the right, leaving the Springfield guard looking for him. Only one man stood between Eddie and the basket—the opposing center who had shoved him hard a minute or two earlier. Eddie went right at him, leaving his feet right in front of the center's face. The center's arms went up and he tried to block Eddie's shot—but he didn't stand a chance. Eddie rammed the ball right over the center's head, banking it off the backboard, his body sending the guy sprawling on the floor up against the mats covering the back wall of the gym. The fans' screams turned to cheers as the referee indicated that the bucket was good and called a foul on the Yellow Jackets' center.

With absolute cool, Eddie stepped to the foul line, bounced the ball twice, and then let it rest in his palm. He felt the shot leave his hand and watched closely as it made its way through the net. Any spunk Springfield had left went down the drain as the ball split the cords. A few minutes later, the buzzer mercifully sounded and all the members of the Green Wave surrounded Eddie, slapping him on his back and hugging him. The final scoreboard said it all: Gallatin 58, Springfield 29.

Meanwhile, downstairs in the locker room, Bill, Roy, and Joe, who were getting ready for game two of the double bill, heard the final buzzer. They could tell by the crowd noise that nothing had greatly altered the outcome of the game since they had gone to change clothes. As Bill laced up his shoes, nobody needed to tell him that Gallatin was in the finals. But right now his primary concern was winning the game against Westmoreland and advancing his team to the finals.

Westmoreland was tough, and because they were Union's strong rivals, everyone knew it was going to be a rough and tumble game.

Bill stood at center court waiting with the opposing center for the jump ball. He easily out-jumped the Westmoreland center, tipping the ball to Joe, who eased down the court, allowing the offense to set up and for Bill to get into position with his back to the basket.

Joe snapped a hard pass chest high to Bill, and without even looking in his direction, Bill fed Roy, who was streaking down the baseline for an easy layup. Westmoreland didn't even know what hit them.

The Union Devils quickly headed down court, playing a zone defense. Westmoreland attempted to drive the lane three plays in a row, but each time, Bill swatted the shots away. *If they're going to beat us*, Bill thought as the Westmoreland guard pulled down one of the blocked shots, *they won't do it down under.*

Bill was equally daunting on offense. Working at the top of the foul line, with his back to the basket, Bill took a pass from Roy. He faked a pass to Joe in the corner, but then without even looking at the basket, in one giant sweeping motion, Bill turned and let sail a mighty skyward hook shot. *Swish!* The ball never touched the rim.

The Union cheerleaders went crazy, jumping up and down while Tyree leaped with sheer joy. Union fans hopped to their feet at the sight of Bill's amazing shot. The Devils took control of the game and never let loose. By halftime, Union had a commanding 30 to 12 lead. Bill had scored as much as Westmoreland's entire team.

The second half began with more of the same. On the opening play, Bill got the jump on the tip-off and nudged the ball to Roy. Bill raced down court as Roy made a fancy behind-the-back pass to Bill as he flew by on Roy's left. Bill took it all the way in and banked the ball off the backboard and through the net. He threw his hand in the air indicating "number one" as he hustled back down court to set up the Union defense. Any indifference Bill had felt earlier about finishing his high school basketball career victoriously was definitely gone. He was in this thing to win!

The Devils kept up the pace. Roy and Joe hit from the outside, running the plays off Bill, who continued to pour in points underneath the basket, grabbing rebounds and putting them back up, tipping in missed shots, and maneuvering himself past the outstretched arms of several defensive players to lay the ball into the net. Bill's face looked as though someone had doused him with water, as perspiration dotted his forehead and trickled down his face and chest, soaking even the large number 35 on his jersey.

The fans screamed like maniacs as the Union Devils continued playing excellent basketball, looking almost as though they were a college team. At one point, Bill went up under the bucket, grabbed a rebound off an errant Westmoreland shot, and whipped the ball on a floor-length pass to Joe, who was all alone under the Union goal. Joe easily laid up the ball into the basket. Union's dominance was almost embarrassing. When the final buzzer sounded, Union had nearly doubled Westmoreland's points. The scoreboard read: Union 61, Westmoreland 37.

Bill and Roy slapped each other's backs, and other Union players were hugging; their sweat-drenched bodies were exhausted, but their spirits were exuberant. "We did it, Roy!" Bill shouted over the commotion of the crowd. "Union is in the finals!"

Principals Malone and Herron looked past the excited players and fans and exchanged knowing looks. In the heat of the moment and the uproar of the crowd in the gymnasium, it seemed that the significance of what had taken place had not yet dawned on most of the people in attendance. But both principals knew they would soon be facing a scenario unlike anything that had ever happened in Gallatin—or in Tennessee, for that matter. The danger and potential conflict loomed ominously behind every congratulatory word, hug, and slap on the back.

Along the sidelines, the Union team was all smiles as they walked off the court. Bill spotted a radio announcer interviewing Eddie Sherlin, who was now dressed in street clothes. Coach Vradenburg and the Gallatin team had returned to the bleachers to watch the Union-Westmoreland game, knowing they would be facing the winner of the matchup. So the guys from WHIN had quickly nabbed Eddie now that the teams that would be playing in the finals were set. A newspaper reporter was standing alongside Eddie, taking notes, and a photographer shot several photos of the impromptu interview. Neither the radio announcers nor the newspaper reporter made any effort to get Bill's or Roy's perspective as they moved toward the locker rooms. And no photographer took Bill's or Roy's picture for the newspaper.

Roy sidled up close to Bill. "They won't ignore us next week when we beat their white butts."

Bill hung his head and shook it. "It's just the way things are, Roy. But when we win next week, they will have to put our pictures in the paper. They might even get one of you scoring." He nudged Roy playfully.

Roy didn't smile. "I'm gonna give them plenty of reasons to shoot our pictures."

As he did in every interview, Eddie tried to acknowledge the source of his ability. "It is really God out there on the court," he told Al and Jesse. "I'm really nuthin'. It's him working in me. That's how it gets done."

The newspaper reporter stopped writing the moment Eddie mentioned God and waited patiently for the star player to say something important or relevant. He likely knew better than to turn in an article to his editors that contained a bunch of "God talk." If Eddie wanted to be a Christian, fine. But, clearly, the reporter wasn't going to let him use their paper as a tool for evangelism.

Eddie was still talking with the interviewers when he noticed a big guy out in the middle of the court, pushing on the chest of the center who had knocked him down during the game. "Excuse me, please," he said to the announcers and the reporter. "I've got to go." Then turning toward midcourt, he yelled, "Buddy! Come on. Let that guy alone. Let's go!"

Outside the gymnasium, kids from Gallatin and Union waited to get on their respective buses. They looked across the parking lot

toward one another, unspoken tension thickening the air. An awareness of the impending potential problems and the magnitude of
the district championship game were setting in. The game between
Gallatin and Union would be a showdown unlike any other ever
played—or any game ever played again in Tennessee.

22

THE AFTER-GAME PARTY was already under way by the time Bill
and Roy arrived at the small, crowded house filled with loud Motown
music and lots of Negro kids dancing. Bill and Roy were looking for
their girlfriends but the two star players could barely make it past
the front door. They fell into conversations with one person after
another about the lopsided victory against Westmoreland and the
upcoming championship game against Gallatin High. Eventually,
they extricated themselves from the questions about how they were
going to shut down Eddie Sherlin or stop that tall center who played
for Gallatin. The two stars picked their way through a crowd of
admirers in the kitchen and continued on toward the living room.

"Well, it's about time," Charlene said to Bill, as he and Roy finally
found their dates.

The living room furniture had been pushed aside to make room for
dancing. Roy and his date, Cecelia, hugged and moved to the middle
of the dance floor, their arms entwined around each other's body
and neither of them moving their feet much. Joe and his girlfriend,
Olivia, a cheerleader, wobbled back and forth in a slow dance, Joe's
hands moving up and down Olivia's back.

"And just where do you think you're headin'?" Olivia asked.

"Down court," Joe replied whimsically, as he moved his hands lower.

Olivia leaned backward, away from Joe, yet not breaking their dance hold. "Oh, yeah? You'd better pass before you foul out," she warned him. "You're not getting anywhere near this basket." She turned abruptly and slapped Joe's hands.

"Ow!" Joe squealed in mock pain. "Hey, careful there, woman. Don't go hittin' the hands. These hands are my career, honey."

"Then keep your career off my rear," Olivia said, clearly indicating she was not joking.

They reestablished their holds and danced slowly over to the side of the room, smiling at each other warmly. For as much grief as they gave each other, they enjoyed being together.

Meanwhile, Bill and Charlene had moved onto the dance floor and struck up a conversation as they danced slowly, but Bill seemed a million miles away.

"Did you hear about Nancy and Tommy?" Charlene asked as they danced.

"No, what about them?"

"They got engaged."

"Really? That so?"

"Uh-huh, and they're planning on getting married right after graduation."

Bill didn't like where this conversation was headed. "Oh," he said nonchalantly.

"Yeah, Tommy's gettin' a job at the shoe factory, and Nancy's going to work for her daddy. They figure in a year or so they can afford one of those real pretty trailers. Maybe start a family. Won't that be great?"

"Yeah, great."

"There's something nice about settling down early, kinda knowing where you are going and how you're going to get there. I know you've been talking about heading north to Michigan where you've spent the past few summers with your relatives. Maybe going to one of those northern colleges."

"Yeah, maybe," Bill said, looking across the room.

"But what am I supposed to do while you are away at some big faraway university? Sure, we could visit, but that isn't healthy for a relationship when two people are miles and miles away from each other. You know what I mean?"

Bill didn't answer.

"Bill?"

Still no answer.

Finally, Charlene took both of her hands and placed them on Bill's cheeks. "What are you thinkin' about, Bill?"

Almost startled, Bill recovered quickly. "Oh, I'm thinkin' about you, Charlene. What else would I be thinking of right now?"

The couple resumed dancing, and Bill looked across the room, catching the gaze of Martha, the girl who had flirted with him by his locker at school. Dressed in another low-cut, tight-fitting sweater and short skirt, Martha smiled and cocked her head slightly in an inviting manner. Bill did not discourage her, even though Charlene was snuggling her body close to his, her lips nearly touching Bill's ear.

"Bill, honey, did you see me waving at you during the game?" Charlene asked.

"Of course I did. I could hardly keep my eyes on the court with you sittin' up there in the stands lookin' so pretty."

"Really? Did you notice who I was sitting with?" Charlene asked.

"Ah, no, I did not." Bill smiled at Martha, who was seated across the room, her legs crossed in such a manner that allowed Bill to view most of her thigh.

Charlene sensed that Bill wasn't paying attention to their conversation, so she suddenly separated herself from his embrace and stepped back so she could see his eyes, only to catch him staring across the room.

Bill tried to cover by reaching for her and turning her on the dance floor, but he was too late.

Charlene whirled around and spotted Martha smiling openly at Bill. Charlene turned back to Bill. "You mean to tell me that you are eying up Martha while you are dancing with me?"

"No, of course not, baby," Bill replied. "She ain't looking at me. She's looking at Darius, over there on the couch."

Charlene looked at Darius, who wasn't even glancing in Martha's direction.

"I'll bet she is." Charlene started toward Martha, but Bill caught her arm. "Let go of me," Charlene fired back at him. "I have a score of my own to settle."

"Now, Charlene, take it easy," Bill said. "It's my fault too. But it ain't nuthin'. Martha and I are just having a little fun."

Charlene shook off Bill's grasp. "I'll deal with you in a minute, but right now I'm gonna have a word with your friend."

She stormed across the living room to where Martha was seductively sitting. When Martha saw Charlene marching toward her, she rose instinctively, ready to defend herself.

"Hey, you little tramp," Charlene lashed out at Martha.

"Who you callin' tramp?"

"You know who. The tramp who's been trying to get my man."

"Your *man*?" Martha repeated. "Who says he's your man? And who is going to stop me if I was trying to get him?"

"I'll be stoppin' ya, that's who!" Charlene pushed Martha's chest violently, and Martha stumbled backward. She regained her balance just in time to see Charlene coming at her again, attempting to pin her up against the wall. Martha ducked under Charlene's arms and ran to the door and out of the house.

Charlene nearly fell over from the thrust of her attempt to pin Martha, crashing into a table and spilling several half-full bottles of Coke that partygoers had placed on it for safekeeping while they danced.

"Come back here, you tramp!" Charlene yelled as she whirled around. But Martha was gone.

Charlene looked for Bill.

He was gone too.

Across town at the Hamiltons' home, the Gallatin victory party was also in full swing. A group of white teenagers were dancing to "Build Me Up Buttercup" by the Foundations, the music blaring from an expensive stereo in the family room. Eddie leaned against a wall, drinking a Sprite, and watched the kids dancing. Friends and schoolmates showered him with congratulations regarding the big win, and a few adult well-wishers peppered him with questions and wished him luck in the difficult game coming up.

Doug, a classmate of Eddie's, wobbled over. "Hey, here's the man of the hour," Doug said a little bit too loudly. "Great game, Eddie."

"Thanks, Doug. I appreciate that."

Doug swiveled in front of Eddie, looking furtively from side to side, checking to see if any adults were watching. Convinced that he was safe from prying eyes, Doug pulled a flask of whiskey out of his jacket. He grabbed Eddie's Sprite and was about to pour the whiskey into Eddie's drink. "I've gotcha something good right here, Eddie. Have a swig."

Whether Doug was slightly slurring his words on purpose or not, Eddie couldn't tell. In either case, Eddie didn't want what Doug was drinking. He pushed the flask away from his Sprite.

"No, thanks, Doug. You need to go easy on that stuff yourself."

"Oh, yeah, Eddie. You know me."

"Yeah, I do," Eddie said. "And you know my brother, Bo."

"Oh, yeah. Bo. Kinda forgot about him." Doug stashed his flask and quickly changed the subject. "You gonna whip them Devils next

Saturday? Those big black boys looked pretty mean out there tonight. Some of those guys must be twenty-two years old."

"It doesn't matter to me how old they are," Eddie said. "If we just play our game, we can take 'em."

One of Eddie's teammates, Henry Horton, a second-string guard, heard Doug talking about Union and jumped into the conversation. "If those coloreds think they can muscle us around the way they did Westmoreland, they'd better think again!"

Doug laughed and Eddie smiled. Eddie appreciated Henry's confidence, but he clearly had no idea how tough the Union basketball team was. Eddie wasn't interested in pursuing that line of thought, either, especially at the victory party, so he eased away from the conversation. Besides, he had spotted Missy across the room.

Missy, looking her Southern-belle best, had long since changed out of her cheerleading outfit and had put on an off-the-shoulder cocktail dress. She looked stunning. Missy ran over to Eddie and wrapped him in a big hug. Then she grabbed his hand and pulled him over to the dance area. "Come on, Eddie! This is my favorite song. Let's dance!"

Missy sang along with the record as she smiled at him and tried to coax him into dancing.

"Missy, you know I can't dance," Eddie protested as Missy shifted his arms to the right and then back to the left, in beat with the music.

"Sure you can, Eddie. Don't be silly. Everyone can dance. Especially nowadays. Come on. All you have to do is get out here and move with the music." She tugged at Eddie, to no avail.

"Oh, you are so boring," Missy said, pouting. She danced toward another boy standing near the wall and reached for his hand, tugging him onto the dance floor. Relieved, Eddie backed up to the wall again. Missy stuck out her tongue in Eddie's direction. He waved at her and took a big swig of his Sprite.

Just then, his sisters, Delilah and Debbie, stopped in front of him. "Good game, Eddie," Debbie said.

"Yes, it sure was!" Delilah piped up. "I was afraid you got hurt when that big guy from Springfield knocked you down. Are you okay?"

"Yes, thanks, sis. I'm fine," Eddie said. "Listen, you all had better get a ride home with someone else." He glanced over to where Missy was dancing, her eyes closed, her body swaying to the music. "I might be getting home late tonight."

"Okay, big brother," Delilah answered. "Can I have a drink?" She motioned toward Eddie's bottle of Sprite.

"Sure," Eddie said. "Not much left in there though." He handed her the bottle.

"Oh, that's okay," Delilah said. "Thanks!" She and Debbie took off with Eddie's Sprite, giggling as they went.

"Hey!" Eddie called after them. "That's my drink."

The girls turned and smiled coyly at their brother, but they didn't stop. Eddie watched as his sisters gathered a pack of freshman girls around them, several of whom he knew had a crush on him. Delilah held out the bottle for all the girls to see. He heard Delilah say, "And you, too, girls, can place your lips on the same bottle where Eddie Sherlin just had his!"

Peggy Sue Herron, daughter of Principal Herron, reached dreamy-eyed for the bottle, but Delilah pulled it back, placing it close to her heart. Peggy Sue stuffed her hand inside her purse, pulled out a dollar, and handed it to Delilah. She snatched the bottle from Delilah's hands, and placed her lips on the rim.

"Oohhh," the freshman girls squealed and cooed as though they were going to faint.

"Oh, Delilah, Debbie," Eddie said from across the room but not loudly enough that they could hear. "What am I gonna do with you girls?"

Just then, Missy bounced back in front of Eddie, her face flushed from dancing. "Are you sure you don't want to dance?" She flashed him a big smile.

"I'm sure," Eddie said, returning her smile.

Missy grabbed both of Eddie's hands. "Okay, if you don't want to dance, come with me. I want to show you something." She tugged him toward the front door.

"Where are we going? Why can't you show me right here?"

"You'll see," Missy replied playfully. "Just hurry before anyone notices that we're gone."

Eddie dutifully followed Missy out the front door and down the porch steps.

"This way." Missy motioned toward the barn. "My car is over here. I know you saw it at my birthday party, but you haven't had a chance to hear the stereo system in it. The sound is amazing!" Missy took Eddie's hand and practically dragged him to her bright red Corvette, which was parked off to the side of the house, along with all the guests' cars. The convertible top was up. Eddie started for the passenger side, but Missy motioned Eddie to get in on the driver's side.

"Start the motor," she said, handing Eddie the car keys. "And turn up the heat. It's cold out here tonight, and I don't want you to get sick." Eddie crawled into the driver's side and Missy slipped into the passenger seat. She reached over and turned on the radio. "Listen to this," she said, the music enveloping them as she leaned back in the seat and rested her head on Eddie's shoulder. Missy closed her eyes and sighed.

Eddie put his arm around Missy, his hand on her bare shoulder, and held her closely as they listened to the music. For several minutes, he simply stared at Missy, admiring her beauty. She looked so pretty in her party dress. Then nervously working to overcome his shyness, Eddie leaned over and kissed her softly. Missy sighed again. Eddie squeezed her tightly and their lips met again, but this time, it was Missy kissing Eddie. They kissed and kissed, so much that the car windows steamed up as though they were covered by a gray fog. Their hearts beat faster as the couple's kisses grew increasingly more passionate, the music filling the car and covering the sounds of their heavy breathing.

Still holding Missy's shoulder, Eddie was uncertain where to safely place his hands. Missy solved that problem for him. As they continued to kiss, she reached up and placed her hand over Eddie's, then slowly slid both of their hands down her bare shoulder to her breast.

For a long moment, Eddie held his hand awkwardly on Missy, right where she had placed it. Then suddenly he recoiled, jerking his hand away as though he had touched a hot stove.

"What's wrong, Eddie?" Missy asked.

"Ah, er, nothing," he replied. He put his arm around Missy again, and they kissed some more. The couple continued making out, with Eddie being careful not to touch Missy inappropriately.

With the intensity of their embraces increasing, Missy placed her hand on Eddie's knee. He flinched but didn't move. But when Missy moved her hand to Eddie's thigh, it was more than he could take. "Whoa, whoa, whoa!" Eddie whispered huskily.

"What?" Missy said, the surprise obvious in her voice. "What's the matter?"

"Just stop right there," he said. "We can't be doing this sort of thing."

"What do you mean we can't? We've been going out together off and on for nearly a year now."

"I know," Eddie said, "but it just ain't right."

"Eddie, we are eighteen years old. We'll be graduating from high school in a few months. Surely, we're ready to move forward in our relationship."

"Well, no, not really," Eddie said.

"What do you mean?"

"We aren't married yet, Missy. And there are some lines we shouldn't cross till we're married."

"Who says?"

"God does," he said bluntly. "I read in the Bible where it says plain as day, don't be having sex outside of marriage. It says fornicators and adulterers God is gonna judge. Don't get me wrong. It ain't cause I don't want to or nuthin' like that. But I don't want to sin against you, and I sure don't want to sin against myself, and most of all, I can't do this thing against God."

"But Eddie," Missy said with feigned modesty. "We're just kissing!"

"No, we're not. And you and I both know it."

Missy sat up straight in the car seat. "All right, Eddie. You don't know what you're missin'."

"Yeah, I do. I mean, no I don't," Eddie stammered. "But I've been around. I know what sex is and what it is supposed to mean. And we ain't there yet, Missy."

Eddie was telling Missy the truth. Because he felt so insecure with the girls at Gallatin High, he had sometimes dated girls from as far away as Portland, north of Gallatin, near the Kentucky border. He'd even once had a relationship with a sweet farm girl who taught Eddie more about the birds and the bees than any health teacher. Although Eddie hadn't always lived the way the Bible instructed, he had recently renewed his Christian commitment and was trying to be as disciplined about his sexual desires as he was about his athletic commitments.

Missy shook her head. She probably couldn't believe that any guy would turn her down, much less the guy with whom she hoped to have a future.

"Okay, Eddie," she said. "You don't have to go all religious on me. If you don't want to have sex, we won't."

Missy tugged on the front of her strapless dress, revealing more cleavage than Eddie was prepared to see. He quickly turned his head and looked out the window as she adjusted her dress. She took out some lipstick from a compact in the car and looked in the rearview mirror as she reapplied the red color to her lips. Then she turned and looked at Eddie.

"But a proper young woman does need certain assurances of love and affection," she said.

"Like what?"

"Oh, Eddie, do I have to instruct you in *all* the lessons of Southern etiquette?"

"Sorry. I guess I'm not like one of your brother's friends."

"Leave my brother and his friends out of this. We're talking about you and me. How do I know you are serious about me . . . about *us*?"

"Oh!" Eddie suddenly caught on to what Missy was intimating. He reached into his pocket and took out the present he had prepared for Missy's birthday but had not given to her. He had hoped there would be another opportunity. Apparently, this was it.

"Do you mean this kind of assurance of love and affection?"

In the dim light of the car, Missy couldn't tell what Eddie was holding, and Eddie was glad she couldn't see the now crumpled, used wrapping paper that covered her gift. "What's that?" she asked.

"Open it and see."

Missy smiled and quickly ripped off the inexpensive wrapping paper, revealing a velvet box. She slowly opened the lid. When she saw the contents, her eyes lit up. "Oh, Eddie!" she gushed. Missy held up the gold necklace with Eddie's class ring attached.

"The chain is real gold," Eddie said proudly. "Twenty-four-carat gold."

Missy held the necklace clasps out to Eddie. "Help me put it on." Missy turned away from Eddie, and he fastened the clasp behind her neck. The ring fell at heart level, resting perfectly between her breasts.

"Do you like it?" Eddie ventured.

"Like it?" She looked at him playfully. "No, I don't like it. I *love* it!" Missy squealed as she crawled over the gear shift, into Eddie's lap and began kissing him passionately again. The windows quickly steamed, but before they could get carried away, they were startled by a sudden rap on the driver's side window. Missy quickly flopped back into the passenger's seat and adjusted her dress again.

Eddie wiped off some of the steam from the window and peered out into the darkness. There stood Henry, the second-string guard.

"Henry!" Eddie yelled. "What in the world are you doing out here?"

"Sorry, Eddie. But I thought you'd want to know. A bunch of guys from Springfield just pulled into town. Sounds like the whole Yellow Jackets team is out there looking for Buddy Bruce, wantin' to tan his hide for pushing their center after the game tonight. From what I understand, Buddy told them that he'd take on the whole crew of 'em down by the lake. So that's where a lot of the guys are headin' right now. Like I said, I thought you'd want to know—you and Buddy being best friends and all."

"Oh, man!" Eddie slapped the heel of his hand against his forehead. "Yeah, okay. Thanks, Henry."

Someone yelled out, "Henry, you ridin' with us? Let's go!"

"Gotta go, Eddie," Henry said, and he took off for the car already backing up in the Hamiltons' long driveway.

Missy put her hand to her mouth. "Eddie!"

Eddie turned back from the window and put his arm around her, wrapping her tightly against him. "It will be all right."

"Buddy can take care of himself," she assured him.

"Yeah, I suppose you are right." Conflicted, Eddie embraced Missy, and the couple began kissing again. Then Eddie yanked away and said to himself as much as to Missy, "I gotta go."

"Eddie Sherlin, if you go out that door . . ." Missy seemed frustrated at what she wanted to say next, but she finally blurted it out. "If you go out that door, you just keep on walking."

Eddie looked back at her with disappointment in his eyes. "I gotta go. Buddy could be in real trouble. He's my best friend. I can't let him down now. Stay here at the house. I'll be back as soon as I can."

Eddie opened the door to the Corvette and stepped out into the cold night air. Missy, livid with anger, screamed after him. "Eddie, how dare you!"

"Go on inside. I'll be back when it's over."

"Don't bother," Missy retorted as she climbed out of the car. "It's over right now." She grabbed the car keys, slammed the door, and stormed toward the house.

Eddie, a little confused by Missy's lack of empathy for the situation, shook his head. He ran toward his car but saw Henry and several other players in another car. The driver revved the motor and honked the horn. "Come on, Eddie. Get in with us." Eddie left his car at Missy's, piled in with the other guys from Gallatin High, and they headed for the lake.

23

DOWN AT THE LAKE, the headlights from several cars illuminated the shoreline. More than a dozen tough-looking teenagers from Springfield stood around a smaller group of Gallatin teens. Everyone was itching for a fight, but nobody was ready to throw the first punch. That changed as soon as Buddy showed up.

The rugged Gallatin teenager pressed into the middle of the gathering, showing no trace of fear. "Someone looking for me?" he shouted.

Anthony, a big guy from Springfield, stepped forward, stopping right in front of Buddy. "Yeah, I'm looking for you. You need to learn some manners, and we're here to help you."

"You and whose army, big mouth?" Buddy asked.

"You think you're pretty tough, huh, big man?" Anthony waved a finger in front of Buddy's nose.

"Get your finger outta my face before I break it off," Buddy snarled.

"Ha, you're the big man in Gallatin, aren't ya?"

"That's right," Buddy said. "Until someone shows me that I'm not."

"Well, we got a big man too. Ronald, come up here," Anthony called over his shoulder.

From out of the darkness behind the cars from Springfield stepped a mean-looking giant of a kid who appeared as though he could play starting tackle for the Green Bay Packers.

"This here's Ronald," he said. "And Ronald doesn't like it when someone from Gallatin goes pushin' on one of our star players. Ronald thinks you ought to apologize. Ain't that right, Ronald?"

Ronald grunted.

Buddy gave Ronald a once-over. No question about it. Ronald was huge. But that didn't deter Buddy for a moment. "You know, you're right. I really should apologize. I was wrong to push your man. I should have knocked his teeth out right there on center court."

Buddy shoved Anthony even harder than he had pushed the center. Anthony stumbled backward but didn't fall. He stepped forward toward Buddy. "You just made a big mistake, boy."

"Boy?" Buddy said. "Do I look colored to you?" He clenched his fists and stepped closer as Ronald moved between them, squaring off with Buddy. They were about to throw punches when they heard a car roar into the lot, screeching to a halt.

Eddie, Henry, and several other Gallatin players poured out of the car. Eddie immediately recognized what was about to happen, so he ran right into the middle of the group of kids. "Hold on, guys!" he yelled. "Cool it for a second."

"Get outta here, Sherlin," one of the Springfield guys said. "This ain't about you."

"Sure, it is," Eddie said. "It's my team too. Come on, guys. Calm down. Let's talk this through. We had a good game. Somebody had to win, and somebody had to lose. That's all there is to it. Buddy just lost his cool after the game. He was trying to protect his friend—me. He meant no harm. And he's sorry now, aren't ya, Buddy?" Eddie looked at Buddy. "Go ahead, Buddy. It's okay. I wasn't hurt. Tell them. It's all just a big mistake and we're sorry. Let's get out of here and go back to the party."

Buddy raised his eyebrows and looked at Eddie like he was crazy. He wasn't accustomed to backing down, especially to a bunch like the gang from Springfield. Buddy had no doubt he could take down Ronald the Giant. But he caught Eddie's look. He breathed out a long gust of air and walked over to Ronald. Buddy extended his hand to shake. Ronald eyed him suspiciously for a few seconds and then took Buddy's hand. The moment Buddy had Ronald in his grasp, Buddy kicked him between the legs as hard as he could.

The giant buckled with a mighty wail and toppled to the ground in pain.

"Buddy!" Eddie shouted. "Are you out of your mind? What are you doing?"

Seeing their hero on the ground, the Springfield guys leaped onto Buddy, one tackling him low, another hitting him around the shoulders, and a third guy wrapping his arms around his head. The Gallatin guys sprang to the rescue, punching and dragging the Springfield boys off Buddy as fast as they could. Once Buddy's arms were free, he went on the offensive, punching madly at anyone who dared get near him.

At one point, Eddie tried to pull several Springfield guys off Buddy. The aggressors let go of Buddy and began clobbering Eddie. Buddy then grabbed one guy by the neck and the other by the waist, pulling them both off Eddie and throwing them down onto the hard ground.

Fists flew in every direction as the Springfield and Gallatin boys fought viciously in the dark. The imbroglio continued until nearly every boy had been slugged several times, with Buddy and Ronald doing the most fighting. The battle finally subsided when one of the Springfield boys got knocked down, hit his head, and didn't get back up. He eventually regained consciousness, but the blow was enough to scare the combatants into calling a truce. Nobody claimed victory, but neither side accepted defeat either.

With the fight finally over, the boys piled back into their cars and slowly pulled away from the lakeshore, all except Ronald and Anthony and Eddie and Buddy. Eddie sat on the edge of the lake, nursing a cut above his eye. "Looks like the bleeding has stopped," Buddy said. He took off his T-shirt, soaked it in the lake water, and handed it to Eddie to wipe the blood off his face. Buddy, now bare-chested, sat down on the ground next to Eddie.

"Aren't you freezing?" Eddie asked.

"Nah, can't feel a thing," Buddy said with a laugh. "How are you doing? Your hands and arms okay? How 'bout your legs?"

"Yeah, I'm all right," Eddie said.

Anthony helped Ronald to their car and then looked back at Eddie. "Hey, Sherlin."

"Yeah?" Eddie turned to see who was calling his name.

Anthony waved to him and yelled, "Good luck on Saturday night. As much as we hate you guys, we hate them more. We'll be rootin' for you."

Eddie didn't answer, but Buddy waved. "So long, boys," he called, as though he and the Springfield boys were now best friends.

Ronald and Anthony pulled away, and it was just Eddie and Buddy sitting on the edge of the lake, staring out over the water, the stars shining brightly in the cold evening sky. "Buddy," Eddie said quietly.

"Yeah, star?"

"Buddy, I really appreciate you stickin' up for me—"

"Hey, no problem. That's what friends do, right?"

Eddie nodded. "But if you ever do something like that again, I'm gonna have to beat your butt myself."

"Ha!" Buddy laughed out loud, nudging Eddie so hard in the shoulder he nearly knocked him off balance. "I'm really scared now. But seriously, Eddie, if one of those colored Union Devils lays a hand on you, I ain't gonna wait till after the game to pay my respects."

"Buddy!" Eddie couldn't contain his exasperation.

"Eddie, somebody's gotta watch your back on Saturday night. This ain't no ordinary game."

"It's just a basketball game, Buddy. Just another ordinary basketball game."

"Just another game? Are you outta your mind? Don't be kiddin' yourself, Eddie. It's Union and Gallatin. There's a reason why we've never played them. This town likes to pretend we got no racial problems, that all the trouble is down the way of Memphis or in

Birmingham. But you know there were lynchings right out here by the lake not too many years ago."

"Lynchings?"

"Yep. The KKK strung up a couple of those darkies just for the fun of it." Buddy rubbed his forehead. "Eddie, that stuff is downright evil."

"So what's that got to do with our basketball game?"

"Don't you see, Eddie? Everyone wants to pretend we all get along fine. That the darkies stay in their place and the whites don't mind and everything is okay. But below the surface, it is like a volcano ready to erupt. Fact is that people are scared. They're scared our whole town is gonna burn down like the tobacco barn did a while back. Do you remember how we were all scared to go out of the house a couple years ago when that King guy got shot? How the darkies were riotin' and burnin' whatever they could? And now, the black school is playin' the white school . . . for the very first time . . . for the title. There's bound to be a riot if you guys win, and people might die if you guys lose."

Eddie rubbed his sore chin and let out a low whistle. "I hadn't thought about it like that. To me, it's just basketball. The sport is the common denominator that brings us all together. Colored or white, it doesn't matter. It's just a game."

"It's not just a game, Eddie. Keep that in mind."

Eddie started to answer, but the flashing red and blue lights of a police car pulling in behind them interrupted him. The beam of a flashlight hit Eddie in the eyes. "Hey, guys," a voice called out from the car. "Time to get home."

"Get that light out of our eyes, and we'll get going," Buddy yelled at the cop.

The policeman got out of the patrol car and walked down to where Eddie and Buddy were sitting. He had a gun in the holster on his right thigh and a billy club hanging from a clip on his left thigh. He was clearly concerned about trouble, but it didn't dawn on Eddie that it might have anything to do with the basketball championship.

"I should have known it was you, Buddy," the police officer said. The officer, Brad Connelly, was only a few years older than Buddy, and it was obvious that they shared some history together. He pointed to the cut above Eddie's eye. "Eddie, someone giving you trouble? Buddy slug you? Some of those darkies hanging around the lake?"

"No, no, I'm fine," Eddie said. "We just had a little encounter with a few guys from Springfield."

"You should have called me," Officer Connelly said.

"What for? We handled it just fine," Buddy said.

"Because it's my job, Buddy."

"Yeah, sure," Buddy said. "Take your squad car and go arrest someone, Brad."

"Watch it, Buddy, or I'll be arresting you next."

"Get out of here, Brad. I beat you up when I was ten and you were fifteen, and I can still beat you, even though you're now the big lawman in town."

"All right, you guys," Eddie said. "Thanks, Officer Connelly. Buddy's had a rough night." He smiled and nodded toward the bruises on Buddy's face. "We were just leaving." Eddie started toward Buddy's car. "Can you give me a ride home, Buddy?"

"Sure thing, boss."

"Oh, man!" Eddie said.

"What's the matter?" Buddy asked.

"Something wrong?" Officer Connelly echoed.

"No. I just forgot about my car. Can you drop me off at Missy's house? I know it's late, and I don't want to wake them up, but my car is still parked there."

"Better you than me," Officer Connelly said, nodding toward Buddy. "If I pull into the Hamiltons' in a patrol car, they'll be calling out the National Guard."

"No problem," Buddy said. "Let's go. Thanks for protecting us, Brad."

"Buddy, there may come a time when you're glad I'm around," he replied. "Especially with all this trouble brewing with the darkies all over the country. Gallatin isn't immune, ya know. This basketball game may be the spark that lights everything on fire. Keep your heads up and your eyes open."

Buddy and Eddie drove in relative silence most of the way to Missy's house. They were both mulling over the events of the evening as well as their conversations. Buddy slowly drove up the long red-gravel lane leading to the house, trying not to alert the family dogs by making too much noise. Eddie's car was the lone vehicle parked outside the house, under a light post.

A pang of regret hit Eddie as he remembered how pretty Missy had looked earlier in the evening. "Thanks for the lift, Buddy," he said. "Catch ya tomorrow sometime."

"You betcha, Eddie. Get some rest. It's going to be a big week."

Eddie got out of Buddy's car and walked over to his own. He looked up toward Missy's bedroom window before getting behind the wheel. Her bedroom was dark, as was the rest of the house.

When Eddie opened the car door, the inside dome light came on, and he spied something shining on the ground. Eddie knelt down to look more closely, and when he saw the source of the reflection of light, he nearly burst into tears.

On the ground lay his class ring and the new gold chain he had given to Missy earlier that evening. It looked as though it had been stomped into the mud. Eddie lifted the ring and chain out of the mud, wiped it off on his shirt, and dropped it into his pocket. *I guess I've blown it*, he thought. *Sometimes doing the right thing doesn't feel so right.*

24

PRINCIPAL HERRON STIRRED IN HIS SLEEP, awakening as he turned over on the bed. He blinked open his eyes and noticed that his wife, Susan, was moving around uncomfortably as well. "Susan?"

"Hmmm?" Susan turned over on her side, her hand searching for her husband.

Principal Herron gazed at his wife in the semidarkness. A classic Southern belle, Susan looked beautiful in her peach-colored, high-necked silk nightgown. "Susan?" he whispered. "Are you awake?"

"Nuh-huhh," she mumbled.

"Did you hear something outside?"

"Outside? Hear something?" she asked. "No, Dan, I didn't."

"I'm going to look around." Principal Herron crept out of bed and threw on a robe over his pajamas and slipped his feet into the brown leather slippers he kept by the bed.

"Oh, no, Dan. Come back to bed." Susan patted the still warm mattress where her husband had been lying.

"I'll just be a minute."

She rolled over and closed her eyes. "Okay. Try not to wake me when you come back upstairs, please."

"I won't," he said. "And I'll ask the intruder to be quiet as well." Principal Herron stepped gingerly out of the bedroom and down the hallway toward the room of their daughter, Peggy Sue. He slowly opened the door and peeked inside. Peggy Sue was asleep, looking as innocent and peaceful as ever, lying in her white nightie, one arm draped around a teddy bear. Peggy Sue, an enthusiastic, almost starry-eyed Eddie Sherlin fan, had taped on the wall above her bed a picture of Eddie that she had cut from the sports page of the newspaper. Principal Herron smiled when he saw the clipping, but he scratched his head when he noticed her holding a bright green Sprite bottle close to her lips as she slept. The strict, former infantry colonel would not have been pleased had he known Peggy Sue had bought the bottle from one of Eddie's sisters.

But while Principal Herron was trying to figure out the significance of the Sprite bottle, a flickering light outside Peggy Sue's bedroom window snagged his attention. He heard the sound of male voices and feet running across the lawn and driveway. He closed Peggy Sue's door and continued down the hall and on downstairs. Without thinking of his own safety, he hurried to the front door, threw it open, and stepped out onto the front porch.

Even with all his experience in the racially charged community, the sight that met his eyes stunned him. Standing in the center of the Herrons' front lawn was a large flaming cross.

Dan quickly assessed the situation, determining that the flames from the cross were not a threat to the porch or to the trees or shrubbery in his front yard. As his eyes adjusted to the flickering light from the fire, he spotted several figures in white hoods and white sheet-like outfits running toward a parked car in the distance.

One of the figures turned and looked at Dan on the front porch. "This better be a lesson to you!" the figure bellowed.

"We're comin' for you next," another sheet-covered person yelled.

One of the figures took off his hood and dove into the driver's seat. Principal Herron couldn't make out the person's face, but he

230

looked a lot like Terry Poster. The engine roared, and the car sped away into the night.

By then Susan had roused and run downstairs. When she saw the burning cross in their front yard, she nearly fainted. "Oh, God, help us! Who did this, Dan?"

She didn't wait for an answer. "I'm going to call the police right now. Or the fire department. Or both!"

"No, Susan," Dan said firmly. "Calm down. We're okay."

By now a large group of neighbors—many of them dressed in only pajamas and slippers, others in robes, and some in overalls and T-shirts—had gathered out in front of the Herrons' home. Not wanting to get too close, most huddled at a distance—out near the street. "What's going on?" a neighbor asked aloud to anybody listening, even though he probably knew the answer to his question.

Some of the onlookers bore scared expressions. Others scowled in obvious outrage. Most displayed a mixture of both emotions. "My Lord!" a deeply troubled older gentleman declared. "What is happening to our town?"

Others were more fearful. "I can't believe this!"

"A man can't even fall asleep in his own bed anymore without this whites and coloreds stuff spillin' into his dreams."

Many of the women whispered among themselves, "Who did this?"

Then a man dressed in only pajama bottoms expressed the fear that was probably in most of the neighbors' minds. "If they will burn a cross on the Herrons' front yard, what's next? Who's next?" A hushed murmur of agreement swept through the group.

"But I thought those Ku Klux Klan people were good, godly Christians," a naive woman said to the man in pajama bottoms.

"What does it look like to you?" he responded. "Does this look like somethin' Jesus would do?"

The woman shook her head and put her hands to her cheeks, acknowledging the truth.

The neighbor turned away from her and called out to Dan Herron, who was still standing on the front porch. "Hey, Dan! It's Pete from next door. Y'all okay in there?"

Principal Herron, his eyes still fixed on the burning cross, had hardly noticed the gathering crowd of neighbors. Hearing his name and the question, he peered into the darkness and saw the group at the end of his yard.

"Yes, we're fine," he called back. "Just a little surprised, being awakened in the middle of the night and all. Yes, thank you. We're okay. This thing will burn down in a while."

"Anything we can do?" the man asked.

"No, thanks. It's okay. Go on home. We appreciate your concern."

Peggy Sue heard the commotion on the porch and came running downstairs. "Daddy, are you okay?" She ran to her father and wrapped herself around her father. "Mama, what's going on? Who did this? What does this mean?"

"It means we have some bigoted, racist cowards in our town, honey," he said. "That's all."

"I'm going to call the fire department," Susan said.

"No, let it go," Principal Herron told her.

"Call the sheriff, Mama!" Peggy Sue urged. "And the fire department. We have to put that thing out before it catches the house on fire!"

"No. No, let it go," he said. "There's no danger of that. Don't worry. Peggy Sue, you and your mama go back inside. I'll stay out here and keep an eye on things." He stared intently at the burning cross. "Don't worry. It will burn itself out."

But deep inside the principal knew that what the burning cross represented in Gallatin would not burn out on its own, that the wretched evil it represented would continue to smolder and reek long after the smell of the burning wood had subsided.

Gallatin pulsated with excitement all week long leading up to the district basketball championship game. Like many folks in small-town America, people in Gallatin and the surrounding area took their high school sports seriously. In 1970, Nashville did not have any major professional sports teams, and Southeastern Conference college teams such as the Tennessee Volunteers, the Alabama Crimson Tide, and the Georgia Bulldogs seemed like untouchable gods who deigned to let outsiders attend their games; therefore, local spectators got wrapped up in high school sports. Football, of course, was king, but when basketball was hot, it was a close second. And in the spring of 1970, basketball was *hot* in Gallatin!

"Good mornin', Gallatin!" Jesse hooted into the WHIN microphone. "What do we got today, Al?"

"Well, you don't even need me to tell you," Jesse's cohost teased. "Everyone in these parts is talking about only one thing—the big district tournament championship game coming up this weekend. And we've got good news and bad news. The good news is that Gallatin can't lose! We have two—count 'em, Jesse—two teams from Gallatin schools in the district finals, Gallatin High and Union High, so we have a lock on the division title, folks. Someone in Gallatin is gonna be taking home a big trophy on Saturday night. That's the good news."

"And what's the bad news, Al?" Jesse set up his partner.

"Well, the bad news is we're talking about Gallatin High School playing Union High School, and, folks, it ain't never happened before and ain't never gonna happen again because, as most of you know, the school district is closing down Union after this term. So this is the very first and the very last time these two teams will meet! And they aren't gonna meet in just a scrimmage game. Not even in a regular season game. No sirree, Bob. They're meetin' in the District Twenty tournament championship game."

Don Savage, the owner of the pawn shop, sat in his rocking chair behind the counter and smiled as he listened to Jesse and Al and thought about the chain he had helped Eddie pick out for his girl-friend. *I hope that gold chain with Eddie's ring hanging on it made her happy*, he mused.

Down at the whites-only barbershop, Bob White unlocked his door and turned on the red, white, and blue barber's pole outside the doorway to let people know he was open for business. He adjusted the volume on the radio so his customers could hear Jesse and Al, but not so loud that the radio hosts would impede customers' discussion of the game while in the shop. After all, arguing over high school sports was a barbershop tradition in Gallatin.

On the other side of the street, Roscoe Robinson, the owner of the Negro barbershop, did much the same thing. In almost every store in town, radios blared. All were tuned in to one topic—the big game.

Jesse pitched his partner a cue. "Yes, sir, Al. Gallatin and Union took care of their semifinal opponents in such convincing fashion it almost made folks feel sorry for Springfield and Westmoreland. Those are two mighty fine teams, but Gallatin and Union are simply a cut above."

"You are right, Jesse." Al picked up the banter. "And this Saturday night, these two teams are going to be evenly matched. The oddsmakers don't even know which way to call it. You've got five future college starters on the Union team, with Bill Ligon leading the way and captain Roy Jackson providing the fire. And then you have Gallatin with Eddie Sherlin, one of the leading scorers in the entire state. In fact, for most of this season, Eddie has been among the top scorers. In mid-February, our hometown boy took the lead, becoming the number one point producer, scoring more than 800 points—33.5 points per game—more than any other high school basketball player in all of Tennessee. I mean the boy can plumb shoot the eyes out of the basket!"

Over at the Dari Delite, Jim Scanlin smiled. He knew Eddie would be ready for this game. And Bo would be right there on the sidelines rooting him on. Jim sincerely hoped Eddie could win this one for Bo.

And down at the Drive-In, all the waitresses were decked out in the colors of Union High School.

Out on the tobacco farm, Mr. Bonner and Roy Jackson's grandfather both sat down to breakfast with the radio tuned in to basketball talk. Farther out of town up on the hill, Charles Hamilton Sr. sat down in the sunroom of his sprawling Southern mansion with the Nashville morning paper and turned not to the stock report but, rather, to the sports section.

Principal Herron walked outside onto his porch to retrieve the morning paper. He stopped short and glared at the blackened cross standing on his lawn. He made a mental note to call someone before leaving for work to have the eyesore hauled away.

At the Ligon home, Bill, Tyree, and Delores listened to the radio as they gulped down their breakfast before heading off to school. "Hear that, Bill?" Tyree asked. "It is anybody's basketball game."

"Hmm, that's profound," Bill replied whimsically.

Tyree nudged Bill playfully. "Well, it's better than them saying that Gallatin is gonna whip our butts!"

Bill smiled. "Oh, no, they wouldn't say that. They know better." He got up from the table, ready to take on the day.

At the Sherlin home, Bo and his parents listened intently to Jesse and Al's analysis of the upcoming game. Delilah and Debbie scanned the newspaper for new pictures of Eddie.

"You can't take those guys too seriously," Eddie said as he walked into the kitchen. "They're just drumming up conversation."

Al intoned, "We'll be open all day for 'Sports Beat Call-In,' so y'all give us a jingle and tell us who you think is gonna win the big game and why. We already got one caller on the line. Go ahead, caller."

"Gallatin's going to win," the caller said.

"Why do you think that?" Jesse asked.

"Because of Sherlin. He's got the touch. Eddie Sherlin is going to score thirty or more points all by himself. That's about half of what they need to win."

Eddie cocked his head and smiled. "Mmm, maybe they know more than I thought they did. See ya later, everyone. We're practicing late tonight."

By Wednesday, besides bubbling with the normal excitement over the basketball game, the entire town of Gallatin braced itself for potential racially motivated problems. Mayor Knapp called for a meeting with Principal Malone and Principal Herron, as well as the chairman of the city council. The mayor welcomed his guests into his office and sat down behind his desk, with his secretary, Elizabeth, poised to take notes.

"Thank you all for coming on such short notice," Mayor Knapp began. "I do appreciate it. I'm sure you are quite busy this week. First, congratulations to both schools and your fine athletic programs. Gallatin is proud of all of our boys—our two favorite sons." The mayor chuckled at his remark, but nobody else in the room did.

He cleared his throat. "Well, now, all right." The mayor rustled some papers on his desk but didn't even look at them. "Let's get down to it. We have a situation comin' up—the two schools playin' on Saturday. 'Course, when you have crosstown teams, it's natural to have a healthy rivalry. In our case we all agreed . . ." the mayor paused and looked up at Principal Malone. "Well, most of us agreed, that having the schools—a predominantly white school and a predominantly colored school—play each other might not be the best idea."

The mayor stood up and walked around the room as he continued to speak. "Over the years, we thought it was prudent to avoid any undue pressure and let things flow their natural course. Take our time,

236

you know, on all this integration talk. But now the government has mandated integration, so we no longer have a legal choice. We've tried the Freedom of Choice program, which allowed parents to choose to send their children to either school, and frankly, I thought it was doing fairly well. I thought we already were integrated in Gallatin. Why, we even have a colored woman on our city council."

Principal Malone rolled his eyes and shook his head slightly. He was about to remind the group that Freedom of Choice was not, in fact, working, but the mayor continued.

"We've been making steady progress on white and colored matters, and things have been relatively peaceful around these parts, except for a short time after the assassination in Memphis a couple of years ago. But we're back on track and doin' well." The mayor took a deep breath, sat back down in his chair, and folded his hands in front of his face.

"But now we have this game . . ."

Even through Mayor Knapp's fake smile, both principals and the chairman of the city council could tell the mayor was worried.

Mayor Knapp picked up a pencil and idly tapped a coffee cup on his desk. "So I ask you, gentlemen, what can we do to help make this an exciting and safe event—something the good city of Gallatin will be proud of for years to come? What are your thoughts?"

Nobody said a word. The mayor looked from person to person. Each face bore a glum expression. "Please," said the mayor. "Mr. Herron, if you will."

Principal Herron sat even more rigidly than usual, his back pressed against his chair. He answered in firm, terse statements. "Sir, in one word: discipline. We have instituted a strict code of conduct at Gallatin High. That includes all student activities on and off school grounds. I expect the basketball team, our teachers, and all of our students to adhere to that code. I have made that quite clear." Principal Herron relaxed his tone and shrugged his shoulders slightly. "While I can't promise 100 percent compliance, due to the unpredictable nature of particular individuals—some of whom are associated with unsavory organizations in our community and in various parts of Tennessee—any infractions will be dealt with harshly and in haste."

"I see." Mayor Knapp seemed taken aback by Principal Herron's brusque, militaristic approach. His face wrinkled with concern, and he tapped the coffee cup more vigorously. But he quickly reasserted his political sensibilities and the politician's smile popped back onto his face. "Well, then. Very good. Principal Malone?"

Principal Malone spoke much more softly but just as emphatically as Principal Herron. "As far as Union High is concerned, we will be meeting several times this week with our teachers and encouraging an open discussion with our students. Regarding the discipline of our team, I have every confidence that Coach Martin and his staff will bring out the best in our boys."

The mayor seemed to relax somewhat. "Well, that's fine. So—"

But Principal Malone was not done. "As far as the community is concerned, you are dealing with decades of anger, hostility, disappointment, and distrust. What kind of symbol this game is taking on beyond mere basketball, I cannot say." Principal Malone looked around to each person in the room and then directed his comment to Mayor Knapp. "Mr. Mayor, we've brushed these issues under the rug for a long, long time. Now, we're lifting up a corner of that rug. I'm not sure what we're going to find or what might pop out."

For nearly thirty seconds, the group sat silently as each person pondered Principal Malone's statements. Finally, the mayor put on a happy face and broke the silence. "Okay. Well, thank you both for your thoughts. We have ourselves a busy couple of days, don't we?"

The mayor stood and escorted his guests to the door, shaking hands with and thanking each person for attending the brief meeting. He smiled broadly. "I wish you all the best, and I look forward to an exciting exhibition of basketball over in Springfield on Saturday night. Good day."

The mayor closed the door behind them. His smile disappeared instantly as he turned to his secretary and said coldly, "Get me Chief of Police Braden on the telephone."

25

MAINTAINING ORDER IN SCHOOLS was always difficult during the early days of spring in Tennessee. Once the dreary winter subsided and the weather turned warmer, kids had a difficult time concentrating on schoolwork. Springtime could easily lull a person into thinking the joys of summer had arrived. But wise old Tennesseans knew that with the warmth also came the potential for quick-rising storms, as well as brief cold spells that could kill the budding growth and spawn destructive tornadoes, resulting in lives lost and the decimation of entire towns and areas of the countryside in a matter of seconds.

The same type of tumultuous atmosphere hovered over Gallatin during the week of the District Twenty basketball championship. Everyone sensed the excitement about what was happening, yet there was also the pervading awareness that something ominous, something awful could happen at any second, blowing the community apart.

At Gallatin High, Eddie was upbeat, as usual. Trying to walk to class was even more difficult, however, due to the constant compliments and encouragements flying his way as he weaved his way through the crowded hallways. "You guys really put it to Springfield last weekend, Eddie. Way to go."

Several students patted Eddie on the back as he walked by. "We're behind you all the way!"

Some of the students' encouragement came tinged with racial overtones, and other comments were outright racist. "You show 'em, Eddie. We can't let a bunch of darkies steal our trophy from us." Eddie nodded or waved slightly to all of the well-wishers, despite their motivations. He didn't stop to talk, though, as he made his way to his first-period class. But just as he arrived at the classroom, the door flew open and several students rushed out into the hall, nearly bumping into Eddie. He stepped aside to let them pass and then entered the classroom. He was surprised at what he saw. The class was in total disarray—students were talking, laughing, and goofing off. Most everyone was standing; few students were actually sitting at their desks. It was more of a party atmosphere than a senior class. Clearly, no teacher was in the classroom and no normal class was being conducted.

Eddie noticed Buddy flirting with a girl on the far side of the room. He walked over and, when it seemed polite to interrupt, asked, "What's going on? Where's the teacher?"

Buddy shrugged. "Not sure. She hasn't shown up yet!"

Eddie left the classroom and went farther down the hallway, looking inside the classrooms as he walked. In each room, the scene was much the same, with the students out of control, rabble-rousing, and having a blast. But no teachers were to be found.

Eddie moved down the hall toward the school's front office. When the office conference room door opened, the mystery was solved: Inside were all the teachers, the office staff, and others, all listening raptly as Principal Herron spoke to them, stone-faced.

Ben, another student, exited the office in Eddie's direction. "Hey, what's going on?" Eddie asked.

"Oh, they're talking about the big game," Ben said.

Eddie looked back toward the conference room. "Really? Why so worried?"

"They're all bummed out about a race riot possibly taking place at the game."

"You're kidding!"

"Nope. They want the state police to surround the Springfield gym on Saturday. They're convinced something bad could happen if they don't keep tight reins on the situation."

Eddie still didn't catch the student's drift. "What situation?"

Ben looked at Eddie quizzically. "Well, some bad stuff has occurred in several other areas of the country where coloreds and whites have played against one another, and you know we've had some cross burnings and things like that right around here. Someone even said there may be a group of people driving all the way from Pulaski to come to the game. And you know that can't be good."

"Why?"

"Eddie, Pulaski is where the KKK first got started. There are still a bunch of KKK members in the area, and they hate Negroes."

"Oh." Eddie nodded. He looked back curiously toward the conference room, where Principal Herron was still speaking in somber tones to the teachers and staff.

At Union High School, the scene was much the same. As Bill walked down the hall, he was surprised at the lack of order and discipline among the students. The hallways were crowded with kids fooling around, talking, laughing, and having a good time. But there were no teachers in the hallways; nor were they in the classrooms.

"Hey, Bill," a student called out. "You're gonna mop the floor with those white boys this Saturday."

Everywhere Bill went at school, students cheered him on and called out words of encouragement. "After this weekend, there will be only one team known in Gallatin. The Union Devils! You show 'em, Bill!"

243

Bill appreciated the enthusiastic support. He saw Charlene walking down the hall with several of her girlfriends, so he thought it might be a good opportunity to talk with her, but Charlene walked right past Bill, as though she hadn't even noticed him.

Bill shrugged. "What?" he called after her, but she didn't turn back to speak with him.

Bill walked down the hall toward the school office. He figured if something was up, his mom would know, since her classroom had a clear view of the office. Bill stopped outside the office door, where he saw Joe. Bill waved to Joe and was about to call out, but Joe put his finger to his lips. "Shhh!" Joe had cracked open the door to a room filled with teachers. His dad was addressing the faculty and staff about the tension surrounding Saturday's game, and Principal Malone's tone sounded deeply serious.

He noticed the door ajar, so as he continued to talk, he walked around the room and spoke from in front of the door. With a barely noticeable shift of position, he reached around and closed the door, nearly catching Joe's nose in it. Joe got the hint. He hurried out of the office and joined Bill in the hallway.

"What's going on?" Bill asked.

"Everyone is talking about the game on Saturday night."

"Isn't that a good thing?"

"Not really," Joe said. "They're talkin' as though by game time it is going to be somethin' like the Watts riots in LA, with people fightin' in the gymnasium. Do you remember how it was after Dr. King was shot, how they banned guns, ammunition, beer, and gasoline here in town?"

Bill nodded.

"Well, they're talking downtown like they might have to do something like that again. They don't want no more of those Molotov cocktails being tossed around."

"That's crazy!" Bill said. "It's a basketball game."

Joe shook his head. "I know that. And you know that. But those KKK-lovin' maniacs are mad that we're even going to be in the same gymnasium with all them white folks. Can you believe that—in 1970?"

Bill nodded pensively. "Yes, it's 1970, but here in the South it might as well be 1870."

The teams tried to prepare for the big matchup as though it were just another basketball game—an important one, but simply a game nonetheless. However, feelings of racial tension slipped in, even on the practice court. As Eddie and the other Green Wave players scrimmaged one late afternoon, Eddie took a shot and missed. A second-stringer rebounded the ball right in front of starter Joey Graves. The second-team guy whipped the ball outside to another sub, who took an easy shot for two points.

Alton Rourke, Gallatin's center, was furious. "Come on, Joey," he yelled. "You gotta box out the defenders under the boards. Keep 'em away from the basket. If you don't, those big gorillas from Union are gonna run all over you."

Alton turned to Eddie for support but found none. The expression on Eddie's face clearly revealed that Eddie was annoyed by Alton's gorilla remark. "What?" Alton railed.

Just then, Coach Vradenburg walked into the gym and blew his whistle.

"Okay, guys," he called. "That's it for today. Hit the foul lines, and as soon as you sink fifty, come on over. I want to talk with you."

When the boys all gathered around, Coach Vradenburg motioned for them to sit on the gym floor. The team sat in a semicircle around their coach, who stood, looking down at his players. "First, I want you to know right up front that I am proud of you. We have had a great year, and I congratulate you. You have handled your success with grace and humility. Character matters, and you boys have it." He paused and looked around the semicircle of players.

"This game isn't about Negroes and whites. We're simply playing another tournament game. A big one, for sure. A good team? Oh, yes. Absolutely. But we're going to play them like any other team. We're going to play tough. We're going to play hard. We're going to play fair. But we're gonna play to win!"

Coach Vradenburg stopped and made eye contact with each of his players. "Does everyone understand me?"

"Yes, sir," several of the boys responded.

"Okay, that's good. Any questions?"

"No, sir."

"All right. Hit the showers and dream tonight about that ball going through the net."

About the same time, Coach Martin called the Union team off the old court across town. The team gathered around their coach.

"We have a big test ahead of us on Saturday night," he began.

"Don't worry, Coach," Roy Jackson jumped in. "We're takin' those white boys down."

The coach raised his hand, indicating for Roy to pipe down. "I'm not worried about the white boys," Coach Martin said coolly. "I'm concerned about us—our team, our school." He paused and looked at his players, wondering if they really understood the significance of this game. "There's going to be a lot of talk between now and the game—not all of it good. You're gonna hear some things you don't want to hear, maybe things you've never heard before. People might call you names or make derogatory statements about your mother or your lineage. None of that matters."

The coach slowly moved his gaze to meet the eyes of each young man on his team. "What I expect from you . . . no, let me say it differently. What I *demand* from you is your best, on and off the court, and that you show sophistication and class."

The Union players listened intently, admiration and respect shining in their eyes.

Coach Martin continued. "Now, folks are talkin' about this game far and wide. A lot of eyes are going to be on you boys. Not only are you representing your school, you are representing a whole lot more—and I don't think I need to spell that out for you. How you handle yourselves will be noted, either positively or negatively. We didn't choose this road, but we are going to run down it, and we won't be backing off. We're going to play hard, and if we do what we do best, we're going to win this game. We're going to win the big one for Union! But let me tell you something, fellows. Win or lose, the way you conduct yourselves on and off the court is more important than the final score. Everybody got it?"

The players responded with positive enthusiasm.

"All right, let's call it a night. Get some rest."

Roy and Joe and Bill exchanged looks as they headed to the locker room. "Obviously, this game goes far beyond Gallatin," Joe said.

"You got that right," Roy replied. "Thank you, guys, for making me stick to my math." He looked at Bill. "I know I wasn't exactly a willing student. But I wouldn't have wanted to miss this for anything."

26

RADIO STATIONS AROUND GALLATIN were buzzing even more as the weekend approached. Everyone wanted to talk about the big game. People kept the radio on wherever they went just so they could hear the latest opinion or prognostication.

On Friday afternoon, Betty Sherlin went to the beauty parlor downtown. It wasn't Betty's custom to have her hair professionally styled, at least not more than once a year. Ordinarily, she did it herself or had one of her daughters trim her hair when necessary. But Sister Althea Jones from church had arranged for Betty to have her hair done before the big basketball game as a special present to her.

"Lots of people are going to be looking at you, Betty," Sister Althea said. "After all, you *are* Eddie Sherlin's mother."

Althea's remark made Betty feel as though she was really special.

"Why, who knows?" Althea gushed. "They might even take a picture of you and put it in the newspaper!"

Betty wasn't sure she liked all that attention, but with Althea's promptings, as well as her willingness to pay for the appointment as a way of expressing her appreciation for all she did at the church, she acquiesced and accepted the gift.

Now, as she walked into the beauty parlor, she wasn't certain she had made a good decision. The place was packed with women getting their hair done in large bouffant styles, as though they were planning to attend the Kentucky Derby. Betty checked in at the front counter and was ushered past a line of large hair dryer chairs occupied by well-dressed women. While Betty was fascinated by the hustle and bustle of the hair salon, decorated mostly in pink, she couldn't help but hear the incessant chatter of voices on the radio that was blaring above the drone of the hair dryers.

A caller was arguing with the radio host. "Gallatin has been just plain chicken all these years. They haven't wanted to play Union because they were too good for 'em. They know they're gonna get beat, and they don't want no colored team showin' them up."

The radio host quickly moved on to another caller, but the women in the beauty parlor picked up on the conversation. In polite conversation, the white women of Gallatin most often expressed a condescending but tacit acceptance of the black people in town, but here in the beauty parlor, the women lowered all façades of civility.

"I will not allow my child to go anywhere near that gymnasium on Saturday," said one woman who was having her hair trimmed. "There's bound to be trouble. Why, you just *know* there's going to be trouble!"

"That's right," another woman said, pulling her head out from under one of the dryers. "You saw what those coloreds did after the Martin Luther King killin', how they burned down that barn at the tobacco company."

"Burned it right down!" another woman exclaimed. "All the way to the ground. Destroyed a year's worth of crops too."

An older prissy woman added, "And the judge gave those boys a reduced sentence because they said they were sorry. Sent them off to military service instead of prison. Can you believe that? Well, pardon me, but does that teach a lesson? I don't think so!"

"And what if Gallatin wins and Union loses this basketball game?" asked a gray-haired woman. "Are the coloreds going to burn down the gymnasium too? Or maybe town hall? Who knows what those animals are likely to do?"

Betty Sherlin took her seat at one of the styling stations. She lowered her gaze to the floor, refusing to look at anyone. Troubled by the conversation she was hearing, she really didn't want to be there, and she didn't want anyone to notice her.

Sitting in Eddie's car in the Gallatin High School parking lot, Eddie and Buddy were tuned in to the radio talk show as well. They cracked up laughing at some of the comments and others almost made Eddie blush.

"Ain't no team, white or colored, goin' to beat Eddie Sherlin and the Green Wave," one caller said. "I don't care who they've got on their roster."

Buddy nudged Eddie's arm. "How 'bout that, brother? That boy knows what's happenin'."

Eddie, who was intently watching the front entrance of the school, smiled but didn't encourage Buddy.

The caller on the radio rambled on. "They could put Lew Alcindor of the Milwaukee Bucks and all the rest of those NBA coloreds on the court, and they still couldn't beat Gallatin!"

Buddy recognized that the caller's voice sounded a lot like one of their classmates. He looked at Eddie in surprise. "Was that *Dewey?*"

Eddie shrugged. "Afraid so. Sure sounded like him." He kept his eyes on the front entrance, searching.

"What an idiot!" Buddy said.

The radio announcer seemed to concur with Buddy's appraisal. "Well, on that point, I'd have to disagree with you, caller, but I appreciate your loyalty to your school. Next caller."

251

Buddy and Eddie laughed at the announcer's quick brush-off of Dewey.

"Hey, wait a minute," Buddy said, sitting up in his seat. "Look. There she is, right over there." Buddy pointed across the parking lot.

Eddie spotted Missy walking through the parked cars. "Great! Thanks, Buddy. Catch ya later." Eddie popped out of the car and headed in Missy's direction.

Buddy just shook his head. "Poor love-struck fool," he said to himself as he watched Eddie weave through the cars in his attempt to catch up to Missy.

"Hey, Missy!" Eddie called. "Hang on a second. I want to talk to you."

Missy stopped, turned, and glared. "Hello, Eddie," she said coldly. "Were you speaking to me?"

"Yeah, I sure was," Eddie said as he bounded up next to Missy. "Listen, I wanted to tell you. I mean, I'm sorry about the other night. I felt really bad that I left you there in the car. But Buddy was in some real trouble. You know he's been my best friend since junior high, and he's been like a brother to me. Sometimes he does stupid things, and he's got a bad temper, but inside he's a good boy. He just needs someone to watch after him sometimes."

Missy stood with her arms crossed over her chest, her head cocked slightly to the left, as though she were bored with Eddie's explanation.

"So the other night, when all those guys from Springfield were coming after him, I couldn't turn my back on my friend."

"But you could turn your back on me."

"No, no, no, that's not it at all. That's just the point. I didn't want to turn my back on you, but Buddy needed me."

"And I didn't?"

Eddie stumbled over his words. "No, I mean . . . you know what I mean, Missy. Anyhow, so I want to tell you that I'm sorry, and I'm asking you to forgive me." Eddie reached into his pocket and pulled

252

out his class ring and the new gold chain. "And I was hoping you would take this back." He held the ring and chain out to Missy.

Missy didn't move. She simply stared at the ring and chain and then back at Eddie, without saying a word.

A loud honk from a car horn broke the silence. Simultaneously, Missy and Eddie looked toward the street in front of the school, the direction from which the sound had come. There, in a shiny, new blue Mustang, was one of the college guys who had been flirting with Missy at her birthday party. He stepped out of the car, smiled, and waved at Missy. He blew the Mustang's horn again and motioned for Missy to join him.

Missy seemed flustered. She stared for a moment at the college boy and then looked back to Eddie. "Look, Eddie, I don't know what I was thinking all this time. Me playing second fiddle to a basketball? It just isn't proper. You're a nice guy, and you're all right to look at too. But you aren't any movie star, and you don't have a lot going for yourself other than sports. Oh, sure, you can get your picture in the newspapers for throwing a touchdown or tossing a ball through a hoop. Who knows? You might even make something of yourself someday." Missy paused, observing the hurt in Eddie's eyes, before looking away.

"But Saturday night when you left me sitting in the car all by myself, I finally realized something about you, Eddie Sherlin . . ." Missy hesitated and then looked Eddie in the eyes. "You and I are cut from different cloth. We have different values, goals, and ambitions. You and I, Eddie, are living in the same town but in different worlds. All you are ever gonna be is just a good country boy." She stopped for a second and then almost spat out her final words. "And that's just not good enough for me."

Missy shook her head, turned on her heel, and walked toward the Mustang, leaving Eddie standing there holding his ring and the gold chain.

"Missy!" he called after her, heartbroken.

But she did not answer. She didn't even turn around. She got into the Mustang, and the college man drove away with her.

Eddie stood for a long moment, looking down the road to where the Mustang had headed. Dejected and disappointed, he slowly took his ring off the chain, put it back on his finger, and stuffed the chain in his pocket. He continued staring down the road until he sensed Buddy standing next to him.

"Are you okay?" Buddy asked him in an unusual moment of tenderness between the two of them.

"Yeah, I guess so. I guess I have to be okay. Maybe she's right, Buddy. Maybe we do live in different worlds, with different values. But I can't compromise what I know is right."

Buddy looked at his friend. "She doesn't deserve you, Eddie," he said softly.

Eddie shrugged. "Thanks, Buddy."

The sentimental moment passed, and Buddy broke the magic. "Hey, do you want me to knock that college boy out?"

"Aw, shut up," Eddie said, walking away.

"What?" Buddy yelled. "What did I do?"

27

IT SEEMED EVERYONE IN GALLATIN knew exactly how the championship game should be played, what each team needed to do on offense, and how to stop the opposition. The players couldn't get away from it. Walking down the street, Bill and Tyree stopped when a car whipped to the curb in front of them and slammed on the brakes. "Hey, hold on there," a man in the car called out to them.

Tyree and Bill looked at the man. The brothers could hear the usual sports talk on the radio in the car.

"How you feeling about that game tomorrow night?" the driver asked Bill.

"Feelin' okay, sir."

"You beat those white boys good, ya hear me?" The man revved the engine, put the car back in gear, and drove off.

"Yes, sir!" Bill said, chuckling as he waved good-bye.

"Who was that guy?" Tyree asked.

"I have no idea. Just someone else livin' out their fantasies or frustrations through a basketball game, I guess."

Farther down the street, the boys were accosted by a group of older Negro men sitting outside the coloreds' barbershop. They too had the sports show on a portable radio that was sitting on a window ledge. "That's Ligon," one of the men said to the rest. "Hey, Bill. Get on in here. Come here, son."

"Sorry, guys. We gotta get home."

"Oh, just come in and set a spell, son," said one of the older men. "Just a couple of minutes. We want to talk to you."

"Yeah," another man said. "We got some things to say about this here game."

Bill looked at Tyree and shrugged. There was no escaping these old men without being rude, so the two teenagers followed the old codgers into the barbershop.

"Here, get on up in the chair, there, Bill," the barber Roscoe Robinson said. "I'll give you a quick trim while the boys have their say."

Bill looked to Tyree for help, but Tyree simply shrugged and sat down in a large stuffed chair. He was looking around at all the short haircuts on the men in the barbershop. Bill had more hair in his Afro than all the men combined had on top of their heads. "Yeah," Tyree said with a chuckle. "He needs a touch-up before the big game."

Bill shot his brother a dirty look as he took a seat in the large barber's chair.

Fortunately, Mr. Robinson was more interested in talking basketball than he was in cutting Bill's hair. "Now, here's whatcha gotta do," he said. "That Sherlin boy is the one you gotta watch out for. Put your fastest man on him all the time."

One of the older men agreed. "Joe Malone is a good defensive player. You keep him in Sherlin's face all night, and there ain't no way that white boy is gonna score no thirty points."

"No, that's plumb nonsense." Another old man jumped into the conversation, talking over the others. "Not Malone. You want someone who will rough him up a little. Someone who will play a physical game. Knock Sherlin off balance a little. Roy is your man."

Bill didn't say a word. He was more concerned about his hair, so he, glancing frequently into the large mirror, kept a close watch on Mr. Robinson's scissors.

"That ain't right!" another man said. "Roy's too slow. The white boy will dribble right around Jackson. You need someone strong, but someone quick too."

The elderly men went back and forth for several minutes, arguing among themselves about who ought to guard Eddie. Finally, Mr. Robinson put a lid on the discussion. "I don't care who you put on Sherlin. The important thing is that you win this game!"

"Dat's the truth right there," one of the older gentlemen crooned. "We gotta win this game. This one isn't just for you, son." He pinned Bill with a look. "It's for us too."

"And ain't we gonna strut down Main Street after Union wins!" one of the old men shouted. "Yes, sir, the Union band is gonna be playing in downtown Gallatin, and it won't even be Christmas season! I can't wait to see the looks on all those white faces when we come by with that big trophy." The entire room full of old men laughed and whooped it up. Tyree was laughing too.

Bill sighed. "Thanks for the haircut, Mr. Robinson. We'd better be goin' now. Mama's gonna be worried that we aren't home yet."

"My pleasure, son," Mr. Robinson replied. "You boys stop in any time, and we'll take care of ya."

Bill and Tyree said their good-byes and stepped out onto the sidewalk, closing the door to the barbershop behind them.

"Nice haircut," Tyree said as he doubled over laughing.

"Yeah, thanks. You were no help at all." Bill fluffed his hair with the hair pick he carried in his back pocket, hoping that Roscoe Robinson hadn't destroyed his Afro too badly.

———

Eddie couldn't escape the hubbub either. He was walking downtown by the city square on his way to Don Savage's pawn shop when a mailman fell into step with him. He walked with Eddie the length of the street, offering his advice along the way. "One more thing,

Eddie, and then I'll let you go. The big guy at Union. Not the center, that other boy. You watch out for him, because he swings his elbows around like a gorilla."

"Yes, sir," Eddie said. He had no idea which player the mailman was talking about, but it didn't matter.

Don had the radio behind the counter blaring so customers could keep up with the latest basketball talk when Eddie arrived at the pawn shop.

"Hey, Eddie, come on in," Don called out when he spotted him. "How's that necklace working for you?" He smiled and winked.

"Hi, Mr. Savage," Eddie said. "Actually, that's why I'm here. I guess I won't be needing the chain after all. We kinda broke up."

"Oh, I'm sorry to hear that, Eddie." Don paused barely a second or two. "Well, it's probably for the best anyhow right now, with the big game and all. You know I was thinkin' that you boys don't wanna try to outrun those colored boys. You might want to think about slowing things down a bit. You had great success in other games when you played ball control and slowed the pace of the game. You took your time to set up rather than shooting every time you got your hands on the ball. You know those coloreds, they're quick and they're shifty, so if I was you—"

"Thanks, Mr. Savage," Eddie said, placing the gold chain on the countertop. "I appreciate your advice."

Mr. Savage nodded and kindly returned the ten-dollar deposit Eddie had put down for the necklace.

"See ya later," Eddie said as he quickly left the store.

He fielded advice from several more well-wishers as he walked back down the street to his parked car. Everybody in Gallatin seemed to have a stake in the game, and everyone was more than willing to offer their advice. It was all too much for Eddie.

He slipped behind the wheel and drove the short distance home. He pulled into the driveway and was about to go into the house when the next door neighbor called out to him. "Hey, Eddie!"

Eddie waved to the neighbor. "Hi, Mr. Nelson."

Mr. Nelson jogged across the driveway. "Well, good luck tomorrow night."

"Thank you, sir."

"Ya know, I've been thinkin' about some stuff." Mr. Nelson scratched his head. "I got me an idea how you can stop that Ligon boy."

"Gotta go, Mr. Nelson! Nice to see you." Eddie then hustled into the house and exhaled a huge sigh of relief. He made his way to the kitchen and heard the radio. "That Union caller should just shut his mouth," someone said. "He don't know what he's talking about."

Eddie walked over and turned off the radio. He opened the refrigerator and poured himself a glass of cold milk. *Finally*, he thought, *I can relax a minute or two without the constant blabber about the basketball game.* He took a big swig of milk. "Ahhhh. Tastes good. Like a glass of milk should." Eddie chuckled at his play on a popular cigarette commercial he had heard on television.

He was about to prop his feet up in the living room and enjoy the rest of his milk when he heard some noise. It sounded as though it was coming from one of the bedrooms.

"Hey, Bo? Is that you?" he called. No answer.

Eddie placed his glass on the coffee table and headed down the hall to his bedroom. "Bo? You home?"

He noticed the door to his bedroom was open. That wasn't unusual, but when he peeked his head inside the room, the spectacle he encountered took him by surprise. Delilah and Debbie were showing Peggy Sue Herron and several other freshman girls his bedroom. The girls were oohing and aahhhing over all the trophies and photos on Eddie's dresser, while his sisters sounded like tour guides at an art gallery. "And this trophy was presented to Eddie Sherlin for being the most valuable player in last summer's baseball league," Delilah said, carefully pointing to the trophy. "And there is his all-county award for football this year and last year. As you can see, ladies, Eddie Sherlin is a superstar in several sports. And on your left . . ."

The girls were só enamored with Eddie's sports paraphernalia that they didn't see the hero himself as he looked in on them. Debbie continued the tour, leading them around the edge of Eddie's bed. "Now, ladies, if you will follow me to this corner of the Eddie Sherlin exhibition, you will find on display the actual gym shorts worn in practice by our star—"

One of the freshman girls spied Eddie and squealed with glee. The other girls followed suit. "Oh, it's him!" one gushed, giddily folding her hands in front of her mouth. The other girls began jumping up and down in the bedroom.

"Uh-oh," Debbie said under her breath.

Eddie glared at her. He sent an equally firm expression to Delilah. "Out," he said.

"Oh, just a couple more minutes, Eddie," Delilah protested. "The tour is almost over."

"It's over now. Out!"

Delilah and Debbie pursed their lips, clearly peeved at Eddie's insolent interruption, but they took his opposition in stride. Maintaining their professional decorum, Delilah continued the tour as they exited the bedroom. "If you will walk this way, ladies, we will show you the exact chair in which Eddie Sherlin sits as he eats his oatmeal every morning . . ." Delilah and Debbie brushed past their brother, followed by the freshman girls, who were still giggling and blushing.

As the girls filed past Eddie on their way to the kitchen, he closed the bedroom door and flopped down onto the bed. *Oh, no!* he thought. *I left my milk in the living room. Who knows what Delilah and Debbie will do with that!*

The Drive-In was hopping even more than usual on a Friday night. Car radios were tuned in to Jesse and Al's "Sports Talk" show on

WLAC, the music station broadcast out of Nashville and targeted predominantly to black people. Kids leaned out of cars, yelling back and forth as waiters and waitresses delivered orders as fast as the kitchen could churn them out. Between the radios and the kids yelling, the sounds created a sheer cacophony.

Several Union High cheerleaders gathered around a pay telephone mounted near the restaurant's entrance. Olivia held her hands around the phone's mouthpiece in an attempt to filter out the extraneous noise.

Over the restaurant speaker system, everyone heard Jesse's voice. "We have a caller from the Oakes Drive-In. What's your name, ma'am?"

"Shhh! Quiet! It's my turn," she said, holding the phone away from her as she shushed the girls around her. Then she turned around and spoke into the mouthpiece. "My name is Olivia." Her voice echoed through the restaurant speaker system, evoking cheers and laughs. Her fellow cheerleaders whooped it up behind her.

She tried to quiet the girls by waving her hand toward the ground, but her efforts were in vain. Everyone was having too much fun.

"Well, I just want to say"—she held out the phone for all the cheerleaders to yell into it—"the Union Devils are going to smash that Green Wave! Go Union!" The girls let out a loud cheer, much to the amusement of Jesse and Al.

Meanwhile, Bill's station wagon was surrounded by a crowd of teenage admirers. After all, three of Union's biggest stars were sitting in the car—Bill, Joe, and Roy. Person after person leaned in the open car windows and offered words of encouragement, hype, or downright nonsense. "Show those crackers once and for all that Union always has been and always will be better than them," a man in his early thirties said. More than a few urged the Union stars to "put those white boys in their place."

It was fun at first, but after a while, Bill grew annoyed. "Let's get out of here," he said to Roy and Joe. He turned the ignition key and cranked up the car's motor.

"What about Tyree?" Joe asked. "Don't you have to pick him up after work?"

"Yeah, I do," said Bill. "Hold on, I'm going to go tell him we will be back later." Bill got out of the car and waded through the crowd of people. He greeted a few well-wishers, sidestepped others who wanted to engage him in conversation about the game, and pressed on inside the Drive-In till he found Tyree serving some customers.

Bill patiently waited until Tyree finished delivering the order before he tapped him on the shoulder. "Hey, Tyree."

"Hey, Bill. Whatcha doin'? It's wild in here tonight."

"Yeah, I know. This place is nuts. Roy and Joe and I are going to go on down the road. I'll be back to pick you up when you get off work."

"Okay, I'll be right here," Tyree said. "I ain't goin' nowhere without ya."

"Right," Bill said. "See ya in a while."

Bill weaved through the crowd of admirers toward his car. Just as he started across the parking lot, he heard a shrill whistle. Bill looked to his left and saw the group of hardened Negro Vietnam vets hanging out at their favorite table. One of the guys motioned for him to come over. "Hey, Ligon! Come here a minute."

Yeah, right, Bill thought to himself, knowing these guys had no concept of time. A minute could easily stretch to ten minutes or even an hour. It was all the same to them. They weren't going anywhere. But out of respect for their courage and the price they had paid in battle, Bill hid his reluctance and ambled to the table. "What's going on, guys?"

The leader of the group, James, an older vet—at least older than the other guys since he had just turned thirty-one—patted a seat next to him. James wore a leather bomber jacket and a bandanna around his head, setting off his curly hair. His face was scarred, but nobody knew whether it was from the war or from gang fights he had been in during his younger years. And nobody asked. Everyone knew that James simply was not to be messed with.

"Ligon, my man. Have a seat," James said, again patting the spot next to him.

"Thanks, but I'm about to take off. My buddies are in the car waiting. I gotta—"

"Have a seat," James ordered.

Bill studied James and made the smart decision. He sat down with the group of vets on the picnic table.

"Ah, that's good," James said. "Now we can talk." He thumped Bill on the shoulder.

"Are you boys ready for this game tomorrow?"

"We're as ready as we can be."

"You sure?"

"Yeah, I think so. It's hard to tell, since we've never played them before, but from what I saw the other night in Springfield during the semifinals, I'd say we can take them."

"That's good," James said. "Because what I been hearing about you boys and your scholarships and your Ivy League schools, I get worried that maybe you aren't hungry anymore." All the vets stared at Bill.

Bill looked James right in the eyes. "We're hungry."

For a long moment, nobody said anything as James looked Bill over from head to toe. "Well, all right then. That's what I like to hear. See, I been hearing some other rumors. People saying things like you boys are gonna roll over and play dead for those crackers—just to keep the peace and all." He laughed and spit, then continued. "Yeah. 'Cause we all know how important it is that we keep the peace and all. We boys here know all about makin' sure that everybody's free." A sneer crept across his face. "We know about freedom, don't we, boys?"

"Uh-huh, sure do," one vet answered.

"But some of those white folks seem to think it's still 1950 and we 'African Americans,'" he said sardonically, "well, they just think we're still easy pickin's, like in the good old days. But we all know the good old days weren't so good for coloreds. And nowadays, we ain't about the nonviolent thing, singin' 'We Shall Overcome' and that sort of nonsense. So me and the guys will be there tomorrow night. And if any of those white boys start anything . . ."

A growl seemed to emerge from the group all at once. James laughed deviously. "Let's just say that if they start anything, we'll be there to finish it. So tell your boys, Brother Bill, tell 'em not to worry. Because me and my boys will be watchin'. You just play your game, and we'll take care of the rest."

Bill forced an uncomfortable smile. "Ah, thanks, guys. Hey, I really do have to go. See you tomorrow night." He slipped off the picnic table and headed back to his station wagon, hoping that the veterans were too drunk or drugged up to remember the conversation by this time tomorrow night.

Over at the Dari Delite, the restaurant was packed with a similar revved-up crowd. Automobiles whizzed by the establishment, with kids honking the horns and yelling out the windows. Radios blared. Every sort of music could be heard—from rock and roll to country and western. An assortment of cars and pickup trucks dotted the property, and kids were everywhere, all talking about how Gallatin High was going to whip Union on Saturday night. Every so often, a cheer went up, "Go Green Wave!"

Eddie pulled in and found a place to park. He spotted a friend and called to him. "Hey, Barry. Have you seen my brother, Bo?"

"I haven't seen him, but he might be around inside. Somebody said he's here," Barry answered.

"Okay, thanks." Eddie stepped into the crowded restaurant and was immediately surrounded by well-wishers. His senses were assaulted by the loud noise coming from the talk radio blaring and the jukebox in the corner playing full blast. Eddie scanned the crowded room looking for Bo and barely noticed Terry Poster and his friends stagger into the restaurant.

"Hey, Sherlin!" Terry yelled.

Eddie took one look at Terry and could tell instantly that Terry was high on something—booze, drugs, or his own testosterone on overload. In any case, he wanted nothing to do with him. Eddie tried to ignore him, but the guy would not be put off.

"Hey, Sherlin!" Terry hollered again. "Over here." Poster and his pals pushed their way across the restaurant and positioned themselves around Eddie, with Terry directly in front of him, face-to-face.

"Hello, Terry," Eddie said quietly. "What can I do for you?"

"What can you do for me? Why, Sherlin, I'll tell you what you can do for me. It might get hot around here tomorrow night, if you know what I mean." Terry laughed, but there was no merriment in it, only menace. "Right, boys?" The guys with Terry, all with short haircuts and wearing white T-shirts, nodded in agreement. "Anyhow, we just want you to know we're countin' on you. And we're gonna be there to help should anything go wrong. So you can beat Union tomorrow night, ya hear? I don't mean win. I mean beat 'em up bad."

"Yeah, Terry. I hear ya," Eddie said. "Isn't it time that you and your buddies head for home?"

"Yeah, I'm goin'. But I'll tell you one thing, Sherlin. You'd better win tomorrow, because if you don't, you are going to be known forever in this town as the stupid white boy who lost to a bunch of coloreds."

With that, Terry's friends nudged him to the car and helped him into the backseat. The driver revved the engine, slammed the car into gear, and peeled out of the Dari Delite parking lot, burning rubber and screeching tires as the car careened out onto the main drag.

As Eddie watched the thugs go, he said a quiet prayer. "God, help them not to kill themselves or anyone else tonight."

"Hey, li'l brother."

Eddie heard Bo before he saw him. He turned and saw his brother wheeling toward him.

"Those boys bothering ya?" Bo asked.

"Nah, they're just a sad lot," Eddie replied. "I don't know whether to get mad at them or feel sorry for them—or both."

"Are you going or coming?" Bo nodded toward an open table.

"Neither. I was checking to see if you need a ride."

"I just got here a while ago. I think I'll hang around a bit longer. The whole town's here. I've never seen folks so excited about a game."

"Yeah, I know." Eddie gave a hint of a smile as he waved to enthusiastic young fans watching him from across the restaurant. "I've had a full day. If you're okay, I think I'll head on home."

Bo wheeled his chair up next to Eddie's knees. He leaned as far forward as his body allowed. "Hey, Eddie. Buddy told me about Missy. I know it's not easy to swallow something like that. But forget it, bro. After tomorrow night, you can have any girl in Gallatin—and their mamas and grandmas too."

Bo laughed, and Eddie cracked a smile. He knew Bo was trying his best to cheer him up. "Thanks, Bo. I think I'll stick to basketball and baseball for a while. They are much more predictable than women."

"Now yer talkin'," Bo said. "Come on, stick around. You haven't done a Friday night here in a long time. The word is that you're getting stuck up, getting above your raisin', thanks to all your success."

"And you're telling them that isn't true, right?"

"Of course, I am. But even the king has to get off his high horse and mingle with the commoners once in a while. Come on, Eddie. Loosen up a little. It's your senior year. It might be your last game ever. Enjoy it!"

Eddie looked at the happy faces all around him. Most of the kids and adults in the restaurant weren't rich; they were just everyday folks from Gallatin. Just like him. "Ya know, Bo, maybe you're right. Come on, let's grab a table."

"You grab. I'll follow."

The Sherlin brothers moved deeper into the crowded restaurant. "Eddie! Hey, Eddie," people called out.

Eddie tried his best to smile and wave at every person who recognized him and even the few who didn't. He lowered his head as the waitress came to the table. After all his success, in many ways, he was still a shy kid.

28

GAME DAY DAWNED BRIGHT and sunny in Gallatin. Knowing that it was going to be a long and exhausting day, Eddie tried to sleep in, but even before the sunshine peeked through the curtains in his bedroom, he was already imagining his favorite sound. *Swish! Swish!*

He knew he might as well get up. Everyone else was still sleeping, so he went over to the school's outdoor courts to shoot some baskets before breakfast.

At the Ligon home, Anna peered into Bill and Tyree's room. Tyree stirred, but Anna was shocked to find that Bill was not in his bed. Nor did it look as though it had been slept in the night before.

"Tyree?" the boys' mom called.

"Huh?" Tyree answered, barely awake.

"Where's your brother?"

"Dunno. He dropped me off after work last night and said he'd see me in the morning. Said not to worry, that he wanted to practice his sky hook shot. Ha, that's funny, isn't it? Practice a sky hook in the dark."

Anna was concerned. Her first inclination, however, was not to worry but to pray. A woman of great faith, Anna knelt beside the

269

couch. "God, wherever Bill is, let your angels surround him and keep him safe. He's belonged to you since he was a little boy and that hasn't changed. Please watch out for him and bring him back home safely." She also decided to make some calls when she was done praying. She lived by the adage that she taught her children: "You do what you can do, and God will do his part."

Bill was perfectly safe but not necessarily comfortable, as he had fallen asleep in the station wagon's front seat. He began to rouse when he heard the sounds of children laughing outside the car. After opening his eyes a bit, he noticed several children pointing at him, clearly amused that he had been sleeping in the car along with a basketball on the other seat. Bill grabbed the ball and shuffled out of the vehicle. He put the ball between his legs and stretched his long arms high in the sky and then bent over and touched his toes, stretching his stiff muscles.

He glanced around, remembering where he had parked—right outside the fence to the basketball court in the whites-only park—the one he and Eddie had once sneaked on and played basketball, nearly causing a bigoted man to go nuts; the one near the old house where he and his family used to live when he had first met Eddie and they played over at his cousin Ella Lee's backyard court.

Bill looked up and saw a couple of curious white kids staring at him from outside the fence, perhaps wondering what a Negro was doing on their court. Bill smiled at them and raised one finger to the sky, as if to say, "Watch this, kids!"

Bill, still in his dress clothes, took several dribbles toward the basketball goal. He took a wider arc and sprinted the remaining distance to the hoop, leaving his feet just inside the free throw line, sailing through the air, and slamming the ball through the hoop.

"All right!" the boys called out.

Bill retrieved the ball, gathered his belongings, got back into the car, and drove home to get some sleep before the big game.

It was a busy afternoon at the Sherlin home as everyone anticipated the evening ahead. Eddie took out his new leather Converse All Star shoes and packed them into his gym bag. He tossed in the other items he needed and retrieved his freshly pressed uniform bearing the large number 22 on the chest. It was almost time to go.

"Hey, it's my turn in the bathroom," Debbie whined as she and Delilah fought for time in front of the mirror, bumping each other out of the way as they excitedly combed their hair and applied makeup, wanting to look just right.

Jim and Betty helped Bo into the car. The entire family was excited about getting to the Springfield gymnasium early so they could get good seats.

Across town, Anna Ligon called out the back door to Tyree, who was shooting baskets in the backyard. "Come on, Tyree. Time to get ready. We don't want to be late."

"Okay, Mom. One more shot." Tyree tossed up a sky hook shot of his own. *Swish!* He threw his hands in the air. *Yes! That's a good sign*, he thought before hurrying inside.

Anna and Delores waited patiently as the boys did their final primping, Bill being especially careful to get his Afro fluffed. He dressed in his Sunday best and checked his uniform twice just to make sure he had everything he needed. If a Negro player forgot an item, he couldn't stop along the way to purchase it. It was unacceptable for a Negro to run into a grocery store or even a gas station operated exclusively for whites. Whatever he needed, Bill had to take with him. Finally, he stepped into the living room carrying his gym bag. "I'm ready," he announced.

Out on the Bonner tobacco farm, Roy Jackson scattered some grain for the chickens before joining his grandfather. "Come on, Grandpa," he said as he helped the older Jackson into Mr. Bonner's car. Mr. Bonner had offered to drive Roy to the school to catch the Union team bus and then take his grandfather all the way to Springfield.

"We sure appreciate your kindness, Mr. Bonner," Grandfather Jackson said as Roy got into the backseat.

"My pleasure, Mr. Jackson. I wouldn't want you to miss out on Roy's biggest game."

At the Hamilton home, a group of gorgeous race horses trotted away from the white fences lining the lane as Missy, dressed in her cheerleader uniform, and her parents rode down the long gravel driveway in Charles Hamilton's favorite automobile—a vintage Cadillac he drove only on special occasions. "This is certainly one of those times that merits a special ride," he said. It may have occurred to Charles that the heavy old car might provide a safer, stronger, more secure vehicle if things turned ugly at the game.

The Herron family had already had a challenging day. Susan Herron was convinced that it was unsafe for Peggy Sue to attend the championship game. Fully aware of the tension surrounding the mandatory integration policies, the moment Susan learned that Gallatin would face Union, she fretted that the game could easily turn into a riot. The cross-burning on her front yard had pushed her over the edge. The day of the game, she admitted her fears to her daughter. "Peggy Sue, as much as I want you to show your school spirit, it simply is not safe for you to attend the game tonight."

"Mother! You can't be serious! This is the biggest game of my life. And it may be Eddie Sherlin's last game. It is sure to be the greatest game in Gallatin history! How can I not be there?"

"I understand all that, but it is simply too dangerous—with your father's position and the animosity in town right now. Perhaps another time."

"Mother! There will never be another time like this, ever again!"

"Peggy Sue, your father and I have discussed it. We are concerned for your safety. I know you don't understand right now, but hopefully someday you will appreciate our desire to protect you."

"I understand that you are ruining my life!" Peggy Sue objected as she ran out of the living room and sealed herself in her bedroom.

"She's a smart girl," Susan said to her husband. "She will figure it all out sooner or later."

Peggy Sue remained in her room throughout the day, regardless of her parents' efforts to coax her out.

When it came time to leave for the game, Principal Herron knocked on Peggy Sue's bedroom door. "Peggy Sue. Sweetheart, we are leaving. Don't worry. You'll get to go to many other games before you graduate."

"I made up a plate of food for your supper," Susan added. "It's in the refrigerator. Now, no more pouting, Peggy Sue." She turned the knob on Peggy Sue's door. "Peggy Sue?" Susan pushed the bedroom door open and looked inside, her husband right behind her.

"Peggy Sue!" Susan shouted.

They stepped inside the bedroom. Peggy Sue was gone.

At Union and Gallatin high schools, the bus drivers pulled up their vehicles to the front of the schools where large crowds of students were waiting. Sixty-six passengers loaded onto each bus, filling every seat.

The players, coaches, and cheerleaders had already climbed aboard their respective buses. The cheerleaders chattered with excitement, but the ballplayers and coaches were subdued, lost in thought, already playing the game in their minds.

Most people in town were getting into their vehicles to head toward Springfield, but many neighbors and fans remained on the streets to send the teams off with cheers. Some of the older neighbors who couldn't attend the game sat or stood out on their front porches to wave at the team as the buses rumbled by. A number of young boys ran down the sidewalks, trying to keep up with the buses, waving and calling out encouragement to their favorite players as the team rolled past.

While his bus passed the Negro barbershop, Bill noticed the group of elderly men climbing into an old car in front of the shop. The barber and his friends paused to wave at the Union bus as it whooshed by.

As the Green Wave team bus rolled through the town square, people cheered as though the players were celebrities in a parade. Shop owners stood outside their front doors and waved. Others were busy hanging CLOSED signs on the windows and locking up the stores. They paused long enough to wave at the passing buses and then loaded up their cars and headed to Springfield.

Four police patrol cars were lined up in front of the courthouse. Chief Braden had put every officer on the Gallatin police force on alert. Nobody had tonight off, unless they had a personal emergency to handle. Every patrolman was in place, either in town or surrounding the Springfield gymnasium in cooperation with the local authorities. When the last school bus passed through downtown, the four police cars, loaded with armed patrolmen, followed closely behind.

As the buses approached Springfield, state police troopers pulled out ahead of them, escorting the buses into town. People in the little town of Springfield had never seen so many police officers.

The team buses rolled to a stop at the back of the school near the locker room entrance where several somber and heavily armed police officers guarded the doors.

Almost simultaneously, Bill and Eddie stepped down off their respective buses. Both boys stood for a moment before entering the school, the stoic expressions on their faces belying their excitement and anxiety.

This was the game the two friends had thought about, dreamed about, prayed about. It was time to play ball.

29

IN FRONT OF SPRINGFIELD HIGH SCHOOL, a mass of spectators unloaded from various buses. Since both teams were from Gallatin, the buses had arrived almost at the same time, setting up a swarm of people converging on the ticket booths. The throng of people—comprised of both blacks and whites—standing in lines and all hyped over the game, set up stressful and dangerous pregame confrontations. People pushed and shoved, trying to get into the gym, vying for a good seat. Several faculty and administrators from both schools stood outside the doors, attempting in vain to calm the crowd. Police officers stood by, watching for any trouble and urging people to stay in lines. Despite the best efforts to maintain order, the crowd surged ahead.

"Hold on, there! Stop your pushing," the doorman shouted. "Back off, or we will close the doors and nobody will get in!"

Al and Jesse were already set up inside the gym doing their pregame show from the scorekeeper's desk behind the center-court railing. "There is an overflow crowd here in the Springfield gym tonight," Al said, "to see who goes home with the championship trophy."

"It's unbelievable," Jesse agreed. "The people just keep pouring in! If you're thinking about coming to the game, let me give you some advice: stay home. There is no more room in the inn. Pull up a chair and listen to all the action right here on Gallatin's WHIN radio."

The radio guys were right. The gym was packed. But unlike last week's semifinal contests, tonight's crowd was divided, black people on one side of the gym and whites on the other. The pre-championship game was a girls' basketball game, so more white women than usual comprised the crowd. Sitting on the girls' bench was Patricia Head, a young woman who would soon make basketball history herself. Trish, as she was known in high school, excelled as a player. Then later, after she married and became the head coach of the Tennessee Lady Volunteers, the world would know her as Pat Summitt, the coach who won eight national championships and had more NCAA basketball victories than any other coach—male or female—in history.

The cheerleaders from Union and Gallatin were busy practicing their routines before tip-off. Teachers, parents, and spectators filled the stands to capacity. Anna Ligon sat with Tyree on one of the lower bleacher seats. Roy Jackson's grandfather and Mr. Bonner slid into their seats on the Union side, just a row up from Charlene and Martha, the two girls who had been wooing Bill's affections. With neither of them able to capture his heart, the two girls became friends and were now cheering for Bill and his teammates right alongside each other. The old men from the barbershop sat together in the center section of the bleachers. Along the top rows in the middle on the Union side sat the group of Vietnam veterans, who stared menacingly across the court at the predominantly white crowd supporting the Green Wave.

Even Bishop Lula Mae Swanson and several elders from the Original Church of God were there. Bishop Swanson sat demurely, impeccably dressed as always in a blue business suit, on the corner seat closest to the exit.

On the Gallatin High side of the court, the Green Wave cheerleaders greeted various people in the crowd. The Sherlin family sat in their usual spot, on the end of the front row, so Bo could position his wheelchair nearby. Buddy Bruce found a seat three rows up the bleachers with several of the football players. He always sat close so he could get to the court in a hurry if a problem came up.

Charles Hamilton Sr. and his wife sat in the heart of the Gallatin crowd, waving at Missy every time she looked in their direction. It was almost as if the Hamiltons were oblivious to the basketball game. They acted as though the entire evening centered around their daughter.

Eddie's neighbors were there, as was Dan Savage, the pawn shop owner; Mr. White, the barber; Mr. Long, the sports equipment store owner; and many of the Sherlins' friends from First Assembly of God church. Even some of the bruised Springfield boys who fought with Buddy and Eddie and their Gallatin friends were sitting in the back rows on the bleachers. Nobody wanted to miss this game.

Principal Herron, in collaboration with Principal Malone on the Union side, stood on the Gallatin sidelines, scanning the crowd for possible problems. As the principal observed the Gallatin supporters, a familiar face caught his attention. Sure enough, it was his daughter, Peggy Sue, sitting with her girlfriends. They were already cheering and laughing and encouraging the team, even though the Green Wave players were still in the locker room. Just then, Peggy Sue turned her head in her father's direction. Her smile disappeared, and she leaned back as far into the crowd as possible to avoid her father's glowering gaze.

Principal Herron felt a mix of emotions wash over him. He was relieved that Peggy Sue was okay, but he was furious that she had disobeyed. He made a mental note to deal with Peggy Sue later.

More than a dozen armed police officers, some in uniform and some in street clothes, stood around the perimeter of the gymnasium, purposely making themselves obvious to all spectators. The message displayed by the strong police presence was clear: don't start anything.

The deafening commotion of the crowd in the gymnasium made normal conversation almost impossible. But down in the Gallatin locker room, only the echoes from the gym above could be heard. The tone was low-key, and the team was surprisingly calm. Coach Vradenburg moved among the players, quietly offering final words of encouragement, checking on injuries, and making sure everyone was ready. There was no need for a big speech. Everything the coach needed to say, he had been saying all week long. Coach Vradenburg took his place near the door, awaiting the signal to head up to the gym.

In the Union locker room, the same noise from upstairs filtered in, especially when someone opened the door, and for the most part, the team members were quiet. Each player sat on the bench, going through his pregame routine. Joe tied and untied his shoelaces half a dozen times, making sure the knots were hidden under the tongues of the shoes. Roy leaned back against a locker and yawned, as though he didn't have a care in the world. Coach Martin paced, occasionally pausing long enough to quietly voice a word of praise or advice about a point in their game plan.

Bill felt nervous, but he portrayed confidence to his coaches and teammates as he sat deep in thought on the bench nearest the door. He was ready to play.

With the girls' basketball game concluded and the floor cleared and swept, two policemen received the signal from the referee. One officer went to the Union locker room, the other went to Gallatin's. The officers opened the respective doors, and both men said the same thing: "It's time."

Eddie jumped to his feet.

In the Union locker room, Bill did the same.

The coaches led their teams out of the locker rooms into a poorly lit hallway that passed in front of the snack bar and up a short staircase to the basketball court. The police in the hallway cleared a path so the teams could pass by the customers at the snack bar without being badgered. Nobody bothered the players, but fans from each team called out words of encouragement to their favorites. As the teams filed out of the locker rooms, the Green Wave players, dressed in white uniforms decked out with green trim, and the Union Devils players, in dark red uniforms trimmed in black, caught their first glimpses of one another. Most of the boys tried to look straight ahead, all except Roy Jackson, who spotted Alton, the tall Gallatin center. Roy shot him a devious smile. Alton returned a quick, irritated look at Roy and then kept his eyes straight ahead.

Standing at the bottom of the staircase, awaiting their guys to file out, the two coaches suddenly realized they had a problem. "Which team goes out first?" asked Coach Martin.

Coach Vradenburg offered a wise suggestion. "We'd better have both teams go out at the same time."

Coach Martin nodded. "Good idea."

The coaches addressed their teams in the hallway. "Single file, boys. Devils over on this side." He pointed to the left wall.

"Waves over here," Coach Vradenburg called. "Stay to the right. Single file."

The two teams formed parallel lines, with opposing players side by side as they moved up the staircase. Eddie stood next to Bill. He quickly glanced over at Bill, but he was looking straight ahead. Eddie returned his gaze forward. Bill sneaked a look at Eddie, who was now looking straight ahead.

Roy Jackson, who was standing behind Bill, kept staring and smiling at Alton. Sensing Roy's gaze, Alton turned his head and asked Roy, "Do you see something funny?"

"I sure do," Roy said and then looked straight ahead.

Alton turned away, his fists clenched, his lips pinched tightly shut, and his face contorted into an angry, disgusted expression.

"Okay, let's go," both coaches said.

With the team assistants holding the doors wide open, both teams jogged onto the gym floor, followed by their coaches. The pent-up energy and excitement in the gymnasium exploded in thunderous cheers as the fans jumped to their feet, screaming approval and applauding their teams. The cheerleaders leaped and twirled, waving their pom-poms as the teams peeled off toward opposite baskets and began their layup drills. The crowd continued its unabated yelling, causing a deafening roar.

On the sidelines, both principals' stoic faces expressed concern. It was no longer conjecture—more than ever they realized how easily this crowd could become a riot. Principal Malone noted the police officers, who were already on their feet at various points around the gymnasium.

As the teams continued to warm up, Principal Herron's eyes narrowed when he caught sight of Terry Poster and his cohorts strutting down the sideline. Herron eyed them all the way until they were right in front of him. "Do you boys have seats yet?" the principal demanded.

"I'm sure we'll be able to find some," Terry responded.

"You've already got them," Principal Herron said, drawing the attention of a nearby police officer. "We've saved them just for you. Right here, next to me." The principal patted the row he had saved. He smiled at Terry and his friends as the police officer nodded toward the seats. Terry glared at Principal Herron, but after a slight hesitation, he and his friends reluctantly sat down.

The gymnasium's scoreboard buzzer sounded and the teams bounded to the sidelines. Several players applied rosin to their hands to counteract perspiration. The coaches raised their hands, calling the players to huddle. While the court was clear, the Gallatin cheerleaders ran out and did a cute cheer, followed by the Union cheerleaders, who performed a similar cheer.

Meanwhile, a final group of stragglers found space to sit on the floor all around the court off the sidelines and even under both baskets. Interestingly, even this group of procrastinators quickly separated along racial lines—with one group sitting on one side and the other on the opposite side.

The buzzer sounded, and the referees waved the teams to center court for the opening jump ball. With Bill jumping for Union and Alton representing Gallatin, the referee stepped briskly in between the two centers and tossed the ball into the air above them. Alton had a couple of inches of height on Bill, and despite Bill's outstanding ability to jump, Alton got the opening tip, tapping the ball to Gallatin's guard, who drove hard up court to the cheers of the Gallatin crowd.

Union started off playing man-to-man defense, so the Gallatin forwards set a double screen on Eddie's man. Union's Joe Malone tried to squeeze by the screen formed by the two Gallatin players but caught an elbow and stumbled into the stragglers under the bucket, leaving Eddie all alone in the corner. A number of Union spectators cried, "Foul!" but the refs didn't see it that way, and Eddie dumped in a wide-open fifteen-foot jump shot. The Gallatin spectators rose to their feet as one, screaming and cheering in delight.

"Come on, Ref," Joe complained as he passed by the referee, with the Gallatin defender in front of him. "Watch the elbows, or it's going to be a bloody night."

"Stop your whinin', ya big baby," Alton said as Joe brought the ball back up court.

Joe didn't appreciate Alton's condescending tone, so with a burst of speed, he dribbled right past him. The Gallatin forward saw what happened and moved to pick up Joe, leaving Bill free under the basket. In a fancy, Harlem Globetrotters–style move, Joe wrapped the ball around his back, whipping it to Bill, who laid it in for an easy two points. The Union supporters roared in approval.

The teams seemed evenly matched, and when the audience could lay aside the tension surrounding the skin colors of the boys on the court, they were seeing some incredible high school basketball on display. Gallatin's offense worked off Alton, the big center, with the smaller guards feeding Alton the ball high up around his shoulders. Then when the defense collapsed on Alton, the big man passed the ball back out to his teammates who had open jump shots. Union's three big guns worked well together down low, controlling most rebounds off the boards.

The game intensified quickly. The spectators on both sides were supercharged and reacted to every play. The cheerleaders from both schools worked constantly, rallying the fans at every score.

The play got rough early on. Joe Malone dribbled shoulder-first right into Henry Hutchins, Gallatin's first substitute. Henry went flying, and the Gallatin fans leaped angrily to their feet, protesting Joe's charge. The referee called Joe for charging, but the Gallatin crowd was calling for blood. The Union fans returned fire, protesting the ref's call, which was actually a good one. A matter of minutes into the game, people on both sides, black and white, were hurling insults, taunting and aiming their fury at one another. Principals Malone and Herron nervously watched the crowd in the stands more than they watched the ball game. They had expected emotions to be frazzled, but their anxiety levels became more heightened when tensions began fraying so early in the game.

Things got worse when Roy Jackson drove the lane and Eddie stood his ground in front of him, taking the brunt of Roy's body blow, which sent Eddie sprawling on the hardwood. The referee blew his whistle and pointed at Roy, calling an offensive foul on Roy for charging.

As soon as he saw Roy ram Eddie, Buddy was on his feet, ready to take out Roy, but several of Buddy's friends held him back. When Eddie bounced up onto his feet, unscathed, Buddy calmed down—for a while.

The next few minutes contained a barrage of missed shots by both teams, with a violent tangle of players under the baskets fighting for rebounds. Alton's height gave him a distinct advantage over Bill and Roy, and it was clear that Roy was growing increasingly frustrated at Alton's ability to snatch the ball out of his hands.

At the first time-out, the teams streamed off the court to wild applause. Missy and the rest of the Gallatin cheerleaders raced out to center court to lead a cheer. Not to be outdone, the Union cheerleaders responded in kind. Students and fans from both schools tried to out-cheer the other school by yelling louder and louder.

Coach Martin pulled his players in tight but still had to yell to be heard above the noise. "If they double team you like that, you gotta switch off. They're getting too many good looks at the basket. And Roy, that center is getting inside on us. You can't let him do that. We can't let them have that second shot, a second chance to score. Keep him off the boards."

Roy nodded as he wiped the perspiration off his face. It was up to him to keep the tall Gallatin center from dominating the game. When the teams broke from the time-out, it was Gallatin's ball. Eddie missed a tough shot, but Alton grabbed the rebound and put the ball back up and in. Bill glared at Roy for letting Alton get behind him again.

The teams traded baskets. Then Joe Malone raced for a loose ball, diving after it and tipping it back into play. It was an amazing effort on Joe's part, but he landed in the midst of the Gallatin cheerleaders, his sweaty body rubbing on the legs of two of the girls who weren't able to get out of the way. The girls were horrified that a Negro had touched them. Joe rolled over right on top of several of the cheerleaders' pom-poms. The Union crowd and even a number of the Gallatin parents reacted with concern for Joe, but Missy and her friends were appalled that "colored sweat" had touched their pom-poms.

Down court, Alton pulled in another rebound and tossed it back to Eddie, who sank a quick jumper. Roy shot Alton a dirty look, but Alton was simply too tall for Roy to handle. In an attempt to take out his frustration, Roy got the ball down low and dribbled straight back into Alton, hoping that he would fall off him and give him an easy jump shot. But Roy was paying too much attention to Alton and not enough to his ball control. Eddie swept by on Roy's side and stole the ball. Eddie fired the ball to Henry, who missed a jumper and the ball bounced high off the rim. Roy and Alton went up for the rebound at the same time. Roy grabbed the ball and furiously swung his elbow around his body, slamming it into Alton's forehead. Alton tumbled to the floor in a heap as blood oozed out around the wound.

Coach Vradenburg and the Green Wave trainer rushed onto the court to attend to the groggy, bleeding player. The refs whistled the game to a halt. The gymnasium erupted in pandemonium! The angry Gallatin crowd leaped up, yelling and screaming, while the Union fans vociferously demonstrated their approval of the rough play.

Police stepped onto the court, facing the bleachers and the crowd. Principals Herron and Malone bounced to their feet. This was their worst nightmare, the scenario they had hoped would not happen.

Terry Poster and his racist cohorts also jumped up and screamed at Roy and the referees. "Get that monkey off the court," Terry hollered.

Union fans heard Terry and yelled obscenities back at him. Principal Herron stepped in front of Terry and pressed his hand down on Terry's shoulder. "Sit down," the principal commanded while applying pressure and forcing the angry boy down to the bleachers. Principal Herron looked up into the stands and caught a glimpse of Reginald Poster, Terry's dad, smirking as though he was pleased with Terry's outburst. To the elder Poster, any bad blood was a plus for his cause.

The Green Wave trainers helped Alton to his feet, still applying pressure to stop the bleeding from the cut on his forehead. They propped him up, one on each side, as he staggered to the locker room. As Alton passed by, Eddie ran over and gave him a light pat on the back.

The referees charged Roy with a technical foul for unsportsmanlike conduct, causing the fans on both sides of the court to respond loudly.

"Throw him out of the game, Ref!" Green Wave fans clamored.

"A technical? For what? That was a good move. That boy just got in the way of a legal rebound," Union supporters hollered.

The referee called both teams off the court while Eddie went to the foul line to shoot the technical. He took a deep breath and poured the ball through the net.

Eddie trotted back to the bench to join his teammates. As he did, a crushed cup landed on the court. Then another flew through the air. Someone also tossed a cardboard tray onto the floor. The crowd was out of control.

Principal Herron and several teachers tried to calm things down. The police once again stepped out onto the court, glaring into the stands and watching for those who were throwing the debris onto the playing area. The Negro Vietnam vets stood to their feet in anticipation of a more overt battle.

The following announcement blared over the public address system: "Ladies and gentlemen, please refrain from throwing things onto the court." Several young boys brought out large janitorial brooms and swept up the garbage.

In the midst of the mayhem, Coach Martin called his players back to a huddle in front of the bench. He didn't say anything directly, but he stared daggers at Roy.

"You said to keep him off the boards!" Roy offered.

Coach Martin ignored Roy's comment. Roy glanced back to the Union stands and caught the eye of his grandfather, who also gave him an admonishing look. Roy ducked back into the huddle.

With time-out called on the floor, Principal Herron walked over to Principal Malone, and they discussed their feelings about the incident. As he talked, Principal Herron looked up toward the Gallatin bleachers. He nodded toward Terry Poster's father, along with four of his tough-looking, middle-aged friends. "If those guys are not card-carrying members of the KKK, the Klan should sue them for back dues!" Principal Malone cracked just a hint of a smile.

With the blood cleaned up and the debris disposed of, the referee blew the whistle indicating that play should resume.

Less than five minutes had run off the clock since the opening jump ball.

The crowd was stunned when the player Coach Vradenburg put in to replace Alton was none other than James "Stud" Johnson. Standing six feet four inches tall and two hundred pounds, Johnson was one of the few black people who attended Gallatin High School. But rather than having a calming effect, his presence on the court seemed to stoke the fires. The game resumed with a heightened sense of anger and resentment. By quarter's end, Gallatin held a two-point lead: 15–13.

"After one quarter, we've got ourselves some kind of game," Al told his WHIN radio listeners.

"That's right, Al," Jesse jumped in. "The fans have not stopped screaming since the opening buzzer. I've never seen anything like it!"

The Gallatin cheerleaders took the court and performed one of their perfectly executed cheers, which ended in a pyramid with Missy perched on top of the other girls. It was all very nice but rather bland and predictable.

Olivia said, "Come on, girls. Let's shake it out there this time." The Union girls kicked things up a notch by performing a sultry routine, with plenty of wiggle and jiggle. Although the Union fans loved it, Mr. Malone was not amused. The Gallatin cheerleaders stared at their Union counterparts. With their hands on their hips, Missy and her troupe acted absolutely appalled.

The second quarter opened with Eddie attempting to be more aggressive. With Gallatin's tallest player out of the game, Union had easy pickings when it came to rebounds. Besides that, the Gallatin offense, trying to work through the center, James Johnson, a second-stringer, gave Bill the opportunity to block more shots. He took full advantage, swatting away several potential two-pointers. The Union crowd crowed loudly.

Union took more chances when they had the ball. Joe and Roy were able to get off more shots from underneath, and Bill sank a long hook shot from the foul line.

Eddie dribbled into a trap while cutting through the key and got sandwiched between Union's two big guys. He lost his balance and was tipping over as he came close to falling out of bounds. But just as he toppled, he drilled the ball backward off Roy's leg. Roy winced and the ball bounced out of bounds.

Eddie's quick thinking worked. The referee blew the whistle and indicated that the ball remained in Gallatin's possession.

Roy glared at Eddie as he trotted back onto the court and then purposely bumped him chest to chest. Roy was bigger and stronger, but Eddie didn't back down. He pushed him away, and Roy came back for more. The referees separated the boys from a potential fight, but since they didn't see how it started, they didn't charge either one with a foul.

The crowd yelled ugly comments at the officials. Buddy Bruce was on his feet, ready to leap over the railing. Eddie cast a warning look at Buddy.

The teams exchanged the lead several times during the second quarter. With only ten seconds left, Union was on top, 29–27. Henry brought the ball in to Eddie, who dribbled rapidly and deliberately up court, looking for an opening. Two Union players tried to trap him in the backcourt, but Eddie maneuvered his way through them. Escaping the double team, however, had taken too long; the clock had nearly run out.

With none of his teammates open, from just over the half-court line, Eddie took a chance. He let fly a desperate long shot, the ball soaring so high in the air that it looked as though it might smack against the large steel ceiling beams. But just as the buzzer sounded, *Swish!* Eddie's amazing shot went through the net, tying the score at the half.

The Green Wave fans went crazy.

Eddie trotted off court toward the locker room, acting as though sinking a shot from midcourt happened every day. His teammates joined him, slapping him on the back as the gymnasium fell into bedlam, with Gallatin fans roaring and applauding and Union fans yelling in disappointment.

The police quickly resumed their positions along the sidelines as the teams went through the doors to the downstairs locker rooms for a fifteen-minute half-time break.

With the last of the players off the court, an awkward tension filled the gymnasium as the spectators stopped cheering and settled into their seats or spilled out of the bleachers, heading for the restrooms or snack bars. Others seemed eager to get outside the school to light up their cigarettes. Each encounter between Negro fans and white fans held explosive potential, so except for those people looking to start some trouble, most everyone moved with a sense of caution.

Jesse and Al, who looked as though they had been in a street brawl, were at their microphones recapping the opening two quarters. With their ties askew, their hair mussed, and their faces slick with perspiration, they were emotionally wrung out. "It's halftime here in Springfield," Jesse told the listening audience, "with the game tied at twenty-nine all. And what a first half it has been! We'll be back with all the highlights after this commercial message."

30

In the Union High locker room, Roy and Bill sat on a bench in front of the first set of lockers toweling perspiration from their faces. "Lucky shot," Roy groused about Eddie's last-second score.

"Yeah, don't worry about the lucky ones. We gotta keep the ball out of Eddie's hands. If he gets hot—"

"If he gets hot, he might just have to run into my elbow." Roy chuckled as he rubbed his elbow, still sore from hitting the Gallatin center so hard. He turned to see Coach Martin, who entered the locker room just in time to hear Roy's comment.

Coach Martin didn't share the humor. "It's funny to see a player in such a good mood when he's only one foul away from fouling out."

Roy sighed. He'd been nailed.

Coach Martin allowed the team to get some water before gathering everyone around him. "Okay, we're going to go with a box-and-one defense. That means I want someone on Sherlin all the time. Roy, that will be you."

Surprised, Roy looked up at the coach. "But I have four—"

"That way the referees will always have their eyes on you." Coach Martin drilled Roy with a look. "And if I see anything that looks like dirty play, I'll bench ya. You hear me, Roy?"

"Coach?" Roy started to protest, but Coach Martin was clearly in no mood to hear it.

"Listen to me and listen well. If you want to be a championship team, you need to win fair and square. It does you no good if Eddie Sherlin goes down and we win the game by ten points or a hundred points if you are branded as a bunch of 'dirty-playin' coloreds.'" He paused and looked from man to man. "Are you hearing me?"

Several of the players nodded.

"Just as we've always said, 'We have to be better than the opposition, and not just better. We have to be *ten times* better than the white team.' Put yourself in the position to be able to compete. Don't waste energy pointing fingers or placing blame. You give it your best shot. You put your best foot forward, and if you do it the way it's supposed to be done, you will land on top."

Coach Martin lowered his voice to the point it was barely audible but no less forceful. "We can win this game. But listen to me, men. We are going to win this game with class—or not at all."

In the Gallatin High locker room, Coach Vradenburg's first concern was for his injured player. "How's Alton?" he asked one of his assistants.

"They took him to the hospital. He needs some stitches. He'll be fine, but he won't be coming back tonight."

Hearing the assistant's gloomy assessment, the players hung their heads in despair. Most had hoped that Alton could get some ice on the cut and be bandaged up and ready to play the second half. Without Alton, Union's height around the boards was going to be even more of a factor.

After the players had toweled off and gotten some water, the coach laid out the game plan. "Okay, circle up here. We're going to protect the middle, so we'll start the second half with a two-three zone. Eddie and Allen up front. With Alton out, we won't have our in-and-out game, so we'll play more of a high pick and roll. Ken, you and Joey bring the ball up court. Eddie, you roll off the screens either way, left or right."

Coach Vradenburg noticed Henry punching his fist against his palm, obviously angry. The coach moved to stand in front of Henry but spoke to the whole team. "Anybody thinking of retaliating? Trying to get back at those boys for knocking out Alton? You will be benched, and you will be dealing with me."

The coach softened his tone and spoke quietly but emphatically. "I'm mighty proud of you men. We are going to win this game the right way—the old-fashioned way—by out-playing the other team, by out-hustling the opposition. If you do what you know is right, you will come out of here with your heads held high."

One of the timekeepers opened the locker room door and popped his head inside. "Two minutes, Coach."

The coach nodded his thanks, and the door closed. "Okay, you can do this." Coach Vradenburg paused as he considered the enormous impact of the game and the pressure on his players. "This may be a life-changer for you and for a lot of other people."

He looked around one last time at his players. "Now, let's go win this game!"

The teams exited the locker rooms at almost the exact same time, following their coaches back past the snack bar and up the staircase to the gymnasium. A crowd of people, including Anthony and Ronald, two of the bigger boys from Springfield who had been in the fight with the Gallatin guys, pressed up against the snack bar as the teams filed by. Anthony spotted Roy and yelled out, "Hey, you cheater. Wanna pick on someone? Come pick on me!"

Roy glared back at the kid.

"Yeah! You there, big man. You're so tough. You with the sharp elbow weapon. Why don't they put you back in the zoo where you belong?"

"Keep moving," Bill said from behind Roy. Roy bristled and was about to respond when he saw Coach Martin shooting him a warning look. Roy kept his eyes on the coach as he moved up the stairs. Bill stayed close to his teammate. But just then, from the top of the stairs, someone else called down to Anthony and Ronald. "Hey!"

Bill and Roy looked up to see James, the leader of the Vietnam vets. "You got a problem, fat boy?" James taunted.

"Me? I ain't got no problem," Anthony fired back. "What's yours?"

"You!" James retorted.

Sensing the danger of this confrontation, the coaches called out to the players. "Okay, let's go!"

The teams burst through the doors and onto the court for some quick warm-up shots. The fans, mostly back in their seats following the break, stood and cheered.

In the hallway below, James threaded his way down the crowded staircase to confront the Springfield boys. A bunch of Union fans leaned into the stairwell to watch the action, and someone yelled, "Fight!"

Several of the police officers guarding the gym and locker room entry doors raced down the steps, with more of the crowd standing up and rubbernecking to see what was going on.

Then the buzzer sounded, indicating the start of the second half. With all eyes still watching the stairway, two police officers escorted the Springfield boys back to the bleachers, while another officer walked James back to join his buddies. One policeman gave an "okay" sign to the referee, indicating that things were under control and the second half could begin. The furrowed brows and tense expressions on the faces of Eddie's parents, Anna Ligon, and the school principals did not convey the same sort of confidence.

The buzzer shrilled again, and the teams went back to work. Bill won the tip on the jump ball, out-dueling James Johnson and tapping the ball to Joe Malone. They ran a play from the top of the key, passing the ball back to Bill at the foul line, where he banked in a jump shot. Union was on the move.

As Gallatin guard Ken Kirkham brought the ball up court, Eddie hustled into position just across the center-court line. Roy Jackson was on him like a glove, shadowing Eddie in man-to-man coverage everywhere he moved. "Hey, Sherlin," Roy said as he squared off in front of Eddie. "I'm going to be your closest friend for the rest of the half."

Roy did a good job too. He played Eddie tight, keeping a hand on him wherever he went, especially when the referee wasn't looking. Eddie was quicker than Roy, but Roy was bigger, and his long arms were in Eddie's face even when Eddie didn't have the ball.

Eddie worked off the picks his teammates placed, trying to block Roy from following him through the key. Eddie got the ball, faked one way, and then dribbled left-handed in the opposite direction, and Roy couldn't keep up with him. But when Eddie went up for the jump shot, Roy recovered just in time to tip the ball enough to knock it out of bounds below the goal.

The Union crowd loved it, and with his face toward the bleachers and his back to Coach Martin, Roy risked flashing the Union fans a cocky smile. They cheered even louder.

Throughout the third quarter, Roy played Eddie closely, keeping up an annoying and constant chatter. More often than not, when Eddie got the ball, Roy was so close to his face that he had to pass to someone else. The man-to-man coverage was working, especially because Gallatin did not have a big man in the center to help draw the guards away from Eddie. The few times Eddie tried to shoot or drive past the defenders, Roy's coverage was too tight or Eddie was double-teamed and his shots bounced off the rim.

Coach Vradenburg sensed Eddie's exasperation and called a time-out. As the cheerleaders led the crowd in raucous yells, the coach gathered his team in a huddle. "If Eddie gets doubled, you guys gotta cut to the basket. Somebody has to be open. And move the ball around. Don't hold it. Keep them running."

The coach looked at Eddie. "You're trying to drive around your man. Go right at him. He has four fouls. He has to back off or he's outta here. Go straight at him."

Eddie nodded, and the team broke from the huddle.

The coach was right. When Eddie went straight at Roy, as much as the Union star wanted to stay with him, he had to back off. Eddie dumped in a long shot from the corner. Union quickly countered. When Eddie came back down the court, Roy was all over him. Joey Graves, one of the Gallatin starters, fired a pass to Eddie, who dribbled into a double team and got trapped. Eddie found a lane and bounce passed the ball back to Graves for an easy two points.

Bill grabbed the ball as it came through the hoop, stepped out of bounds, and whaled a long pass down the court to Joe Malone at the top of the key. Joe took two dribbles and put the ball up and in.

Back and forth the game went.

Near the end of the third quarter, Roy covered Eddie like a wet blanket as Eddie backed in toward the basket, keeping the ball just far enough away from Roy's long arms. Eddie turned quickly for a jump shot. But he faked it. Roy leaped high in the air to block Eddie's shot, but the expression on his face said it all. He had been fooled. Eddie brought the ball up in front of him, making an off-balance shot as Roy came crashing down on top of him. The referee blew his whistle, and Roy cursed under his breath for allowing Eddie to fake him out. The gym buzzer sounded its jarring tone.

"That's the fifth and final foul for Roy Jackson," Al told the radio audience as the referee indicated the call to the scorekeepers. Roy walked off the court to the cheers from Union fans, who applauded his strong showing, and jeers from the Gallatin crowd, who were glad to see Roy out of the game. To make matters worse, Eddie sank the foul shot, tying the score once again.

The teams continued to trade scores back and forth, but neither team could break out in a strong lead. The clock ticked down and the buzzer sounded, ending the third quarter.

"Unbelievable!" Jesse was nearly yelling into his microphone. "After three quarters of play, we're still tied up!"

"That's right, Jesse," Al chimed in. "We've got only eight minutes to go in this ball game. Eight minutes to decide who will walk out of here with the district tournament championship. And we are starting the game all over again. Tie score. It all comes down to this, folks!"

The noise was deafening. The gymnasium seemed to be rocking as the place prepared to come unglued. Both cheerleading squads had given up their efforts to perform cute routines. They were simply screaming and chanting cheers, the crowd yelling right along with them. Even Buddy Bruce was hollering as loud as he could. On the other side of the gym, the Vietnam vets were standing and chanting something. The barbershop men were standing and waving, their voices hoarse. Up in the Gallatin stands, the KKK racists glared at the Negroes across the court. Betty Sherlin hugged Delilah and Debbie. "Pray, girls, pray!"

The fourth quarter began with Joe Malone bringing the ball down court, looking carefully for the open man. Every shot mattered. Every move was crucial. Bill was still finding ways to get open under the bucket. He made a hook shot. Then a quick fake and move to the corner for two more points. He caught a quick pass from Joe and drilled a turn-around jumper from the foul line.

Gallatin matched Union shot-for-shot. Eddie got free in the corner, and James Johnson whipped him a quick pass. Eddie drove from the corner but couldn't find an opening, so he passed to Allen Cook, who sank a sensational fall-away jump shot.

Bill dribbled toward the basket then zipped a behind-the-back pass to Joe, but the pass caught Joe off guard. He fumbled it, knocking the ball out of bounds.

It was Gallatin's ball.

Ken Kirkham, spying Eddie open, brought the ball down court and passed it to him. Eddie faked a set shot and then dribbled around his defender, straight toward the basket. Only one man was in his way—Bill Ligon. Both players went high in the air. Eddie leaped as high as Bill, although Bill was nearly five inches taller. But Bill had position on him. He blocked Eddie's shot, their bodies slamming together.

Eddie tumbled to the ground, flying into a group of fans on the floor under the basket. Bill stumbled backward as well, landing awkwardly right next to where Eddie had fallen. Eddie caught Bill's eyes for just a moment. The two star players stared each other down, neither backing off an inch. For a fraction of a second, perhaps they both remembered two childhood friends—one colored and one white—and a time in each of their lives when one had fallen and the other had helped him up.

Not tonight.

Both Bill and Eddie struggled to maintain their composure as they hustled back onto the court. The Gallatin fans were outraged that no foul had been called. Union fans snarled in return.

Since Bill had blocked the shot, it was Gallatin's ball. Allen Cook brought the ball in to Eddie. Still fuming over the blocked shot, Eddie dribbled all around the top of the key, looking for an opening, wanting to shoot. But he was covered well and dribbled right into a double team. Eddie didn't want to be tied up in a jump ball, so he forced a shot that missed badly.

Bill snagged the rebound and saw Joe streaking toward the Union bucket. Bill hit him with a pass about ten feet above the foul line. Joe took it the rest of the way, faking his defender to the left and cutting back to the right to score.

Coach Vradenburg called a time-out.

The Union fans were going wild, sensing that victory was within their grasp. Several of the rowdy vets were taunting the white fans, and the white fans responded in kind. Things were getting ugly again.

The Gallatin team huddled. In an unusual move, Eddie sat down and grabbed a quick sip of water.

Coach Vradenburg came over to him. "Are you hurt?"

"Naw, I'm okay," Eddie said, rubbing his shoulder where he had hit the floor. "Just needed a breather."

The coach nodded and returned to the huddle, drawing a play on his clipboard and showing the other players.

Just then, Eddie heard a familiar voice calling his name from behind him. He turned and spotted his brother, Bo.

"Eddie!" Bo called again.

"Not now, Bo," Eddie said, shaking his head.

But Bo would not be deterred. "Eddie!" he yelled again.

Eddie turned around to face his brother.

"Listen, Eddie. You gotta let it go, man. Don't let them get to you. Don't let them get you out of your game." Bo shook his fist. "Eddie, you can do it. They're not giving you the middle, but you can hit those long shots. Just like when we were kids, you and me, out behind the house. Do it like you've always done it." Bo stopped and gulped hard. "Eddie, I love ya, buddy. Win this thing. Win it for you, win it for the school, but win it for me too."

Eddie nodded and turned back to the court. He closed his eyes, and for an instant, he was back behind the house, hitting the twenty- and twenty-five-footers.

The buzzer sounded and Eddie opened his eyes to see the team breaking the huddle. "Let's go, guys," he said as he rejoined the team. "We're gonna win this thing."

It was midway through the fourth quarter and the scoreboard read Union 60, Gallatin 56. As the players returned to the court, the crowd's roar, like Niagara Falls, reverberated throughout the gymnasium.

Bill looked over and spotted Eddie heading to the far sidelines. But on his way, Eddie stopped and stared up for a moment at the net, almost as if to say, "You are mine."

He trotted over to the edge of the court. The ball came into play, and Ken Kirkham found Eddie along the sideline. Eddie took the pass and dribbled around to the front of the basket. Joe Malone was playing him loose, assuming that Eddie was too far away to dare a shot from that distance.

Joe was wrong.

At least thirty feet away, Eddie went up for the shot. The ball arced to the basket, never touching the rim. *Swish!* Eddie's favorite sound.

To Eddie, it seemed that he was all alone—out behind the house as an eleven-year-old boy. *Swish!* His teammates got the ball to him and from the deep pocket corner—*Swish!* Eddie scored again.

Athletes refer to it as "being in the zone" when the rest of the world fades away and there is nothing but the goal. Eddie was in the zone. The Gallatin crowd was going wild. *Swish!* From everywhere and anywhere on the court, wherever Eddie shot—*Swish!*

The Union Devils scrambled in every direction, trying to shut down Eddie by keeping him from getting the ball. Roy Jackson, sitting on the bench, shook his head and yelled instructions to his replacement. "Stop him! Foul him. Do anything you gotta do. Just don't let him shoot!"

Missy and her cheerleaders jumped for joy. Even the racist boys were overcome with school spirit, cheering, not just because Eddie was white, but because he was part of the Green Wave. The vets stared in disbelief. The kid was a shooting machine. The Sherlin family cheered wildly. They'd seen Eddie shoot like this before. Several people on the Union side slumped in their seats. The barbershop guys sat stunned.

Bill Ligon raced from one spot on the court to another in a desperate attempt to stop Eddie. Suddenly, Union couldn't do anything right and Gallatin could do no wrong. Thanks to Eddie's performance, Gallatin not only pulled away, they pulled out of sight. Union was running out of time.

As the clock ticked down, the Union players double-teamed Eddie, but he still scored. Finally, Eddie shot an impossible thirty-footer, with two guys all over him. Eddie watched the ball sail through the air as though it were moving in slow motion, the game-ending buzzer sounding the second after the ball left his hands. *Swish!*

The Gallatin side of the gymnasium erupted in a thundering roar. The noise combined with the long, loud growling buzzer brought Eddie out of the zone and back to reality. Despite his teammates jumping up and down, patting him on the back, and the cheerleaders shaking their pom-poms and screaming, it took Eddie a few seconds to realize the game was over.

Al and Jesse frantically tried to tell the story to their radio listening audience, but they couldn't come up with enough superlatives to describe Eddie's performance. "What an exhibition of shooting marksmanship!" Al gushed. "I mean, Eddie Sherlin just went into a zone and took over this game!"

"I've never seen anything like it," Jesse concurred. "Absolutely amazing!"

Eddie looked up at the scoreboard. The final score read: 74 to 60. Gallatin won by fourteen points. Eddie scored twenty-seven points, nineteen of them coming in the second half, thirteen in the final quarter. He spotted his family in the bleachers: the girls were cheering wildly and his parents were smiling broadly. And Bo, from his wheelchair, was beaming like Eddie hadn't seen him smile in a long, long time. Bo's expression made it all worthwhile.

Missy and the cheerleaders were ecstatic, still yelling and whooping it up. The Gallatin bleachers vibrated from the excitement of the fans. Even Terry and his racist buddies were cheering, although Terry's cheers sounded more like taunts.

The Union fans were crestfallen.

The Vietnam vets had spotted Terry and his buddies, and they were spoiling for a fight.

On the Union bench, the boys were crushed. Joe Malone hung his head, fighting back tears. Roy was angry with himself for fouling out. "If only I had been in there, maybe I could have stopped him."

But nobody really believed that. Bill covered his head and face with a towel. He didn't want to see anything or anyone, and he didn't want to be seen.

Bill Bunton, the announcer, stood at the scorekeepers' table, microphone in hand. "Ladies and gentlemen, let's give a big hand to the tournament runner-up, the Union High School Devils. What a game! Give 'em a hand!"

The Union supporters cheered madly, and even many people from the Gallatin crowd joined in, acknowledging the hard-fought efforts of the Union team. The announcer handed the microphone to Principal Malone, who thanked the team, the coaches, and the spectators for a great season. The crowd applauded halfheartedly as the principal handed the mike back to the announcer.

"And now," Bill Bunton said, looking out at the still turbulent crowd, "how about a big congratulations to your district tournament champions, the undefeated Gallatin High Green Wave!"

The Gallatin crowd broke into a rambunctious cheer with loud, sustained applause and screaming by those who still had a voice. The cheerleaders kicked and jumped and rustled their pom-poms as Coach Vradenburg stood and accepted the large trophy from the district officials. Coach Vradenburg encouraged the team to stand as well, acknowledging the audience's ebullient praise.

The Union cheerleaders turned away in heartache, tears streaming down their faces. The Union crowd flinched at every clap and cheer from the Gallatin side, almost as if being slapped in the face. In their minds, they had lost much more than a basketball game. Many of them were terribly sad; some were downright angry and belligerent. Others turned their backs on the celebration.

In the gymnasium, as well as in the parking lots outside, the police were on high alert, watching for unruly behavior or anything that might precipitate violence or destruction of property. The authorities were mindful of the Molotov cocktails, burning crosses, and fires that had destroyed thousands of dollars' worth of property in the recent past. "And now," the announcer called out above the noise.

"It's time for the all-tournament team. These boys are the best of the best. As I call your names, fellows, please come to center court so we can let you know how much we appreciate you." The announcer paused and looked over at the team benches—one jubilant and one devastated.

"The first player on the all-tournament team: at guard, from Gallatin High, Eddie Sherlin!" The Gallatin crowd erupted again as Eddie, with tears of joy still in his eyes, trotted out to center court.

"And at forward," the announcer continued, "from Union High School . . . Bill Ligon!"

The Union crowd applauded, joined by some of the Gallatin spectators. Anna, Tyree, and Delores enthusiastically applauded for Bill. But Bill didn't move. He remained seated on the bench, his head hidden under a towel.

When Coach Martin saw that Bill was not getting up, he leaned down to his star player. "Come on, Bill. Get out there."

The announcer and the crowd waited an awkward moment. In the Union section of the bleachers, Bill's family watched anxiously, feeling bad for him, but nonetheless not wanting him to be disrespectful.

Under her breath, Anna Ligon prayed. "Help him, Lord."

After a few seconds, Bill slowly rose to his feet. The Union side applauded enthusiastically, but the Gallatin folks seemed irked by Bill's slow response.

When Bill stood up, he slowly let the towel slide off his head and onto his shoulders, and for the first time it was obvious to the crowd that he had been crying. Watching Bill as he walked across the court, Eddie realized how awful Bill felt. Eddie understood that Bill's disappointment went far beyond basketball. Not only had he lost the game, but he would have no opportunity to redeem himself. There would never be another Gallatin-Union face-off. Childhood memories of the two of them playing basketball together flashed through Eddie's mind. He and Bill were on the same side, really. Their skin color was different, but they were both created in God's image. They were a lot alike.

Bill stopped at center court, fighting back the tears and trying to regain his composure. He glanced up and noticed Eddie's compassionate eyes welling with tears as much as his own. Eddie took a step toward Bill. The entire crowd froze. Bill couldn't contain himself any longer. He began crying again, and his tears flowed freely. For an awkward moment, Eddie looked at his childhood friend. He knew what to do. Somewhere in the recesses of his mind, little children were singing: "Red and yellow, black and white, they are precious in his sight, Jesus loves the little children of the world."

Eddie threw his arms around Bill's sweaty shoulders and hugged him.

The spectators in the stands and packed along the sidelines stiffened. A white boy hugging a black boy? In 1970? In Tennessee?

But Eddie didn't let go. Instead, he held Bill tighter as Bill sobbed and sobbed. Eddie's emotions overcame him, and he started crying too. Bill's arms wrapped around Eddie, and the two players stood at center court embracing and bawling.

"It's over, Eddie," Bill said as he wept on Eddie's shoulder. "It's all over."

"Aw, man, don't worry about it," Eddie consoled him.

"Shoot, Ed. It's over," Bill repeated. "Good game, but it's over."

Bill and Eddie were so overcome by their emotions that they did not even notice that the entire crowd in the gymnasium had fallen silent. Deathly silent. Everyone no doubt was wondering, *What's going to happen?* Yet no one spoke a word. The coaches, the principals, the other players, Eddie's family and friends, Bill's family and friends, the radio announcers—everyone seemed speechless and appeared to be holding their collective breaths. The announcer, poised to introduce the remaining members of the all-tournament team, lowered the microphone and simply watched and waited in awe at what everyone sensed was a holy moment.

And the moment continued. For thirty seconds . . . sixty seconds . . . a minute and a half . . . two minutes or more. The same gymnasium that had been roaring with sound all evening long was eerily silent, as strong men and women, students, teachers, grandparents, and children alike watched the tender scene unfold. The innocent friendship Bill and Eddie had enjoyed as children—the love and respect they'd had for each other, a secret to most of the community all these years—still resided in their hearts, just waiting for the opportunity to reappear.

In the midst of the awe-inspiring silence, somebody—to this day, nobody is certain who that somebody was—started to clap. Then somebody else began applauding. And then another and another.

Anna Ligon began crying as she started to applaud. Jim and Betty Sherlin stood up and applauded, as did the Sherlin girls, Delilah and Debbie. Principal Malone was clapping as more and more people joined in. People on both sides of the gym stood and began applauding. Missy and Olivia and their squads joined in the wonder of it all, with some of the girls hugging one another, while others joined hands. James and the rowdy Vietnam vets stood and clapped, several of them locking arms around one another's shoulders. Some of the white and Asian vets in the crowd saw the Negro veterans applauding, and they too stood to their feet and began clapping.

As the applause continued, Principal Malone and Principal Herron walked toward each other as though they were going to shake hands. But they didn't. Right there along the sidelines, for all the world to see, the two men embraced in a huge bear hug. Before long, almost everyone in the gymnasium—even Ronald and the Springfield boys—young and old, black and white were all applauding. A number of people were sobbing tears of joy and relief.

About the only people who were not pleased were Terry Poster and his dad, along with their racist friends. The kids sat back in their seats in amazement, while the adult KKK guys, appalled by what they had just witnessed, headed for the door. *Darkness must flee wherever the true light shines.*

On the bench, Roy sat bewildered. He leaned over to Joe, who was still applauding. "Why is Ligon hugging Sherlin?"

Joe smiled at Roy. "God only knows."

Roy looked back into the stands and saw his grandfather and Mr. Bonner standing and applauding. Grandfather Jackson smiled broadly at Roy and motioned for him to stand up. Roy dutifully obeyed his grandfather; he stood, looked around, and then began applauding with everyone else.

Finally, the two tearful young men at midcourt broke apart but still kept one arm around the other's shoulder. Eddie smiled and waved. Even Bill managed a smile.

For the longest time, it seemed nobody wanted to leave the gymnasium. There was an unusual presence in the place. Everyone was aware of it, even if they couldn't understand it, explain it, or describe it. Peace—a peace that passed all understanding—permeated the air. Some people sat down on the bleachers and simply basked in the moment. A large number of Negroes and white folks shook hands before leaving. A few people even hugged—white people hugging colored people, colored people hugging white people.

When they finally did leave the gym, many people walked arm in arm. In a very real way, the tension and stress that had been building all week long in anticipation of Gallatin and Union's first—and last—meeting on the basketball court had dissipated. All the racial overtones the game had carried were now suddenly and strangely and almost supernaturally gone.

"This is the start of something big," a little boy said.

And it was. Gallatin was never the same. A spirit of racial understanding had been born.

Establishing a new attitude of racial equality was no slam dunk. It took years of hard work and reconciliation to develop mutual respect and cooperation between the races, but that night was a turning point in the relationships between blacks and whites in Gallatin—and in all of Tennessee.

31

MORE THAN FORTY YEARS LATER, people in Tennessee still talked about that hug. The two old friends, Eddie and Bill, now in their sixties, shared a special reunion when they met in downtown Gallatin to reminisce. They walked the town together, talking as they went.

"Isn't it amazing," Eddie said to Bill, "that people still remember that game and the two of us embracing afterward? Although we didn't realize the significance of our actions at the time, something happened in our town that night. We were a part of something really special, something good."

"Yeah, I ran into a guy from the Gallatin class of 1981 the other day," Bill said. "A black guy. He knew more about that hug than he did about the game. He thought that Union had won. So I didn't tell him any differently."

Both Eddie and Bill burst out laughing.

"Yep. Folks are convinced that what we did at center court that night had something to do with making things better around here," Eddie said. "That somehow it opened the way for racial reconciliation in our neck of the woods."

Bill nodded and rubbed his chin. "There may be some truth to that. After all, not long after that game, they not only integrated the schools, they also integrated the Palace Theater and everywhere else in town. We got black kids and white kids going to the same movie house and sittin' together on the same levels now, and some of 'em even eating popcorn out of the same popcorn buckets."

"I hear that they can sit anywhere in the theater," Eddie said with a smile. "And believe it or not, I've even seen a white boy and an African American girl walking down the same side of the street, holdin' hands, right here in downtown Gallatin."

Bill shook his head. "Hard to believe, isn't it? Nowadays, kids of all races go into the diner and sit wherever they want to, with whomever they wish, and nobody even blinks an eye." Bill cocked his head, and with a twinkle in his eyes asked, "Are we that old, Eddie?"

"Ha! Nah, we're not old, but we've come a long way, and we've had an amazing journey. You and I realized as kids that we were no different from each other, except you had a darker suntan than I did."

Both men chuckled.

Eddie continued. "Basketball brought us together. And in an odd way, basketball brought our town together."

"That's right, Eddie. Look over there." Bill pointed to a school bus that had stopped to unload some kids coming home from school. "Black kids and white kids getting off that bus, and nobody thinks nuthin' of it. That would not have happened in our high school days, but now it is commonplace. That's progress, Eddie."

Bill stretched his long legs against the curb. "And despite some difficult obstacles to overcome, the integration of the schools went fairly well that fall."

"That's right," Eddie agreed. "And just two years later, your brother, Tyree, and the integrated Gallatin basketball team won the Tennessee state championship."

"Yes, they certainly did. They were unbeatable once Union and Gallatin joined forces as a team. Of course, you and I didn't get to see much of that."

"Right, you were off to college. What was the name of that dumpy little school you attended, Princeton or something?" Eddie smiled and nudged Bill's shoulder playfully.

"Nope. Turned Princeton down. Had the entrance packet and everything, but I went to Vanderbilt instead. I got in academically first, and then later they gave me a basketball scholarship. I was glad to be playing in Nashville because they broadcast the Vandy games on television. So there I was, a couple of nights every week, the only black fellow on the team, on live television."

"Ah, so that's how the Detroit Pistons found out about you? All that TV time!" Eddie teased. "And you signed with the Pistons, pursued your dreams, and played professional basketball. Good for you, Bill!"

"Thanks, Eddie, but what about you? Instead of attending college and playing basketball at the University of Tennessee, you pursued your dreams and signed with the Pittsburgh Pirates baseball team, right out of high school. I don't know how you did that. Gallatin High didn't even have a baseball team, but the pros recognized your ability. How did they know you could hit?"

"Turns out, I couldn't," Eddie joked, and both men laughed. "But my dad was mighty proud of me." Eddie shook his head. "Isn't it amazing, Bill, how much we can do if we just lay aside our differences and try to understand one another? Who knows what we could accomplish if we'd work together instead of against one another?"

"We still got a long way to go, Eddie," Bill said. "We ain't in heaven yet."

"I know that's true," Eddie mused. "Here we are, both of us back in Gallatin. We've had some success, and we've both made some mistakes. But if people can just learn to love one another, and forgive one another, no problem is insurmountable. What was that song you guys used to sing? 'We Shall Overcome'? We really can overcome the pain we've all experienced in the past, and any problem in the future, if we will help one another. I believe God will guide us as we do that, if we will ask him."

"I know that's right, brother. Preach it!" Bill patted his friend on the back.

"Naw, I ain't no preacher," Eddie said. "I'm just a sports nut, like you. But here we are, back in our hometown, where we still have a chance to make a difference every day."

"That's pretty cool," Bill agreed. "But speaking of a difference, I wonder if we played some ball today if we might have a different outcome?"

"I don't know, but let's find out. Look where we've walked."

The two friends were standing in front of Gallatin's park, the same park where they were not allowed to play together as boys, close to where Bill formerly lived. Some young boys, black and white, were playing basketball on the new asphalt courts. They looked to be about eleven years old.

"Let's ask them if we can join them," Eddie suggested.

"Are you kidding?"

"Surely we can keep up with a couple of kids."

"Okay." Bill called to the kids on the court, "Hey, do you guys mind if we play too?"

The boys stared skeptically at the two sixty-something men wearing street clothes. They exchanged doubtful looks. Finally one of the boys called, "Sure, you can play—if you can shoot."

"Oh, we can shoot, all right," Eddie called. He and Bill hobbled over to the court.

"I'll take the big guy," one of the black boys said.

"Aw, come on, you always give me the short guys," a white boy said.

Bill interrupted them. "But sometimes those short guys can really shoot." He looked over at Eddie and winked.

Eddie and Bill joined in the boys' game and were holding their own with them for a while, until Bill went up for a jump shot from above the foul line. Eddie leaped up to block Bill's shot, and both men tumbled to the asphalt. Eddie bounced back up, but Bill was slow in moving.

"Oh, you got me that time," Bill said. "Ow, my achin' back."

Eddie stood over him and reached out his hand. "Come on, you're not hurt."

"Are you kiddin'?" Bill protested. "I can hardly move! Let's go get somethin' to eat."

"Sounds good. Let's go over to the Dari Delite and grab a burger." He smiled. "I hear they're lettin' black folks in there these days."

"Naw, man," Bill said, as he let Eddie help him up. "Let's go to the Drive-In and get some good fried chicken. If we can get in, that is. Since you white folks discovered what good fried chicken tastes like, we African Americans can't hardly get in over at the Oakes Drive-In. Hmph. Integration, they call it."

Bill threw his arm around Eddie's shoulder, and they waved good-bye to the kids as they walked away.

A black boy and white boy stood together, watching the two friends walking into the sunset. "Old people," they both said, shaking their heads.

"Who can figure them out?" the white boy asked.

The black boy raised his eyebrows, glanced heavenward, and said, "God only knows."

Ken Abraham is known around the world for his collaborations with popular celebrities and fascinating, high-profile public figures. Many of Ken's books have attained *New York Times* bestseller status, with three books reaching the number one spot on that prestigious list.

Ken's collaborations have been featured on *20/20*, *Dateline*, *Larry King Live*, *Good Morning America*, *CBS This Morning*, *The Today Show*, the Fox Television Network, and the Family Channel.